TESTIMONY

TESTIMONY

The Word Made Fresh

DANIEL BERRIGAN

Foreword by John Dear

ORBIS BOOKS

Maryknoll, New York 10545

Copyright © 2004 by Daniel Berrigan, S.J.

Published by Orbis Books, Maryknoll, NY 10545-0308.

All poems are taken from *And the Risen Bread: The Selected Poems of Daniel Berrigan, 1957–1997*, ed. John Dear (New York: Fordham University Press, 1998). Used with permission.

"The Promised Land of Rabbi Abraham Heschel" was originally published in *No Man Is an Island: Abraham Joshua Heschel and Interreligious Dialogue*, ed. Harold Kasimow and Byron L. Sherwin (Maryknoll, N.Y.: Orbis Books, 1991). Used with permission.

"In Better Hands Than Our Judges" was originally published in *Sojourners*, June 1990.

"Thomas Merton, Friend and Monk" was originally published in *The Catholic Worker*, December 1993.

"An Ethic of Resurrection" was originally published in *National Jesuit News*, November 1982.

"Keeping the Flame Alive" was originally published in *The Catholic Worker*, June–July 1997.

"The Colors of Corita Kent" was originally published in a longer form in *The Critic*, Summer 1989.

"A Chancy Encounter with an Angel" was originally published in *Sojourners*, April 1993.

Queries regarding rights and permissions should be addressed to:
Orbis Books, P.O. Box 308, Maryknoll, NY 10545-0308.

Manufactured in the United States of America

Library of Congress Cataloging-in-Publication Data

Berrigan, Daniel.
  Testimony : the Word made fresh / Daniel Berrigan ; foreword by John Dear.
    p. cm.
  ISBN 1-57075-545-0 (pbk.)
  1. Nonviolence–Religious aspects–Christianity. 2. Christian life–Catholic authors. I. Title.
BT736.6.B465 2004
261.8'73–dc22

                                        2004009729

for

Elizabeth McAlister

Peacemaking is hard,
hard almost as war—
the difference being one
we stake life upon.

Contents

IV. SERMONS AND HOMILIES

V. CHRISTIANS IN A WARMAKING STATE

Foreword

John Dear, S.J.

Aᴙᴏᴜɴᴅ ᴛʜᴇ ᴛɪᴍᴇ I entered the Jesuits in the early 1980s, the New York province of Jesuits organized a conference on nuclear weapons in New York which featured several generals, "just war experts," and Daniel Berrigan. This was the age of Reagan, who joked into what he thought was a dead microphone that "the bombing of Russia will begin in five minutes." For a brief time, church leaders debated the "issue" of war and peace as the Catholic bishops prepared to publish a "balanced" letter upholding the just war theory and nuclear deterrence while tolerating some unknown philosophy called "Gospel nonviolence."

The generals gave their speeches, and the Jesuits applauded. The just war theorists outlined the conditions in which Christians could dismiss the Sermon on the Mount and support war, even the use of nuclear weapons—and the Jesuits applauded.

Then Daniel Berrigan spoke.

"The Christian response to imperial death-dealing is in effect a nonresponse," he said. "We refuse the terms of the argument. To weigh the value of lives would imply that military or paramilitary solutions had been grotesquely validated by Christians. There is no cause, however noble, which justifies the taking of a single human life, much less millions of them.

" 'Witness of the resurrection' was a title of honor, self-conferred by the twelve apostles," he continued. "They were called to take their stand on behalf of life, to the point of undergoing death, as well as death's analogies — scorn and rejection, floggings and jail. This is our glory. From Peter and Paul to Martin King and Oscar Romero, we are witnesses of the resurrection. We want to test the resurrection in our bones. To see if we might live in hope. We want to taste the resurrection. May I say we have not been disappointed."

His words were like a lightning bolt in the long dark night of war. I remember reading them in the Jesuit newspaper a few weeks after I entered the novitiate. They struck me with the force of power, authority, and truth. He seemed to make the Word of God fresh all over again. This is what Christianity is about, I realized, saying no to the crucifixion of humanity, and yes to God's way of nonviolent love. Here is a modern version of the ancient testimony of Peter and Påul.

Dan's testimony left everyone at the conference dumbfounded. There was little applause. The Jesuits walked away, resentful that Dan had spoiled their military consultation by bringing up that small, impractical, irrelevant matter of the Gospel.

The word "testimony" has a noble history in our Christian tradition. After that first Pentecost, the early apostles took to the streets and gave testimony to "what they had seen and heard." They were "witnesses." As witnesses, they were arrested, put on trial, hauled before judges, and forced to testify to the reason for their illegal actions. Throughout Christian history, the saints and martyrs have been hauled into courts to give testimony to the truth. Testimony remains a basic requirement for Christian living in times of violence, war, and nuclear weapons.

Daniel Berrigan has spent his life offering testimony to the truth of Gospel nonviolence and witnessing to the resurrection. In courtrooms and jail cells, before the media and large audiences, on street corners and in retreat houses, to friends and opponents, from Catonsville to King of Prussia, from Sharpeville to Selma, from Vietnam to El Salvador, he has proclaimed the Word of God: "Love your enemies, do good to those who hate you, blessed are the peacemakers, put down the sword." His life fits into the Acts of the Apostles, one of his favorites, with its rhythm of arrests, jails, courtroom scenes, and eloquent testimony.

In 1968, Dan shocked the world with his brother Philip and the Catonsville Nine by burning draft files with homemade napalm in a dramatic act of nonviolent civil disobedience. Since then he has continued to be a lightning rod of truth, an apostle of peace, a prophetic sign of God's judgment on our culture of war. In 1980, Dan, Phil, and the Plowshares Eight hammered on an unarmed nuclear nose cone, sparking the first act of nuclear disarmament, the first of over eighty such "Plowshares actions," fulfilling Isaiah's vision of "swords into plowshares." Dan has published over fifty books, including an unprecedented series of scripture commentaries on the Hebrew Bible seen through the lens of Gospel nonviolence. Today, Dan continues to teach, lecture, lead retreats, write poetry, and offer his testimony to peace. With our friends in New York City, he risks arrest repeatedly against U.S. warmaking, especially at the notorious S.S. *Intrepid,* a museum displaying U.S. weapons of mass destruction in the New York Harbor.

This book offers a powerful, shining testament of peace and nonviolence to a world of war and violence, a strong and soothing word of hope to a world of despair, a bright spotlight of truth to a world of darkness and lies. Here Dan tells us, like those first disciples, what he has seen and heard. He stands as a modern-day witness to the resurrection.

Encouraged by our friend and editor Robert Ellsberg, I read through many of Dan's files — his talks, essays, poems, and reflections — and culled these testimonies, including excerpts from that 1982 Jesuit conference talk entitled "An Ethic of Resurrection." Most of these writings have never before been published. Together, they offer an eloquent appeal to the truth of Gospel nonviolence.

Dan's testimony is as good as Gospel witness can be, ranking with the sermons of Martin Luther King Jr., the *Catholic Worker* columns of Dorothy Day, the essays of Thomas Merton, the pastoral letters of Oscar Romero, and the courtroom statements of his brother Philip Berrigan. They inspire us to give our own testimony, to take new risks for the Gospel, to cross the line in opposition to imperial warmaking, to become witnesses to the resurrection. When I read his reflections on Isaiah or Jesus, his essays on Dorothy Day and Thomas Merton, his analysis of the culture's "normalizing" of death or the church's violation of its vocation to resist evil, I feel "cut to the heart" as the crowds did when Peter first spoke about the resurrection. Like them, I ask, "What can I do? How can I take another step on the road of discipleship? What testimony can I give to this world of war and nuclear idolatry?"

Dan's testimony comes at the perfect time. I hope every Christian across the land will read it, share it with others, take it to heart, and recognize here a modern translation of an old story. I hope we will all act on Dan's testimony and become witnesses to the resurrection by dedicating our lives to the abolition of war, injustice, violence, poverty, the death penalty, and nuclear weapons. Every Christian should welcome Dan's testimony, share his hope, and risk the resurrection in their own lives. If we take Dan at his word, if we take the Word of God seriously as he has done, we too will become peacemakers, and be the blessed sons and daughters of God. We too will not only contribute to the disarmament of the world, but to God's nonviolent transformation of the world.

Nothing could be more meaningful. Dan's testimony pushes us to the great work at hand. It is a word we all need to hear. It may help save us.

Thank you, Dan, for your testimony, your life, your friendship. You make the Word of God believable.

1

They Shall Beat Their Swords into Plowshares

*Everything enhances, everything
gives glory—everything!*

*between bark and bite
Judge Salus's undermined soul
betrays him, mutters
very alleluias.*

*The iron cells—
row upon row of rose trellised
mansions, bridal chambers!*

*Curses, vans, keys, guards—behold
the imperial lions of our vast acres!*

*And when hammers come down
and our years are tossed to four winds—
why, flowers blind the eye, the saints
pelt us with flowers!*

*See, the Lord's hands heap
eon upon eon,
like fruit bowls at a feast.*

1

Courage Is a Verb

In Other Words, Do It!

And God will judge between the nations, and will render decisions for many peoples. And they will hammer their swords into plowshares and their spears into pruning hooks. Nation will not lift sword against nation. Never again will they learn war. —Isaiah 2:4

∼

I SUPPOSE in the estimate of everyone there are one or two commanding texts, whether in the Hebrew Bible, the Koran, the Gita, or the Christian Testament, that beckon us from "the paralysis of analysis," as Dr. Martin Luther King would say. Beckon us, that is, to doing it.

At that point, perhaps we touch on the point of faith itself, as Kierkegaard wrote. Surely he was the great and dour decrier of a Christianity that remained "an inert truth," as Whitehead would put it; or a Christianity that remained merely "notional," as Newman would put it. In any case, a religion dead and buried in the mind. A religion that put to naught an essentially commanding word and summons.

Do it! To me, this text of Isaiah has been pure summons. A vigorous text, designed to set the human in motion. Stand there indeed, but do something!

∼

The congruence between the times in which the oracle was first issued and our times is striking, unsettling, close. Isaiah spoke in the eighth

---

Daniel and Philip Berrigan and the Plowshares Eight hammered on unarmed Mark 12A nuclear nose cones at the General Electric plant in King of Prussia, Pennsylvania, in the first "Plowshares" disarmament action on September 9, 1980. They originally faced three to ten years in prison for their civil disobedience, but after years on appeal, the Pennsylvania Court of Common Pleas in Norristown sentenced them on April 10, 1990, to time served. Since then there have been over eighty Plowshares actions around the world. For a chronology see www.plowsharesactions.org.

century B.C.E., a time of imperial darkness, of wars and rumors of wars, of duplicity in high places. Isaiah entered deliberately this scene of desolating power.

His method was, to say the least, unsettling to conventional religion and politics. A religious figure, and most political! Isaiah refuses to separate public responsibility from the voice of God within.

It was all quite simple. He had seen God, therefore.

It was a terrifying equation — and remains such. He had seen God, therefore he had a message for the king and the people. The premise and conclusion were forged with a fiery, dangerous simplicity, the simplicity of a saint or a madman.

∼

Isaiah seemed to have enjoyed a vogue, for awhile. He was heard in places of power, he had audience at the throne, for awhile. Then the war with Assyria broke; it proceeded bloodily, and was hardly resolved. Prelude to more violence, never an end of it. A war like every other war.

And the fortunes of Isaiah were altered. War was resumed. A "Second Isaiah" enters. The message darkened. Now the prophet spoke only of doom and defeat, words perennially unwelcome to imperial ears. This other prophet said, in effect, the first war was only a first act. You shall now be invaded, Samaria will fall.

So it transpired. And worse. Eventually, a siege was laid to Jerusalem by Sennacherib of Assyria.

∼

In those terrible years, this voice was, in one way or another, a presence to be reckoned with. The imperial adventurers, whether foreign or domestic, felt the sting of his prophecy. He played a variety of roles. Sometimes he reminds us of a court fool, sometimes of a dog at the wheels of a rampaging chariot, sometimes he is an honored oracular presence. He dwells at length on bad outcomes to dubious enterprises. And oftener than may be thought healthy, he derides the foolish inflations of ruling ego.

∼

And then, something else.

An oracle that seems to issue from a burning bush or a fiery epiphany. Isaiah announces — the impossible. The necessary impossible, the absolutely crucial impossible; the impossible that must come to pass.

That which shall come to pass, precisely because it is impossible.

"They shall beat their swords into plowshares." It is as though he were holding in suspension two fiercely incompatible elements. One is icy, one fiery. A terrifying experiment! The necessary must somehow be joined to the impossible. Something new, something beyond all effort and imagining must come to be.

Swords into plowshares. The oracle is absolutely crucial to the prospering of cultures, of nations, to the survival of individuals, to honor, to religious faith, to a civilized sense of humanity. To the fate of the earth.

But the oracle is also impossible of fulfillment. (Who then, who now, believes it could come to pass? After Vietnam, after Grenada, after Panama, after Nicaragua, after El Salvador, after Iraq? Who believes?)

Therefore, the conclusion of Isaiah. Because the task is crucial, necessary, and because it is radically impossible—therefore it must be done. The oracle will come true. God has sworn it.

"They shall beat swords into plowshares." The words surpass the human, even while they engage the human. Even while they commit, invite, command, exact vows, demand conversion of heart.

〜

It is in the unlikely coincidence of these two, the human that surpasses the cultural understanding and thereby betrayal of the Bible, that the truth of God is addressed.

Indeed, the oracle surpasses the cultural grant to the human. Is anyone in need of instruction on our helplessness, our lassitude, our sleep of death, our psychic numbness, our inertia of soul, before a dreadful nuclear predicament? Our successive and savage incursions from Vietnam to Iraq? Is anyone in need of instruction, as our planet, insulted and raped, wounded in its elements of fire, water, air, land, cries out for redress, sinks in exhaustion, can no longer replenish, heal, sustain, our heedless tribe?

And yet, and yet. The oracle, like a resurrecting command, beckons forth this very helplessness, this acceptance of dumb fate, this rehearsal of death. You are not helpless, you are not objects of fate, you are not dead. Your despair is to your shame.

"Your sins are forgiven. Arise and walk."

〜

Further, understand that it is not God who through some magic or other will beat swords into plowshares: it is yourselves. It is you—whom the times have beaten, literally—your spirit, enterprise, imagination, your very humanity—into the form of death, into the form of a sword. The blade lies at your own throat. You taste the death before death which we name despair.

Disarm. Take care of the widow, the orphan, and the poor.

It must be done, and it cannot be done. And if it is to be done, it must be done because God wills it, and it must be done by us.

~

The task is literally impossible, to our resources, to our will. Sixty years of cold war, successive American wars, nuclear threats — these testify, pitifully, cynically, to the impossibility.

Disarmament? Nuclear? Conventional? Disarmed hearts? The summons lies beyond all political wit and witlessness. It is impossible to Russians, Americans, French, British, Chinese, Germans, Israelis, Indians, Pakistanis. Impossible to Harry Truman and George Bush. Impossible to uncommitted nations and passionately communist and capitalist nations. The "kingdoms of darkness" and the purported "kingdoms of light" are equally plunged in darkness.

And perhaps most striking of all, beating swords into plowshares is impossible to conventional Christianity. During these awful years, in most of the nuclear nations we have hardly seen a suffering or witnessing church. No Isaiah arises in the churches. No oracles cast light on the benighted nations. Indeed, the churches show little or no interest in echoing the oracle of First Isaiah. Let it be said plainly: The churches, by and large, have aided and abetted, have co-conspired, have laid a blessing on the forging of swords. A blessing that is a curse.

~

And yet the oracle sounds in our ears with absolute assurance. "They shall beat swords into plowshares, spears into pruning hooks." They shall do this; which is to say, ourselves, in this generation, in our lifetime, during our adulthood, in no other. Shall our children be safe, our world salvaged? It is literally, and brutally, now or never.

~

I fear to fall into another sort of fatalism here. As though in saying "now or never," I were saying something like this:

"The famous clock of the nuclear scientists has been ticking away, a time bomb. We stand to lose everything, unless we muster our resources and lay our effort to a nuclear accommodation, an Icelandic freeze, so to speak. All are agreed there are too many nukes. Very well, let us reason together. Let us find an acceptable number of nukes to live with. Let us seek a marriage of convenience in Armageddon."

I do not mean this. It is too easy in principle. It is also frivolous in political understanding and doomed in practice. The oracle of Isaiah stands against all such absurd "peacekeeping," a nuclear winter in the soul, desolate terror as a way of life.

~

I do mean this. Isaiah stands against this; so does God. The oracle proceeds neither from expediency nor psychological necessity nor imperial arrogance, however veiled; not from armageddonists nor from nuclear nightmares or daymares; not from the spirit of blackmail, rancor, ideologies bloody or bloodless. It proceeds from a different source than these polluted ones. It proceeds, Isaiah says, from the fidelity of God joined together with human courage.

~

The word implies a promise. Disarmament shall happen; wars shall cease; the outcome is irresistible. No human will, no malevolence, no nation, not the most powerful imperium, can prevent it. The tone of Isaiah is absolute, assured—for the promise is uttered by God, and God is faithful.

~

I have an image, awakened by the text. First of all, a hand. Or better, many hands. The hands of women and men and children. Hands of farmers and workers, writers and artists, ministers and students, old and young, hands of pacifists and former warriors. Indeed, the text implies that all hands are symbolized by just two, the one unlikely, the other consistent. First, the converted warrior, the veteran who casts his medals away; and then the farmer, cultivator, nurturer, cherisher, the "compleat ecologist," the lover of children and of all the living.

In any case, such hands, armed only with hammers, come down with force against a bared weapon. They bend it around, blunt its cruel edge, neutralize its threat. And more, for they are not mere destroyers. They transform instruments of death and maiming and blood, transform them into something new, useful, prohuman.

In the act, those who forcefully lend the sword its new shape are themselves transformed.

~

As a little child, each spring, I stumbled along after the plow as my father turned the earth up, one furrow upon another. A mild, breathing sense of life arose in the suave air, after the killing North Country winter. The plow hummed along. I imagined that the giants of the earth were turning over in sleep, just before awakening. Or I thought of the furrows as great coils of woven rope, weaving, binding all things in one. The blades of a plow wove the tegument of the world together. It was all one—seasons and furrows, families and beasts, plantings and harvest.

The child, it must be admitted, was not notably useful to the work. He went along, free and feckless, a contemplative of the new season, wandering, humming to himself, falling behind, catching up. Sometimes he had a sense of walking on black waters. The furrows dipped and rose, his unsteady feet were treading a kind of heavy earthen surf.

Above all, he remembers breathing the earth, that overpowering odor of "wet and wild," the released soul of the soil.

~

That world of the child, measured by later times, was small, restricted. It held before him a truth, which the times would reveal as partial indeed. Which is to say, he thought the whole world was like his world. He thought plowing the earth was the normal function of humans, that the odor of the earth was of soil, not of blood or brimstone.

He had much to learn.

Years later, he saw his four brothers enlisted for war. And the truth, the reversal of the oracle of Isaiah, struck. The war was, in the cruelest of phrases, world war, total war. "For the duration," they said, the able bodied must lay down the plow and take up the sword.

Even that awful fact did not exhaust the event of war. In effect, the plows were not abandoned to rust and rot. "Lend lease" the plows, was a war cry. So the plows were beaten into swords. Overnight, swords sprang up in the furrows, those first shoots of a harvest of blood. It was wartime. Swords had become the very symbol, the only accoutrement, of the human. The swordless, the unarmed (and much more, the disarmed), were simply less than human. They were stigmatized, the shirkers, deserters, draft evaders. They were hounded, ostracized, jailed.

And if here and there, in Europe and Asia, a plow turned up the earth in those years, it turned up — corpses, land mines, and the discarded, rusted tools of peace.

~

During the war, the nation was conferring a new name on my brothers. They were no longer farmers, steel workers, students. They were warriors. That was their honor, the new vocation conferred on them by holy mother state. That this was a shocking contrast to former, life-giving work was ignored. Their lives took on a new static beat, the beat of a muffled drum, or a muffled heart. Their lives, like their clothing, went from multiform to uniform. So did their minds, cowed and obedient, their civil baptism. Now they were pledged to kill, or to support those who killed, or to die.

~

The boy learned something else. He learned a cruel new climate in which he must henceforth somehow live. The air froze, the wind was always from the north. It was not yet a nuclear winter, and yet the air was like a sword at the throat. No more springtime. The future would offer no climate of peace, only war, always war, hot or cold. Hot war, Korea, Vietnam, Grenada, Panama, Nicaragua, Iraq, Afghanistan, a litany of loss and shame; and cold war in between and ever since. Never a season for plowing, always the season of the sword.

~

He had much to learn, and he so slow a learner! It came to this: As long as the sword was in hand, the human vocation was violated. The God he had been taught of, whose name he reverenced, God of peace, God of life, this One lent neither presence, approval, nor blessing on the course of the world. It was perpetual wartime. Other gods, Mars or Vulcan or Jupiter, were in horrid charge, worldwide.

This is the way it went in the boy's lifetime.

For decades, the gods mocked and mimed the former times, the times of peace. They plowed the earth with a sword blade. Then they sowed the earth with dragons' teeth — nuclear mines, bunkers, laboratories. And there sprang up a new and unheard-of race — nuclear warriors.

~

Thus was a new history forged, an utterly spurious normalcy, a new sin. The new sin was the original sin in a new form, newly original.

And most appalling of all, conceived in the sin of war, a new species of human was born. This genetic mutation celebrated the new times of the gods of war. The newly born were the normalized inhuman.

This phenomenon, the "new human," as presented and authenticated, was a permanent figure of terror. He, she, it made no difference. They had never known a time of peace or the art of peace. The human was now one with the warrior.

All other forms of the human, those which long centuries of travail and glory had created, were placed in question. And that was the least of it, and only the start, making traditional and honored forms of the human obsolete. What must occur, as the leaders well knew, and the people came to know, was ordered: The formerly human must be derided, and then declared extinct. We must be get used to murder. The prohibition against murder must be removed from the Decalogue. The Sermon on the Mount must be expunged. The believing human, the compassionate human, the just human, above all, the peacemaking human — these must become peripheral to the main chance. They must be held suspect, indicted or jailed. They are to be judged — in the human race, but not of it.

And what of the nations, more specifically, of the warmaking nations? Under such assault, for a long generation, the assembly of humans became, in concert, a suicide club, a mutuality of perfectly balanced hostilities, teetering, bickering, lying, invading, cozening, controlling. The nations fulfilled to the letter, the dark description of the inhuman in Paul's letter to the Christians of Rome.

The ecology of the world too was monstrously altered. It became a forest of drawn swords, laid to the throats of the living.

∼

And still, that oracle of Isaiah.

Heartening, despite all. The oracle was issued in a time analogous to our own. The time of Isaiah was just as dangerous, petrifying to the spirit, mindless, captive to illusion, appallingly belligerent. Indeed, successive wars have merely underscored once again the ancient stereotype and impasse. A world at war, a world prepared for another war, a world grown inept in the uses and skills of peace.

An unlikely time to issue a word of hope!

∽

Indeed, the worst time, Isaiah dares imply, is the apt time! The kairos of God, the epiphany of God's hope, is exactly the time when our hands drop in helplessness, when all resources fail. The time when little can be done, when the new gods own the world—this is exactly the time of the toppling of those unsteady thrones!

If only we believed!

∽

I summon to our side the suffering servants of the oracle, those who have taken the hammer in hand, and beaten the nuclear sword into a plowshare. I summon Helen Woodson, mother of seven. Sentence: twelve years. Summon the Fathers Kabat, Carl and Paul. Sentences: twelve and eight years. Summon Larry Cloud Morgan. Sentence: eight years. Summon Richard Miller. Sentence: four years. Summon Darla Bradley, Jean Gump, Larry Moreland, Ken Rippetoe. Sentences: eight years. Summon John Volpe. Sentence: seven years. Summon my brother Philip. Accumulated sentence: eleven years. Summon Sisters Carol, Ardeth, and Jackie. Sentences: two and three years. Summon all the Plowshares resisters across the land, sisters and brothers in Australia, Germany, Netherlands, England, Scotland, Ireland.

Presente! I summon them to our side, to our worship and intercession — sisters and brothers, Christians and Jews, prisoners and ex-prisoners, witnesses of the oracle. Summon them all — parents and grandparents, nuns and priests, Catholic Workers, missioners, chaplains, teachers. Summon them to our side. Ignored as they are by the media, derided by prosecutors, scorned and punished by judges, their fate of no great concern to churches and synagogues.

These women and men have made a beginning in the sorry and thankless task of fidelity to the oracle. No great claim, and yet through the courage of a few, the claim is verified once more. They have made a human future less unlikely for all. They lay their hammer to the sword, and the beginning of a new creation has dawned in our terrifying world.

The sword is turned aside, the plow renews the earth.

We Are Filled with Hope

The Tale of the Plowshares Eight

O UR RESOURCES (to begin at the beginning) are biblical and ecumenical. Our resources are also American. And upon each of these it seems profitable to reflect, and with these to walk. In the footsteps of ancestors of both kinds of history, Christian and secular. And so, never alone.

Our attention was drawn to General Electric and its weapons complex in King of Prussia, Pennsylvania, late in 1979. As I recall, the friend who opened the matter was a Mennonite lawyer, John Schuchardt. He pointed out that we and many others had stood and withstood at the Pentagon, the air- and sea- and land-based military centers, for many years. But no one had confronted the industrial complex. These scientists and engineers, in utmost secrecy and unaccountability, continued to stoke their forges, beating the world itself into the shape of a nuclear sword.

Vigilers, leaflets in hand, had stood outside the plant for a number of years. But now, Schuchardt felt, a more vigorous intervention was called for. The secrecy surrounding the weapons production was in effect, an enormous protection for high crime. Under such conditions as prevailed, in contravention to all public exercise of vote, debate, citizen alertness, literally anything could continue, any crime, any violation of international, national, divine, or human law, quite out of sight and mind.

The point was not that the forges of Mars at G.E. were off limits. Everything nuclear was off limits. The point was that Mars had made himself both invisible and unaccountable. No one knew what went on in such factories and labs; not even the workers were privy to the whole as they played their part. By and large, as we were to learn, the workers had only piecemeal responsibility; they created, as they insisted at our trial, only bits and parts of the bomb; and so laid claim to a more or less tainted ignorance.

Given the situation as "normal" (nuclear normalcy—a grotesque oxymoron), a question arose. Where had democracy gone? What meaning could responsible citizenship hold? By hook and by crook a sleazy authority got hold of our dollars. They contemned and ignored our vote. Vote? In regard to nuclear weapons, we had, all said, no more voice in our future or that of our children than Soviet citizens of the time. Indeed nuclear arms were proving the great political equalizer. East and west, all people, children and adults, were in the same boat, and the boat was leaking at every seam.

Once this was pointed out and reflected on, a great light arose in our souls. We had seen something. We had always seen it. But now we saw it as though for the first time. We were like the Texan bishop Mattheisen, who rode past the immense Pantex plant in Amarillo hundreds of times. Every American nuclear weapon was assembled there, and the bishop rode past. And then one day he saw it, through those who had vigiled and prayed and been arrested there. He began to visit the prisoners, to inquire about their families, to carry the sacraments behind the walls, to ponder these events. And as he recounts, his life has never been the same.

We also had seen something. In consequence, in the spring and summer of 1980, we spent many months at prayer, reflection, discussion. We were seeking in scripture a metaphor, an image that might lend strength to our nascent purpose.

Finally it came to us through Molly Rush, mother of eight, grandmother, found of the Thomas Merton Center in Pittsburgh. She suggested the great image from Isaiah, chapter two: "God will wield authority over the nations and render judgment over many nations. They will hammer their swords into plowshares and their spears into pruning hooks."

All great moments are finally simple. Why not, we asked our souls, why not us, our hands, our hammers? And if not us, who?

So we took our small courage and small household hammers in hand. And on September 9, 1980, we entered the G.E. Reentry Division plant, in King of Prussia, Pennsylvania. It was, I need not add, a watershed hour for our lives, and who knows, perhaps also for the lives of others.

We reflected long and hard on those hammers. Each of us had sometime or another, clumsily or with skill, used a hammer. It seemed a tool of the common life, a symbol of the urge to humanize creation. Its modest heft, its adaptability, its gentle scope, makes it a traditionally peaceful tool—for building homes and schools, hospitals and churches, for making toys, shaping metal, repairing and mending and enhancing the earth.

And more. Both Isaiah and Micah drew on the hammer, as an implied symbol of spiritual rebirth, of conversion to compassion and justice, of a new face put not just on things, but on the soul. A new face tuned toward God and one another.

And closer to our topic (the hammer after all is lifted, and falls; and falling, turns one thing into another) — the hammer, falling on the weapons, transforms it. Thus the hammer becomes a symbol of the outlawing of war.

If war were outlawed, we asked ourselves, what would the world look like? What would that other, improbable, even unimaginable shape be?

Isaiah is a visionary, and a practical one. He sees what few saw in his lifetime, and only a few since, only a few kings and courtiers and academics, students and churchgoers and consumers. He sees a new form of things, the shape of a world that has turned away from killing, turned its face toward "the stranger, the widow, and the orphan."

What he sees is what we all can see, but only in proportion as we have absorbed his vision. He sees a world in the form of—a plowshare.

But the plowshare was not yet forged. Isaiah's vision was not of a peace already accomplished. Nor did his vision arise from citizenship in a peaceable kingdom. Indeed the Israel of this time was eerily like our own country. There was no peace, only war abroad and injustice at home.

Thus came his vision of peacemaking — in a strangely unpeaceable time. His century, the eighth before the common era, was turbulent in the extreme, with wars and rumors of wars. Jerusalem was under siege, the king was preparing a violent defense. Isaiah said no. In the grand tradition of the prophets of action, Isaiah intervened directly in political, military, and diplomatic events. He predicted the invasion. It happened twice.

But it was not merely his predictions that rubbed the powers raw. Bad news they could absorb—because it seldom or never fell on their heads. Isaiah dared go further. Someone, he declared, was responsible for making the news bad. He denounced the selfishness and violence of those in power. Wars were not inevitable. Neither was domestic misery. These were the creation of those who would put thrones above lives, riches above honor, excess above human need.

Do not place your trust in armies and chariots, he cried again and again. No trust in secret deals with powers. Whatever the pretensions of the nations, he insisted, God rode the cockpit of history. More chariots, multiplied warriors? These were the fits and starts of madmen. They would never serve or save or succor. They could only multiply destruction and disorder.

Let the great ones ignore or revile or punish, Isaiah persisted. The crimes of the powerful, he declared, were paid for by the sufferings of the people. Before God, this was intolerable.

Politically passionate, mystically intense, Isaiah reminds us of other, no less grand spirits of our day: of Adin Ballou and Martin Luther King and Dorothy Day and Gandhi. And indeed of Jesus, who claimed Isaiah again and again as his spiritual ancestor.

Our heroes resemble Isaiah in this. In life and death, they are alternately hated and feared, loved and celebrated. Thus a familiar tradition, implying the rejection of his own people, has Isaiah martyred at the end.

Turn, turn, turn. Isaiah is a very whirling dervish of a new order. He turns and turns, in the flames of vision; turns himself and others to the God of peace, away from the bloody cliché of war. And when his dance is over, he falls dead, in perfect trust in God. In life and death, in rhythms of resistance and submission, Isaiah enters and becomes his own vision.

Swords into plowshares. It seems remarkable, a proclamation both simple and audacious, and all in the teeth of contrary evidence. Isaiah and his contemporary Micah echoed the same image of transformation. Each spoke, historians tell us, in a time of whetted swords and rusted plowshares, a time of immense violence and social conflict and neglect of the poor. No plowshares worked the fields, or very few. Little attention to the turning up of the soil, the nourishing of the people, the lives of children. Much attention to the arming of nations; to swords, their forging, multiplying, whetting.

And in consequence of the social and military crimes, Isaiah saw something else: false worship. God could not be honored while the poor were dishonored. There could be no simultaneous sword making and true worship, anymore than there could be a balancing off of swords and plows, of guns and butter. One could not be violent and nonviolent together, anymore than one could be worshipful and blasphemous together.

Isaiah sensed it. The soul is not built upon such divisions. Neither is the community. In its debased balancing act of moral contradictions, the nation could only bring itself and others to ruin, betrayal, flight from sanity.

Isaiah is, among other things, an acute psychologist. Again and again, he sees the nightmarish schizophrenia of soul and body politic that follows on the attempt to unite essential contradictions, to make of war a virtuous cover for arrogance, avarice, and conquest.

Against the filthy tide, he commended sanity and good sense. Only when the sword took another form could healing occur. Once the plowshare was busy, the neglected earth would grow fruitful again. When structures of injustice and avarice were transformed, something of momentous public consequence would follow. There would be no more poor because there were no more rich.

In so speaking, Isaiah flew in the face of something commonly understood as the facts, or realism, or big power diplomacy, or a slavish judiciary, or just war theory, or the curious game know as "interim ethic." He spoke as one who had better access than the conniving or compromising wisdom of the world. He spoke in consequence of a piercing intuition of history, of those who were its true makers and breakers.

These were, to put matters bluntly, neither kings nor pharaohs nor judges nor commissars nor juntas nor shahs nor presidents nor their armies or chariots or horses. Not their bunkers or laboratories or their nukes.

Those who made history pursued a far different task. They broke swords. Those who made history made plowshares.

Once the swords were rusty and the plowshares busy, we had an apt symbol for the conversion of society, its structures, attitudes, politics, priorities. No useless chatter about "reform," a kind of luxurious berth on a *Titanic*. No, men and women must bend the instruments of death, structures of injustice, into a new form, a form in accord with the holy, which is to say, the fully human.

What new form? A plowshare was primordial, useful, appropriate to hand and earth. It was apt for the works of life, and the Giver of life. The image turned the blade aside, the old lethal stereotype of the settler sword; the sword that settles matters, once and for all.

The plow was in harmony with the neglected and despised human, as with the neglected and despised earth. No one need be ashamed to put hand to the plow, that modest and appropriate instrument. But those who wielded the sword must be ashamed indeed, for they lost, first of all, their own humanity, in making a brother an enemy, and of the enemy, a corpse.

Word for word, we eight friends studied Isaiah in that summer of 1980. We knew we had come on our image.

We were intrigued by the verb of the text: "to beat, to refashion, to re-shape, to forge." It was a word freighted with action. It implied effort, cost, mental and physical drive. No miracle or magic are supposed. No act of God intervenes. Nothing happens as long as we humans are un-concerned, cowardly, blunted in conscience, selfish, seduced by national myth, deaf to human suffering, politically naïve or neutral, obsessed with law and order and money and security. No act of God intervenes, as long as believers regard themselves as citizens of a state first, and be-lievers second, or third, or last of all (which perhaps puts matters more honestly).

Hands, heart, courage, patience, peaceableness—all are presumed. Short of these, the sword remains the master and mastering image, the enslaving image of life in this world. Short of these, no sword in history has ever changed form or function. No nation in history has seriously disarmed, by edict of the armed. Few nuclear weapons, since Los Alamos designed the bomb named Fat Man to fall on Hiroshima—only a few of these have been dismantled by nuclear nations. And more, and worse, are being built.

Indeed the weaponry breeds outlandish illusion, perennially dusted off by political charlatans. The weapons make their believers "drunk, reeling in their vomit," to use the words of Isaiah. They weave a tale of a benign superstate, arming with reluctance, to a minimal degree only, with due regard for the lives of noncombatants, against implacable outsiders, for a time of crisis only. Thereupon, the crisis past or resolved, this entity resumes its tranquil way in the world.

Thus the illusion.

Isaiah is lucid. Swords beget not plowshares, but more swords. Nukes beget not disarmament, nor even "arms control" (those words signi-fying very little). Nukes beget nukes. Nuke beget star wars. This is a nuclear law. Terror, a more honest word than deterrence, but the same thing, is the iron destiny of the world, and of the peoples thereof.

In brief then, the supremely practical vision of Isaiah, which our times make ever more urgent, is a call to rebirth of spirit and practice, to renewal of the skills of the human.

Is the call issued in an inhuman time? No matter. Issue it anyway.

The renewal includes in the nature of things, such neglected virtues as compassion and justice toward the needy, the outcast and victim-ized. And above all, and first of all, "Don't kill. Have no part in killing, either enemy or criminal or the aged or the disabled or the unborn." Everything depends on this.

On September 9, 1980, disarmed by Isaiah, carrying small household hammers and vials of our own blood, eight good friends strode in G.E.'s squat, cost-efficient anonymous factory in King of Prussia, Pennsylvania. The factory was the matrix of the Mark 12A, a first-strike "reentry vehicle" deployed currently on Minuteman 3, and arming the Trident fleet, the MX, the warships. The time was approximately 8:50 a.m. The shifts of workers were changing. We easily slipped by a "security" notable for its laxity. We went unerringly toward a huge room whose entrance sign read "nondestructible testing." We found before us the nose cones and components, and began their conversion. And perhaps our own as well.

Hammers and blood. The blood, we thought, was a reminder of our common life, our common destiny, the bloodline that joins us to one another, for good or ill. The blood, as Exodus reminds us, is a sign of life, and therefore of the Lifegiver, and therefore sacred. A sign also of covenant, a common understanding, that the blood of Christ, once given, forbids all shedding of blood. "This is the new covenant in My blood, given for you." A gift, a wellspring of justice and peace. No more genocide in our name, no suicide and murder by Mark 12A, Trident, MX, Cruise.

The rest is a kind of history. We had agreed that if stopped short of our purpose, we would simply drop the hammers, pour our blood around, form a circle of prayer, and wait for the consequence, which as we knew, is never slow to arrive.

But we went (I believe we were led) against all expectation, straight as unbroken arrows, to our quarry. I speak, I believe, for the others also. We were led there in spite of our second thoughts, our fears, fears of injury, fear of consequence. We were led almost in spite of ourselves.

We walked unhindered into a "high security" setting. There was no security worth the word. That was simply the fact; no security surrounding the weapons. And it continued to be the fact in over ninety Plowshares that have followed our own, in our country, Germany, Australia, Scotland, England and Ireland. No one to this day has been injured. And this in spite of warnings in many of these plague spots that "lethal force is decreed" against intruders such as ourselves. One cannot but reflect that the myth that "the weapons are secure" is matched by the myth that "the weapons supply security."

In both myths, I suggest that the controlling factor is fear. Fear that keeps us in place, in lockstep. We learned this on that morning. Neither guards nor dogs nor hoses nor guns confronted us. But the fear that such dangers lurked in the building was almost as paralyzing as the dangers themselves. The dangers were nonexistent, as it turned out. Fear of the dangers could be mastered, we discovered, only by walking — with or without the fear. But walking.

Indeed the weapons are a monstrous monument to fear, as it moves both within the soul, and outward, to make of the nuclear nations, lethal camps, socialized death rows. And makes of people, hopeless and baffled victims.

Fear, nihilism, despair, anomie, and then the weapons that curse the human venture and lay their indelible stigma on our lives, a stigma of fear, nihilism, despair, anomie.

The weapons are a kind of demonic anti-sacrament, a sign of a mystery, of the sin that gives up on life. Despair of sisters and brothers, of human variety and beauty, of contesting forms of organizing societies. Most grievously of all, despair of the possibility of peacefully settling human differences.

The logic of hope, we thought, runs counter. What has been ill made, immorally made, illegitimately made, secretly made — made without accountability or public debate or plain horse sense — this can be unmade.

This too we learned on that day. As we started a long trek down a corridor that seemed like a veritable last mile for humanity, we believed then, shakily, and our faith grew less shaky with every step we took.

And then, in sight of the horrid weapons, faith exploded into an epiphany. We had dared look Medusa in the face, and behold! We were not turned to stone. We raised our hammers, and the sound was like the knell of the Kingdom come. We were putting death to death.

Say it again. We believe a mysterious providence accompanied us into that antiseptic charnel house, that nuclear Auschwitz. We believe that same Providence led us to the deadly bric-a-brac, offered us ten or twelve minutes of noninterference, guided our hands and arms, protected us from injury.

We had accomplished something, the first act of nuclear disarmament in thirty-five years.

Even while we hammered away, a knot of workers stood by, transfixed, aghast. The plant manager arrived, to blurt out the old canard, also repeated by the then secretary of war at the Pentagon, "That's no way to get peace!"

And later, plant security, local police. The FBI, nonplussed at our timing and precision, asked fretfully, "How did they know where to go? They couldn't have done this without a leak!" Our agreement couldn't be more profound. We were led in that place of moral incoherence and blindness straight to the heart of darkness. And there, perhaps, were enabled to strike a small light.

The official aftermath was roughly predictable. Hot wires to Washington and G.E. headquarters, illegal maneuvers, FBI prowling about, worried paper shuffling. We heard all day from our holding cells the frantic ringing of phones. We endured equably, as the down payment on our crime, eleven hours of enforced lockup and fasting. And then toward evening, finally, an arraignment and a swollen vindictive indictment. Thirteen charges, no bail. Deterrence indeed!

We finally came to trial in the winter of 1981. Many offers of reduced sentence, or no sentence at all, had been set floating about, if only we would plead guilty. Such goodies we saw as seldom sway before felonious eyes. Ample time in court to say our say to very hearts' content. No jail time, no fines, no parole. Plead guilty, walk free.

Indeed our brains reeled at the contradictions implied in the proffer. How to plead guilty to nonviolent activity, on behalf of children, the future, the ecology, the plowshare that opens and releases life?

Thank you but no thank you. We were tried finally, in Norristown, Pennsylvania, a locale whose brand of justice would recall rural Mississippi in the late nineteenth century.

We defended ourselves, perhaps with more passion than prudence. At sentencing, our judge, quite beside himself after two weeks' exposure to our unchecked spirits, declared his regret "at not being able to send you all to a Siberian prison camp or a Puerto Rican leper colony."

I was unfamiliar with the first alternative. But I had worked and lived briefly with lepers in Hawaii. Upon receiving news of this vindictive racism, a group of lepers wrote the judge, inviting him to "visit us, and perhaps yourself be healed."

Constrained by law to a less draconian course, this juridical wonder then sentenced us variously to two to ten years. The appeal began.

The foregoing treats clumsily of our religious beliefs, how these might be thought to impinge on our public conduct, with respect to the law and its claim. I should like also to refer to our culture or secular history as U.S. citizens. This history too is writ large on our souls.

We see ourselves as Christian first of all, but not to the exclusion of all. Our guide in this matter of a double strain of ancestry is the apostle Paul, among others. He speaks of the respect for "whatever is good, whatever noble, whatever just." Indeed, Americans to the bone. (I dare speak here for the other defendants, for those in prison tonight, for my brother Phil and my sister-in-law Elizabeth, for the Douglasses, Ellsbergs, Dellingers, and so many other noble unhousebroken spirits.)

We see ourselves as conservatives. We love our country and its people. Root and branch, for good and ill, weal and woe, we belong here. We take to ourselves a history of heroes and martyrs, civil libertarians, cross-grained writers and solitaries and pamphleteers, town criers, tea party tosspots, stamp act resisters, seditious printers of broadsheets, poets, myth makers, chroniclers.

Also and of course, native Americans, slaves, indentured servants, artisans, radical farmers, multitudes of women, labor organizers, students, people of the cloth, political prisoners, philosophers. All those who from the start saw, dimly or ecstatically, something new. And declared it, pursued it, embodied it, dared be imprisoned for it or die for it. Taxation without representation is tyranny! Don't tread on me! Don't mourn, organize! Bread yes, but roses too!

We see ourselves in this bloodline. It is a line, it goes without saying, that prefers to give its blood rather than shed blood. We prefer, it goes without saying, such preference.

Thus perhaps we offer an illustration of our claim, to be conservatives. In such times as we endure, we see the good sense of such a claim. We claim, clumsily, to be conserving innocent blood. And to that degree, conservative. Those who save lives.

Obviously, we are not in the camp of Tories or Reaganites or Clintonites or Bushites. But something like this: We are modest custodians of a tradition that honors life and defends the wretched of the earth. And since all of us stand at the edge of the nuclear precipice, and to that degree all are defenseless and victimized—to that degree we must defend all the living.

We tried to say something of this on the fateful morning in 1980, and at the trial, and at our sentencing. This is from our statement; on this, we rest our case:

We commit civil disobedience at General Electric because this genocidal entity is the fifth leading producer of weaponry in the U.S. To maintain this position, G.E. drains three million dollars each day from the public treasury, an enormous larceny against the poor.

We wish also to challenge the lethal lie spun by G.E. through its motto, "We bring good things to life." As manufacturer of the Mark 12A reentry vehicle, G.E. actually prepares to bring all things to death. Through the Mark 12A, the threat of first-strike nuclear war grows more imminent. Thus G.E. advances the possible destruction of millions of innocent lives.

In confronting G.E., we choose to obey God's law of life, rather than a corporate summons to death. Our beating of swords into plowshares today is a way to enflesh this biblical call. In our action we draw on a deep-rooted faith in Christ, who changed the course of history through his willingness to suffer rather than to kill. We are filled with hope for our world and for our children as we join this act of resistance.

3

In Better Hands Than Our Judges'

Statement at the sentencing of the Plowshares Eight,
Norristown, Pennsylvania, April 10, 1990

⌇

DEAR FRIENDS (including Your Honor, Ms. Prosecutor), so many who have gathered from near and far; our honored lawyer friends; also our dear ones already in prison, Karl, Anne, Elmer, all here with us; also Helen, Ladon, Jerry, Greg, Larry, and Jean. The very summoning of your names confers courage and steadfastness this day.

Indeed such a day invites and sharpens memories. In this court we were convicted a long decade ago of various charges. The charges, it was clear, were a juridical effort to name not so much our crimes as ourselves. (One is tempted to say in light of the biblical events commemorated this Holy Week, the charges were attempts not only to name, but to nail us.)

I urge you to view with alarm, therefore, the felonious faces you see before you this day. The defendants, according to this court, are breakers and enterers, conspirators, destroyers, worse and worse and so on and so on. God preserve General Electric and this honorable court from such as ourselves!

When one thinks of it, this naming and nailing of people has been going on at a great rate in our lifetime. One thinks of the naming of Nelson Mandela by the South African state some twenty-six years ago. He was called dangerous, violent, a conspirator plotting the overthrow of law and order. One thinks of the repeated naming and nailing of Vaclav Havel by the Czechoslovakian state over the years. He was called disruptive, an enemy of the state, a hooligan. One thinks of noble Sakharov and his long ordeal, condemned and vilified as traitor to the state.

One thinks inevitably this week of another naming and nailing. It occurred in a court very like this, in the first century of our era. The Accused was hauled in, successive judges had at Him, as did the tempestuous crowd. He was named repeatedly, scornfully by the Roman state and its satellite religionists and thugs: would-be destroyer of temple property, withholder of tribute money, blasphemer, pretender to a lost throne. The charges were sharp as nails. The names attached to Him quite literally held firm. He was convicted and capitally disposed of.

And yet, and yet. Even though the law has claimed so often to speak the last word concerning the accused, to name the final name, to drive the nails deep—yet some event down the road of time, an intervention, a change of heart, a change of climate, these keep intruding. A far different word is heard. It slowly attaches itself to such as Mandela, Havel, Sakharov, Jesus, and countless other noble criminals. This seems to be a constant of history, whether in our lifetime or long before.

No court in fact seems able to speak a last word or to drive a final nail, even in a coffin. The names fade and fall to rot in the rude weathers of time. The nails rust and spring apart. Which is to say, justice, in contrast to the law, tends to get heard eventually, to forge new names on behalf of the vilified, to raise the very dead.

I have often thought of the strange figure named "Justice" that one encounters everywhere in our world. The eyes of this woman are blindfolded. She bears a scales in hand, as though, prevented from seeing the world, she still could weigh, estimate rightly, set wrongs right.

She also bears a sword, for she is vowed to truth and consequence.

Blind justice. The image, I think, conveys a great irony. She is blind, one thinks, in order that justice may not be swamped by the passing show, by the passions and storms that shake the earth we walk. Justice is blind in order that justice may see, longer and deeper and within and beyond the passion and prejudice of the hour.

She is blind for another reason as well: in order that justice may hear more acutely, as the blind often do; may hearken to the voices of the ancestors and the unborn, the inarticulate and victimized and scorned. She must hear what others are deaf to, as she must see what others are blind to.

And Justice holds in hand a scales; in order that she may touch and sift and weigh (and often find wanting) the law of the land (the lawlessness of nuclear weapons, let us say, the lawlessness of G.E.); that she may judge the tyrannical burden of that law, as it weighs heavy on our conscience, on our courts, on our churches, on our poor; as under that burden the world itself falls to knee in fear of nuclear Armageddon.

That blindfolded Justice! How deeply the vision penetrates, how nicely she sorts out and balances innocence and guilt, crime and consequence. How, contrary to expectation, special interest, greed and fear and folly, Justice cries aloud — for Justice. And in consequence, justice at last! Vile verdicts are reversed, vilifying names are renounced, murderous nails are loosened!

Given patience and steadfastness in the accused, this comes to pass. Justice is attained. Sometimes in one's own lifetime, sometimes after.

Thus Mandela becomes an only hope of a tormented and degraded society. Havel is elected president of his country. Sakharov is rehabilitated in death.

And the nails spring from the hands of the mysterious victim of Good Friday.

On a larger stage, our own lifetime, the murdered Jesuits, the murdered women of El Salvador are invoked and honored, the children dead in a bloody swath from Bethlehem to Soweto, rise and sing. Our cloud of witnesses, witnesses for the defense!

Such are the outcomes, eventual and chancy and altogether wondrous, wrought by Justice. Such also are the momentous reversals suffered by lawless law and disordered order.

Such reversals we note and rejoice in. How the vile names come unstuck and the murderous nails fall to rust, how the law is struck blind, how blind Justice penetrates the heart of truth and, in God's good time, rights the wrong!

This, April 10, 1990, is the day of the law. It is by no means to be thought the day of justice.

And yet we have a slight implication of justice, even today, even in this town. G.E. is also in the dock; not for its great crimes, for its lesser crimes. For crimes of greed, not for crimes of war. For domestic crimes, petty crimes, in contrast to its monstrous crimes in prospect and preparation.

This is the best the law can muster, the feeble picayune best. But in the great matters before this court, the law is helpless; it is in collusion with General Electric, and acts as the legal cover of a momentous criminal entity.

Let this be said. The judgment rendered out today, the judgment meted out to G.E. and to the Plowshares Eight, these are in better hands than ours, better hands than our judges'. In the hands, let us pray, of a holy Defendant once reviled and misnamed in an earthly court, named and finally nailed in infamy.

His wounds, we believe, are healed, and glorious. And His name is above every name, every earthly power and dominion — including the power and dominion of this court, or of any earthly court.

It is to Him, finally, we proffer our argument. The argument goes this way.

If the children of the world will be accounted safer for our imprisonment, so be it. We go in a good spirit.

If the earth will be accounted free of nuclear illness and insult for our imprisonment, so be it. We go in a good spirit.

If first-strike weaponry is to be judged within the law, and we outside the law, so be it. We go to prison in a good spirit.

4

Hiroshima and the Church
of the Blind Gods

IT WAS A DAY to stop the heart in its tracks.

The president was jubilant; the generals exulted. Later, in a more serious mood, Truman summed things up with laconic exactness: "We had the Bomb and we used it."

August 6, 1945. The day we dropped the atomic bomb on Hiroshima. Three days later, we dropped a second bomb on Nagasaki.

What Truman did not see, what very few saw except a number of pacifists, was that the humanity, the self-understanding of Americans, had undergone a sea change. The Bomb exploded in Japan, but the fallout is here. Today, it continues to fall.

The effects were not immediately apparent. Japan surrendered. America gave a great collective sigh of relief, the G.I.s came home, cold war replaced hot, Russia was contained, the churches sang a muted "Te Deum."

But a shadow lay over the sun. What was learned could not be unlearned. This was sterner than a law of nature; it was a law of conscience. We had stolen fire, and the payment came due—a Promethean wildfire.

Who could have told on that August day when the guns went silent, when a living city joined the cities of the dead, who could have known what a monstrous future we had hatched? The president rejoiced. We had traded lives, theirs for ours, and won. We had delivered the Russians an exemplary lesson. The future belonged to us.

The Bomb had proven itself; it was the very apotheosis of political savvy. It was manifest proof of destiny, even of divine favor, of the unassailable superiority of Western technique. It reminded God of something: that we were god-like—not God's rivals, but God's guardians in the world.

Thus from the beginning, a religious aura attached itself to the Bomb, and lingered there. A serious case could be made for the assertion that on Hiroshima day, the bomb gained a capital letter and the biblical God lost one.

It is desperately important today that we look the reality of nuclear war courageously in the face, that we announce one to another what we have seen there. Even if the sight turns us to stone—the sight not only of apocalyptic horrors, but also the sight of ourselves—a people, who seriously, with forethought, are preparing their own demise.

A grinning irony, a kind of wolfish death's head looks back at us. At the moment when we declare ourselves masters of fate, Merlins who hold the key to the Arcanum of the universe—at the moment our doom gathers.

Masters of fate? Merlins? We are immodest. The universe will cut us down.

The first fruits of our skill and overskill, the people of Hiroshima are long dead. A few still cling to the tree of life, scarred and ailing. But there will be also a second harvest as a greater storm shakes that tree. We shall live to feel it.

One has only to hear the latest scares conjured by the Pentagon, to witness the scrambling of politicos scoring points at death factories and weapons fairs.

Americans are now capable of vaporizing every living being on earth some seventeen times over; our opposite number can dispose of every one of us some eight times over. Enough? Will the generals and their henchmen in the labs and think tanks and Congress declare a standoff, hang up their bombs and go fishing? Like hell they will.

All these decades after Hiroshima, we have by no means renounced that crime. We are fervently preparing to destroy more than a distant city. The nuclear stakes have risen. We are now preparing simply to end the world.

We are proceeding on this mad course with a persistence, skill, investment of resources, income, and scientific talent incomparably greater than is expended on housing or schooling or health or food or all of these taken together. The dollar goes where death goes, and in the megadeath industry of death, the dollar goes far indeed.

The changes in Americans since Hiroshima, changes inevitable in peoples East or West, will gird us for all-out nuclear war, for such changes are above all a spiritual phenomenon. To be understood, they exact of us a painful self-questioning.

What is our responsibility toward the innocent, the children, the unborn? What sort of world do we want (if indeed we want a world at all) for ourselves and for them? Finally, perhaps most austerely, what do we believe in, what does our God look like?

At Hiroshima, the nuclear blade entered our very souls. All these years later, we lead the world in weapons manufacturing and sales. It could be said the weapons lead us. The weapons lead our leaders. The weapons grow wise and oracular. They dictate foreign policy and domestic spending.

Our true sanctuaries and synagogues are now the bunkers and Trident bases and Strategic Air Command fields. In them, the high priests of our destiny assemble: the money moguls, the political shamans, the generals incanting exorcisms against our enemies. They surround their idol, the Bomb. They invoke a tribal god-on-our-side. They pour the bowls of blood—the blood of the poor, of soldiers, of civilians, of women and children, of the ill, the aged.

They pour the blood of the unborn. They pour healthy blood and tainted; a great and growing flood of the latter pours out—cancerous blood, blood of the fallout.

And of money tribute, no end. Billions upon billions. Those gods, faceless, impervious, steely—their appetite is that of a thousand Neros. They will have the world raped and polluted and dumped at their feet.

Thus goes the liturgy in the caves. The sponsor of such worship is the "Church of the Blind Gods," whose worship has spread with the virulence of a plague. Faith in the Bomb has absorbed other faiths, silenced them, inducted them, shamed them with its success in the world, its adherents under every sun, its command over the best and brightest; finally with its ineffable slogans: "War Is Peace," "Duplicity Is Truth," "Secrecy Is Candor," "Terror Is Peace," "Law Is Order."

The Church of the Blind Gods! It is aggressively ecumenical; its icons, drawn from every nation and religion, gleam in the caves and bunkers. There, the faithful may invoke Jesus-with-the-Bomb, Luther-with-the-Bomb, Calvin-with-the-Bomb, Penn-with-the-Bomb. In the old images of the saints and martyrs, the instruments of their death were held in hand.

But the Bomb has lent them a sterner visage. They stand there in the darkness, aggressive, steely. Their eyes follow you like a war poster: "The Blind Gods Want You!"

Whom the Blind Gods want, they get. Especially the blind.

As we remember the dead of Hiroshima and Nagasaki, we pledge, "Rest in peace. The Crime will never be repeated." We give our lives for that pledge.

5

The Cause Is the Heart's Beat

1999—SIXTY YEARS A JESUIT

A huge percussion
brought back and back;

memory. As though
the heart of things

beat on, despite.

   I wish I knew
where that sound wends its way.

I don't. The drummer boy
mum, muffled, won't tell.

He goes, all said,
spellbound.
   (Or can't).

Like the next beat,
he walks in and out of.

Hear it;
   Yet, yet to be.

OUR DRUMMER BOY doesn't know, but his rhythm is one with the beat of "the heart of things." The heart beats on, despite all.

I like that. It keeps a needful obscurity.

In my neighborhood in New York City dwells a small community of Japanese Buddhist nuns and monks. On the anniversary of the Hiroshima bombing, they walk down Broadway, silent, banging their drum. From the aerie where I dwell, it sounds as though they caught the rhythm of "the heart of things," and were echoing them.

30

The sound, I take it, is subversive. Muffled, steady, this is the message of the beat: You artificers of death, take note, Hiroshima lives. No silencing the heart of things, even with an atomic bullet.

These same Buddhists have attended several of our courtroom scenes in the past twenty years. One Plowshares trial in Portland, Maine, still sounds in memory — a muffled beat of drums in the square outside the courthouse.

To the prosecutor of the Plowshares defendants, the sound was baffling, outrageous. Distracted from her fervent quest of punishment, she arose to demand that the judge order the drums silenced or the drummers punished or — something. Anything to quell that persistent, muffled, gentle thrumm.

Hizzoner, a character out of Grand Guignol, unexpectedly demurred. The drums, he pronounced, were a form of free speech, albeit unusual. They could continue.

So they did, that gentle intrusion, the sound of the heart of things, the truth of things. Thrumm thrumm . . . If sounds were bees above a poisoned flower, veering away in an instinctive daring arc — that would be it.

Thrumm thrumm . . . questioning the rancor, the untruth, the coverup, the trial and travesty. The wrong parties accused and silenced and criminalized, the "justice system" in servitude to artificers of death and their poisoned flowers of violence.

The drumbeat . . . Beware, beware!

The heart of things! During the 1980s and 1990s, the quest brought my brother Philip and me to Europe and nuclear weapons brought us to courts and jails, brought him to prison repeatedly.

In 1980, we undertook the first Plowshares action. By the year 2000, some sixty-five of these had taken place in the United States, Germany, Scandinavia, Australia, England, Scotland, and Ireland.

In 1981, eight of us were sentenced to three to ten years for our act of antinuclear effrontery. The appeal dragged on for a decade. Finally in 1990, we were summoned for a showdown. Unexpectedly, the judge listened attentively to our friends and ourselves, our pleas based on conscience and faith, on international law and the "argument from necessity." The judge then sought the view of the current prosecutor. She declared that "the state of Pennsylvania has no current interest in this matter."

Mirabile! The judge confessed that "I have undergone a change of heart. I came into court this morning determined to send the defendants to prison. But enough is enough. They are free, with time already served."

In the course of the proceedings, I noted an unusual exchange. The prosecutor passed a book to Ramsey Clark, then to myself, with a request that I autograph it. The book was my first collection of poems, *Time without Number.* She had won it as a prize in her college years.

A small miracle, I thought.

For sure, there aren't any large ones.

> A Chinese ideogram
> shows someone
> standing
> by a word.
>
> Fidelity. Freedom
> consequent
> to the accepted necessity
> of walking
> where words
> lead.
> Wherever.
>
> Hebrew prophets and
> singers also
> struck the theme;
> bodies belong
> where words
> lead,
>
> though the com-
> mon run of exper-
> ience be—
>
> stature
> shrinks as
> words
> inflate.
>
> The synthesis—
> "no matter what" (or
> better) "never
> the less."

For the last twenty-five years I studied and wrote on the Hebrew Bible, publishing studies of the major and minor prophets. Each was the fruit of days of reflection offered across the country, and courses taught at universities.

Revise, sweat, burn midnight oil. There was no end of it. I was pursued by a demon or a fireball. Or writing was an exorcism. I struggled to rid the text of rhetoric, puffing, self-justification, parti pris. How let words, images, events, parables, speak for themselves? It was purgatorial.

Then, an innocent in a bear pit, I opened the historical books — Judges, Samuel, Kings. Degradation met my eyes, chicanery, betrayal, wars of extermination, crimes of high culture, from Saul to David and Solomon and beyond. Ancestors and their shame — and the ever so slight relief offered by colluding court prophets.

And what of the god of kings, this Jawe apt to stir up or mimic the worst instincts of his human clones?

Most commentators offered little or no help.

The prime delinquents among Catholics were the scholars of the Ecole Biblique in Jerusalem. These were a species of cautious taxidermists and diggers. They forbid utterly the rabbinical method of midrash. Safe, sure, and ultimately deadly, the motto of their efforts went something like: "The text is the text is the text."

Dead on the page. It was as though the Christian testament cast no light on the ancient texts; as though, for example, the Sermon on the Mount had never been recorded, old enmities canceled, the powerless and poor and meek declared blessed.

This brand of exegesis allowed for no point of contact or contrast.

I came to think that geography was a clue to the lethal wariness of the method. The biblical scholars in Jerusalem were foreigners, and Christians. They dwelt in a furnace of conflict, cut off from the political realities of the day, the inhuman Palestinian camps, the demolished homes, the detentions and torture. No wonder the scholarship was — safe.

Were there embarrassing likenesses in the text, say between the god who ordered the death of the Egyptian firstborn and the pharaoh who ordered the death of the Hebrew firstborn? Were there nagging contradictions between the god of the prophets and the god served by David and Solomon? Did the morality of the god of jihad differ in any significant way from that of the baals?

Was the god of the Hebrew kings in fact a projection of royal ego, lust, violence? And if this be true, was it not incumbent on believers to deny this deity a capital letter, since the Christian Gospel commended love of enemies, forgiveness, reconciliation, compassion toward the vulnerable—such virtues as are terra incognita to the god of the kings?

In the Jerusalem Bible, such questions never arise. In my ever so humble opinion, they must.

FIVE SENSES OF THE TIMES
WE ENDURE

1.

When I look back, I see

I've spent my life seeing—
under that flat stone—what?
why that star off kilter?

Turn turn, I intoned, and
out of the stone there stood
What-Not in a white garment.

Jacob's ladder descended
(angels holding steady)—

I mounted, and I
saw What

2.

A rabbi intoned on the way;
"What then did you hear?"

"Death knell, birth cry, both
wrung from his throat."

3.

The taste was gruesome and sweet;
first, a prison privy.
They pushed you face down
in the common woe of war,
the shit of conquering heroes.

But then, in a desert place—
honey from a lion's jaw.
I tasted at long last

alleluia!

4.

In no time at all
death, and you're compounded
princeling and jackanapes
with common carrion stench.

Which isn't the point I believe.

Like a bride, her bridal flower
in two tremulous hands,
I carry in memory—
odor of wild roses
wet with Block Island fog.

5.

It was touch and go all the way.
I saw along the way
blur of blood, then closer
a wounded wayfarer—
hands, feet, heart's pocket
rent savagely.

"Touch!" he cried. "And live!"

Mirror mirror—
him I saw, and myself
rent. And in went.

Since the mid-1970s, I have lived in a Jesuit community in upper Manhattan. Over the years, our members have been graduate students, teachers, counselors, social workers, hospital chaplains, pastors, a lawyer for civil rights cases, a masseur, and the director of an international peace organization, the Fellowship of Reconciliation.

Until recently, we counted in our midst four convicted felons for peace who had risked prison for disarmament, a number unmatched in Jesuit communities across the world. Of this felonious record, need it be added, we are inordinately proud.

Until recently our dwelling was a rather gone-at-the-heels relic of WWI vintage. When we moved in toward the late '60s, the building was half empty, dangerous and drug ridden. The amenities, heat, lights, water, were of ancient vintage and uncertain function. A priest was mugged at knifepoint in the wobbly elevator.

Now, as in Yeats, "all, all is changed." The neighborhood has blossomed with spiffy shops of every kind. The lobby is secured. One encounters well-dressed and well-heeled newcomers, sporting on leashes canines of exotic vintage.

The building has changed hands at least three times since our arrival, each exchange falling to a richer bid and a larger consortium.

The latest, aptly named "The Expansion Group," disdaining compromise, has hailed us in court seeking our removal from the premises. It seems that twenty or so Jesuit priests, whose lease is under the protection of "rent stabilization," are a serious impediment against the megadollars that would accrue, if only we could be evicted.

In the first round of contention, a remarkably able and principled judge ruled that the landlord's case was without merit.

The Expansionists promptly appealed, and within months we were in court once more, this time before three judges. To the date of this writing, the outcome remains unclear.

One matter is sure. Were we to lose the appeal, our community could not remain intact in Manhattan. Current rents are dizzying.

For consolation, we reflect that we are tasting, in small measure, the treatment meted out to the poor in our city—and in every city.

Meantime, we go on with our work and prayer and life together; perturbed to be sure, queasy at times, but at peace.

And so it goes, in this not so new millennium.

The work of peacemaking is more urgent than ever. The nuclear weapons, the wars, the Pentagon budget, the international arms trade, the forces of violence are more hideously pressing than when we began opposing the Vietnam War. America wobbles and feints from crisis to crisis, bombings and lethal sanctions prevailing over good sense or compassion or the will to settle differences peaceably.

Wisdom for my eighth decade would counsel something like this: Nothing you do counts for much.

And the conclusion matters not a whit. Nothing, no sacrifice is in vain; I believe this with all my heart.

Or this wisdom: The closer one's activity relies on a biblical ideal, from Abraham to Jesus, the less one will know of its outcome or result— let alone of the weasel word so dear to the culture—"success."

As the new millennium begins, I am recovering ever so slowly from spinal surgery. If health had permitted, in the winter of 1999 I too would have registered outrage at the American plague of depleted uranium warfare. I would have joined my brother and the Plowshares Four, pouring my blood on the hideous "Warthog" flying battleships in Maryland.

A species of cold comfort descends. Dismayed witnesses as we are of a violent, larcenous, spiritually bankrupt national system, we come to realize that only saints and mystics live humanly.

One does what one can. I teach, lead scripture retreats, write books. And am arrested with regularity by the guardians of law and order, whether at the "School of the Americas" in Fort Benning, Georgia, or in New York City at the infamous war museum, the S.S. *Intrepid,* or the U.S. Mission to the UN.

I believe, with Karl Barth, that "to clasp the hands in prayer is the beginning of an uprising against the disorder of the world."

Of such is the realm of heaven.

> Some stood up once
>   and sat down.
> Some walked a mile
>   and walked away.
>
> Some stood up twice
>   then sat down.
>   I've had it, they said.
>
> Some walked two miles
>   Then walked away.
>   It's too much, they cried.
>
> Some stood and stood and stood.
> They were taken for fools,
> Then were taken for being taken in.
>
> Some walked and walked and walked.
> They walked the earth,
> They walked the waters,
> They walked the air.
>
> Why do you stand? they were asked, and
> Why do you walk?

Because of the children, they said, and
Because of the heart, and
Because of the bread.

Because
The cause

Is the heart's beat
And the children born
And the risen bread.

II

The Way, the Truth, and the Life

You come toward me
prestigious in your wounds,
those frail and speechless bones.

Your credentials:
dying somberly for others.
what a burden—
gratitude, fake and true vows,
crucifixes,
and then the glory gap—
larger than life
begetting less than life,
pieties that strike healthy eyes
blind: believe! believe! Christians
tapping down the street
in harness to their seeing eye god.

Only in solitude
in passing tic of insight
gone as soon as granted—
I see you come toward me
free, free at last.

Can one befriend his God?
The question is inadmissible I know.
Nonetheless a fiery recognition
lights us:
broken by life
making our comeback

6

The Face of Christ

SOME YEARS AGO I stood on an ancient outpost of western Ireland, off County Mayo. It was an island named Caher, or "Saints' Island." Preserved there are several quite remarkable relics, including a monastic ruin, circumscribing an altar of stones.

And scattered across the modest hills like a procession is a series of standing stones. These stones invited attentiveness as I made my way across the green land. The thin slabs, I was told, had been carved by monks and set in place, fronting the harsh climate of the northern seas.

And there the stones stood and withstood for some fourteen centuries.

Each stone is incised with a different symbol; some of great simplicity, others more cunningly carved; runes, Celtic curlicues, spirals interlaced, even a fish or bird.

The tallest of the stones is not very tall, a matter of five feet or so. But it stops one in his tracks. For it bears a curious emblem, different from all the rest. A small medallion, perhaps five inches in diameter—a human face amid all the symbols.

The face of Christ. The first face of Christ, I was told, in Europe. A momentous breakthrough indeed. For the previous five centuries, images of Christ were symbolic, borrowed from nonhuman creation—cross forms, pelicans, dolphins, elegant or rude, carved or painted or set in mosaic.

One wonders why the literal image was so tardy in arriving. Was Christ's humanity too problematic? Or was the manner of his death—excruciating, disgraceful, a capital execution—beyond bearing in permanent form?

Whatever the cause, generations of Christian artists turned to symbols, groping toward, even while distancing from, our central mystery.

One speculates that during those centuries, a question was hovering on the air, gathering force. Granted that the Gospels offered no physical description of the Savior, it remained true that in Christ, God wore a human face. And what was the art, the faith, the community to make

41

of that? Was the accessible Incarnate One to remain inaccessible to art—or accessible only through hints and emblems?

On Saints' Island, a literal finisterre, a land's end which must be thought of also as a new beginning, a source—a handful of anonymous monks took tools in hand. Christ inaccessible? From the promontory they cut and hauled a slab of stone. Then they incised an image both momentous and modest—the face of Christ, the art of Europe.

In regard to this event, I may have heard a memory drawn from folklore rather than from literal fact. There may have existed other, even older images of Christ, of which we know nothing, they having crumbled or been destroyed.

All this may be true, but I find it of small interest. The standing stones of Saints' Island beckon one, not to speculation or art history, but to pondering, to a deep heartfelt pause of breath, to a center all but lost. On a little wind-scoured, uninhabited island, one may for a time cast off the folly and fury, the anomie and despair of the Western adventure in the world.

The power of the place, the images, the trajectory of ruins and crosses! A place of healing, inevitably. To the island each summer comes an aquatic procession of the ill, brought there in curraghs, to touch the ruined altar called the Bed of Saint Patrick.

It was midwinter when we landed, a friend and I. The winds blew and blew, merciless, cleansing. It seemed to me, as I moved about like a sleepwalker, that I and those I love, who stand perilously near the end of things, stood for a time at a place where beginnings are, where new beginnings may yet be possible.

For an hour or so I wandered among the sentinel stones. Then I stood for a long time facing the face of Christ. And I thought of the fate of that crude and astonishing image, how it was multiplied, modified, stolen and borrowed, conjured and defiled, again and again in the hearts and guts and hands of Christians.

Artists and saints and martyrs seized the image for their own. So did scoundrels and conquistadors. Century after century, sometimes secretly and under threat of law, sometimes in rich processions, they bore the image across borders and continents, invoked its power upon causes shameful and holy, upon wars and crusades and pogroms, upon plagues and catastrophes in nature.

In the image of that image, what crimes and follies, what astonishing heroism, what poetry, what visions! They summoned the face in heroic witness, in courts and prisons and places of execution.

Thus the powers of this world, as well as the powerless, seized on this modest icon. Our own, our own! Uprooted from monkish soil, set like a stone sail in a preternatural barque, blown by winds of time far from its planting—the image became the common property and possession of humankind, transformed mightily, jealously. A terrible beauty was born.

Thus we have had, in turn upon bloody turn, the Christ of bosses and barons, of thieves and diplomats and generals, of entrepreneurs and oligarchs. And finally in our own lifetime, a Christ of Armageddon, itching for showdown. A Christ who saves some, we are told, by destroying all.

You do well, I counseled my soul, to pause here, to take in account the unaccountable power of this newborn image, a face just issuing from a womb of stone, all but lost in time, scored and scalded by weathers.

The small medallion, no larger than a hand's palm, is pressed like a stigma on the imagination of the unborn and the dead, on all who perilously and vulnerably walk the gauntlet of the living.

It has come to this, I thought. A face which once signaled the beginning now would seem to signal the onset of the end, or an hour perilously near the end. Set up long ago on a headland by a few peaceable monks, a guerdon, a legacy signifying peace, all, all is changed. The face has become a very Medusa, a Gorgon, a nuclear Chimera.

The gentle face of new beginnings has become a clock face, warning of mere minutes before midnight, the face of the nuclear countdown.

In America that face of Christ, like a brand on the soul, is impressed in fire on the incumbents of the Christian White House, the Christian Pentagon, the nuclear think tanks and bunkers and bases. In such places Christians, as is said, are "doing their thing." Within walking distance of the living, highly qualified scientists and engineers seriously envision the end of the world. Their ideology and weaponry are hyphenated horrors.

And they pursue their crimes, as many among them assert straight-faced, in honor of the face of Christ. The end of the world, they assure us, is a religious undertaking of the religious West. Let the godless take note.

Christians, I reflected, have honored the face in numberless icons, in worship and prayer and vows. We have also, alas, committed unspeakable crimes while invoking that face, have shielded ourselves from consequences behind that face.

And now Christians would obliterate all faces—in virtue of that face. Thus in cold point of fact, we are coldly informed. The end of the world will be a religious act.

Such folly is so near madness, near the end of all art, the end of all life, as to impel us for sweet sanity's sake, back to our beginnings.

I turned away, toward the ruined sanctuary. I saw then something else, something implied powerfully in the setting. The monks of Caher Island, raising their small chapel, did not place the image of Christ within its walls, under its roof. The standing stone was set at distance from the sanctuary, out of doors, facing the sea, exposed to the wild weathers, unprotected, taking its chances against ice and fire, season and century.

Clinging to their inhospitable island like sea birds to a cliff, lost to the world and its bloody ways, seeking in solitude the Spirit of wisdom and self-knowledge—what a healing the monks offered—and offer! Yin and yang, faith and compassion, gathering into one the fragments of soul, fragments of community. They made peace with the warring halves of our humanity, whose divisions and wounds are our present travail.

Fourteen centuries later, the monks may even have worked such healing for me.

For us? We must resist with all our powers the apocalypticism that would make of gentle Christ the warrior of a mad Christian star war.

7

The "I Am" Sayings of Jesus

In Christ, God Imagines God

THERE IS MORE than one way of identifying ourselves.

"Say something of yourself, your name, what you do, why you came, what you hope for," is a suggestion to get a retreat under way. Thus we draw closer to one another.

It is also a way of self-understanding. We ask ourselves, we ask one another, "Why are we here?" Normally we respond by describing our family, our work, our community, our faith. Then we ask why we come to this place. And the answers engage our hearts, our hopes.

The answers also imply a nascent confidence in one another, a bond already formed or forming. In one way or another we say or imply that being in this place, with one another, for a time, is an excellent, indeed crucial way of surviving the world.

There is a subtler way of doing something like this. It is not so much naming ourselves, our hopes, as imagining ourselves, our hopes. Often it is done with body language, wordlessly, a dance, a song, a poem. There is a tradition in the church of *les grands silencieuses*. All their long lives, hermits, Trappists, Carthusians, Carmelites, let their prayers, prostrations, fasts, solitude, speak for them, say who they are.

When speech is used, the most powerful (and highest) clue to "who I am" is imagery, metaphor, a poem. This is one way of understanding certain passages of John's Gospel. In a series of declarations, many of them metaphors, Jesus describes himself: "I am the bread of life," "I am the light of the world," "I am the door," "I am the good shepherd," "I am the resurrection," "I am the way, the truth and the life," "I am the vine."

The images imply a profound communion between spirit and visible creation. In one image the communion is celebrated between aspects of earth's creation and spirit (I am the way, I am the vine). In another, between an artifact of one's hands and spirit (I am the door), or between a human occupation and spirit (I am the good shepherd). We all but conclude that spirit can only be imagined—and we are right!

Or again we might conclude that every humble or human thing is apt to lead beyond itself, or within itself—to spirit.

In this reflection we mention only in passing the incendiary implication of Jesus borrowing a phrase like "I am," unadorned, naked. Thus he takes to himself four times in the Gospel of John (8:24, 28, 58; 13:19) the divine Name announced to Moses (Exod. 3:14). He claims for himself the faith of the people of covenant. The daring words have struck fire, and not by any means a friendly one.

We have what seem to be two steps in Jesus' self-revelation. First, the naked phrase of the Jewish testament is taken to himself, quoted as true of himself. And as if this were not daring enough, we have something more. Second, the unimaginable Jawe becomes subject of an imaginative addition: God is not simply "I am who Am." We are offered a series of images, a series of imaginative approaches to the mystery.

And this is sublimely fitting, if one pays heed to the claim "I am" as pressing upon us. For according to the claim, Jawe, the God who is One, is now incarnate in this world. In Christ, God knows God, a knowledge infinitely beyond the human—and yet now announced by a human.

In other words, in Christ, God imagines God.

We are right also in venturing that poetry is not necessary; prose is necessary. Which is to say, prose is an instrument of efficiency. It belongs to the "things which are seen." Prose is useful, moves things, gives orders, is logical, serves for argument, settles conflicts or makes war, is privy to special interests, makes money, passes information and the rest.

Poetry on the other hand, is unnecessary in the sense that God is unnecessary. Poetry is useless in the sense that God is useless. Which is to say, God and poetry are not part of the kingdom of necessity, of a world of law and order (of lawlessness and disorder) and sin and war and greed we name "the Fall."

Merely naming that world is not enough. It leaves us in the same world, the same plight, fallen amid the ruins. For we cannot name a prelapsarian world and still be true to our world. Events have caught up with our history. The first parents dwelt in a garden, but we are in another world.

The poetry of John does something more than naming that world. It imagines a Fallen world, and thus is liberated from its malice. Thus the "Word," the "logos," "came among us" who are the Fallen. He entered not an Eden, but a world of sin and death. Of which matters He was destined to learn much, most of it awful, wrought in His own flesh.

It was a sorry drama that ensued, a tragedy of whose end we know something. "His own did not receive him."

To say "I am the way" is to say "I am the way out. Come, imagine a way out. Then put foot on it."

To say "I am the truth" is to say "I am not the untruth. Come speak the truth."

To say "I am the life" is to say "I have risen from death. Come, don't get used to death, don't inflict death, get up, resist death, rise from death."

To say "I am the light of the world" is a way of saying "People lose it, lose their bearings, their direction, lose their humanity. I have struck a light. Come, light your mind and heart from mine."

In a sense, the primal command to "name all things" was badly understood, partially taken. Naming things, in the sense of a mere catalogue, devoid of affection or connection, ends in this: We consume instead of eating. That was the first sin, we are told. The first parents did not imagine creation, they only named it. They could not imagine boundaries as well as freedom, taboos as well as trees.

I hope all the preceding is not an interminable detour round a rather simple point.

In the statements beginning "I am . . . ," Jesus does not so much name Himself as imagine Himself. In doing so, he gathers us in, takes us along; sometimes implicitly, sometimes by name. He takes us far, farther perhaps than we would be willing to go on our own, far into nature, into the unknown.

Let us call it a Zen voyage, perilous, exhilarating, ironic. What would it be like, He implies, to live in a shepherd's skin or (more properly) in the skin of "the good shepherd"? What would be the actions of such a good pastor? What would be the outcome of tenderness and solicitude in such days as we endure, when our charges are not sheep but children, the innocent, the victimized, the noncombatants, women, the aged, the refugees—from El Salvador and Bosnia to Nicaragua and Guatemala to Afghanistan and Iraq—all the endangered?

What would it be like to be "the branches of a vine"—when the weathers of the world are as they are, sharp, unpromising, assaulting, all against fruitfulness, capacity, and love?

What would it be like to be a light, when darkness covers the earth?

Christ speaks so confidently "I am . . . ," rather than, "I look like . . . ," or "I resemble." Can He speak this way because, in fact, He has done something of this sort, plunged to this depth of imagery, so that the images proceed from a life lived, rather than from a Godly superiority, over our benighted selves? Because perhaps He has taken to Himself the torment and wounds of this world, and in so doing, imagined a better, and in so imagining, has created a better world?

And more; in not one of His statements or images does Jesus name Himself as one member of a species. There is a crucial, though subtle matter here.

Which is to say, "I am not just any vine in a vineyard, 'a' vine, one or another among many. No, I am *the* vine." Which is to say, "I am all vines, I am the vine of all times and places; the Alpha and Omega vine."

"Is this impossible? Only to prose, to logic, to necessity, to the Fall, the nonimagination. To these, it may be impossible, but it is not beyond imagining, at least my imagining. For I am the—mythic vine."

"The mythic vine." Which is to say something quite simple. There is a vine about which stories are told. The soil of this vine is the imagination of people. There gathers about the image all sorts of implications, as generations come and go, telling once more to children, the story of "a" vine which in the telling and retelling has became "the" vine.

In time, the vine became the people themselves. According to Isaiah and Jeremiah, they were one vine, they were an entire vineyard, kept by Jawe. They produced well at one time, at another they fell to ruin and decay. But no matter weal and woe (and these were all part of the story), the image was like a deep root. It went to the heart of the world, it could not be uprooted.

There were other implications too. The harvest time, the fruit of the vine became the symbol of the rejoicing of the last days. It was the cup of blessing, the fruit that rejoiced the spirit.

By the time of Jesus, to say "I am the vine" is a stark claim indeed. It amounts to this: that the speaker is the protagonist of a myth. He has placed himself at center stage in the tribal story.

(Wallace Stevens ends a poem with a phrase: "the the." A poem is about "the." I used a phrase in a poem, comparing a poet to "an old woman's fingers in a flea market." Which is to say, a poem concerns "thisness," "thatness," the pointed finger, choice, the ah! I've got it!)

The images of the "the" (vine, way, shepherd, etc.) are not statements of orthodoxy but of inclusion. Which is to say, Jesus does not "imagine" Himself in the world as one who is out to win adherents or to get people in line. His imagination doesn't function like a policeman's superego. Nor, be it added, does ours, when ours is exorcised of illusions and fantasies of domination.

The image, "I am the door," implies this nonnecessity, this welcome and inclusion. The implication is: "I am the open door, not the closed door." Or, "I open a door long closed, locked. You are not trapped in the kingdom of necessity, the Fall. The door is now open."

We would say today, Jesus knows something about first things first. Let us start here with the improbable, if not the impossible. If He started by being "useful" to a project, founding something, proving something, squaring off against other orthodoxies, and so on, we would know rather shortly that something else of crucial import was being neglected, ignored, even despised. Something so simple as the truth.

But He says simply, "I am the truth." That image, it might be thought, of "the" truth has its own native power; it sounds all the more powerfully on the polluted air of the kingdom of untruth, the Fall.

No need to enlarge on this; a nation rather continually at war will suffer a huge loss of capacity. The Greeks knew it; in war, the first casualty is the truth.

Implied here is "I speak the truth." And more, for he claims more: "I embody the truth." And then of course (we say "of course," it trips off the tongue; but what a cost implied!), "I live the truth, I follow through on the truth."

And from this good beginning all sorts of good things might be thought to follow; including a community dedicated to "the truth."

It seems to me this is something of the way the imagination, including the imagination of Christ, works: two steps. The first is to draw attention, to point, so to speak, to "finger" images until one makes sense. Then, "that's the one." "The" image is now isolated, to help us become mindful, as the Buddhists say.

"I am the way." We are not to miss, as they say, the context. He is imagining himself in a Fallen world. Chaos is implied, distemper and confusion. In such a world he offers a "way" that, as we say, actually goes somewhere. Among the many ways, one deserves special attention. His way.

Therefore He is justified in saying—"the way." And this in a world of great confusion as to ways false and true, conflicting signs, false road maps, of dead ends and land's ends, of detours and pitfalls, chasms and cunning twists.

On those ways, that tangle and web of purpose, appetite, misery, stretching across time and this world (the time after the Fall, the Fallen world) travel the wanderers and the lost ones, thieves and robbers, priests and Samaritans, the wounded, the afflicted, the homeless, the mentally bereft, the shoppers and campers and so on. In this world, He makes his way, and makes way for us.

Make straight the way! was the cry of Isaiah. Even for the wayward? Yes. His cry might have been an ancestral command issued to John Baptist and Christ. So the image was passed on and arrives on other lips.

That is the first point of the image; to draw attention, to make us mindful. There is a way to go in the stalemated, bewildering world. It is "the" way, in proportion as it makes sense, offers companionship, leads us home. The way is the way of the heart; the world and time (even a Fallen world and the time of the Fall) is the terrain of the heart of Christ.

I confess I do not know what all this means. I have a suspicion (and a hope) that the image is true.

We are not to miss the context. To announce "the way" in a Fallen world is hardly to propose a "way back" to some garden of innocence. The announcement is not nostalgic, in other words. To the contrary it deals with memory, and remembering. (Nostalgia is a way of forgetting, of amnesia; but memory, as we say, "brings to mind," "recalls," "calls us back"—mainly to our true selves.)

Context is everything. The word on the page, even the image on the page, can be received as abstract, weightless. But the context of "I am the Way" is a real world, as real as our own, which is to say (risking the otiose), the realm of the Fall.

This "way" leads somewhere; the arrival is one with the way. The image grew from the action. To comprehend the image, it is necessary to take into account the action. Which is to say, Christ walks the way before

He commends it to us. The Gospel tells us so. He set His face steadfastly toward Jerusalem. Which is to say, toward death.

Now if that were all, Jerusalem and death, we were then allowed to grow nostalgic. But since that is not all, we are instructed to "remember Me," something entirely of another order.

The way passed through a Fallen world, toward a Fallen city. In point of fact, that meant "the way," whatever adherents or enthusiasm it had gathered in the countryside, was to come to an abrupt halt in that city.

Jerusalem, for the likes of Jesus, was land's end, time's end, life's end. It was the city of death; which is to say, of capital punishment, of foreign intervention, of religious collusion and temple religion. Such people as ran affairs there, we are told, bickered a great deal among themselves. But they were quite in agreement on one matter; any "way" that challenged their affairs—or worse, derided them and their authority—should reach a literal dead end.

The Way was to halt there. But it did not. Something quite different transpired. The Way resumed from there, "to the ends of the earth," we are told.

Once the Way is proclaimed, we too may take our soundings, so to speak. Our way, as we walk it today, is manifestly one way among many. There is the Buddhist way, the Hindu way, the Muslim way, the Jewish way. From a cultural point of view, there is the American way, much commended in song and story, by media and mammon. A way which leads straight in our time to the disasters named Vietnam, Salvador, Guatemala, Bosnia, Afghanistan, and Iraq.

And then among us Christians — what to say? — there is the way of Mr. Bush and of Dorothy Day, of Bonhoeffer and of, God help us, Hitler. Divisions, conflicts, warmakers, peacemakers, the many ways, including the abhorrent, the perilous, the heroic, the modest, the demented.

But for ourselves, here and now, a question or two may help clarify matters. Is our way also THE WAY? Does it make sense, offer companionship, lead us home? If so, is it parallel to, does it converge on THE WAY?

"I am the Vine." "You are the branches." In the other "I am" images, our part was only implied. One might say, it was left to us to imagine where we fitted in, or responded or took part. He left it in all courtesy to our own imagining.

Here, something else. We are part of the image, the "sarmenta," the tendrils and branches; also the harvest, the grapes. But this inclusion is a matter of emphasis rather than of "here we are, there he is, all nicely distinguished"; no matter of "we are something, He is something else." As though it could be said, the vine stops here, the branch starts there.

Nature does not work that way. There is an equation, a continuity, a "we" that includes Him. There is root and vine and branch and fruit, one living being.

There is a kind of ecology of the spirit here. He and we, deep in the earth, dependent on the earth, one with the earth; and deep in one another, dependent on one another, one with one another.

Context is everything. It is hardly by happenstance that "I am the vine, you the branches" is the last of the "I am" statements of Jesus. This one is placed by John at the opening of holy week, the supper of Holy Thursday. Which is to say, the image is to be verified, tried, and convicted (and to that point proven truthful) in a Fallen world.

In such a setting, the image is manifestly political as well as pastoral, tragic as well as comforting. It is as though the vine and branches were bare survivors in a vineyard torn to pieces; a battlefield littered with up-rooted vines, the dismembered dead. Creation would have the vineyard brought to harvest; but in the world of the Fall, wine turns to blood.

The fruit of the vine is indeed the cup. But it is also, in a surreal and tragic transformation, something else. "This is the cup of My blood, poured out for you."

Somehow, the fruit of the vine has been harvested, trodden, aged. It has reached this cup, this evening meal. And there, it has been transformed—"The cup of My blood."

As if that were not enough, pressed down and flowing over.

It is not enough. As the Vine included us, the branches, so the cup of "My blood" includes us, by fervent implication. The cup contains blood, the blood is "given, for you." The giving of one's blood supersedes the letting of blood. Violence yields to nonviolence. The illustration is clear and passes into instruction.

Say it again and again, in a world dissolved in a welter of blood-letting: "The cup of My blood, given for you."

In the words spoken, the cup passed, the covenant is made new, and the former texts are clarified. "Greater love than this no one shows, that one yield up one's life for a friend." "Peter, put up your sword, for those who live by the sword will perish by the sword." "Blessed are the peacemakers; they will be named sons and daughters of God."

God speaks to each of us as He makes us,
then walks with us silently out of the night.
These are the words we dimly hear:
"You, sent out beyond your recall,
go to the limits of your longing.
Embody Me.
Flare up like flame
and make big shadows I can move in.
Let everything happen to you; beauty and terror.
Just keep going. No feeling is final.
Don't let yourself lose Me.
Nearby is the country they call life.
You will know it by its seriousness.
Give Me your hand."

—from "The Book of Hours"
by Rainer Maria Rilke

8

Love Your Enemies

There Is No Just War;
the Gospel Is Always Relevant

"God has wished to bring us forth by a word of truth."
—James 1:18

"And the Word was made flesh and dwelt among us."
—John 1:14

WAR, ABORTION, THE DEATH PENALTY. In the judgment of anyone with eyes to see, these have become simply another form of "daily behavior." We confront these crimes day by day in the media, in the images of a permanent war against the living—the disposable, the vulnerable, as the Nazis defined these, "the lives of no value."

I invite you to reflect on one aspect of the "daily behavior" of American authorities, indeed of our citizenry—war preparation, in view of warmaking. Total war as simply routine activity, with its own by-laws and suspension of laws, its secrecy and duplicity and media control, war as domestic consumption and chief export, war ruling decisions regarding money and resources and scientific talent, war as a kind of universal solvent, applied to relieve unemployment and domestic turmoil.

I regard war as a brute fact of our lifetime, and more, as a metaphor, an emblem. War reveals the contempt for life implied in current forms of the wasting of life—abortion, capital murder, medical experimentation, warehousing of the aged, denial of housing and education and food and healthcare and a clean environment.

In wartime, crimes against the living are not only to be taken for granted, but are considered inevitable, even praiseworthy.

War also is a kind of periodic explosion in nature, of the spiritual ills that fester beneath the skin and skull of the culture, ills like racism, sexism, greed, and duplicity in high and low places.

One of the cruelest aspects of war and a war atmosphere is the mental confusion it induces. Decencies that prevail in peacetime no longer hold firm. The center, the clarity, breaks up. Compassion? We grow stern and set. We have an enemy to deal with.

Two examples of this dramatic shift, the Dr. Jekyll who seizes the soul of Mr. Hyde, occur to me. The first is a matter of history. A meeting of Christians from several countries took place in England just prior to the first World War. They discussed forming a group of peacemakers, tentatively to be named "The Fellowship of Reconciliation." Sensing that their countries were massing for war, the members resolved to return home to oppose the draft, to speak and act on behalf of peace.

In the midst of their discussions, war was declared. The news changed everything. Dr. Jekyll took over. The participants were issued orders to return home and face induction in the military.

Two pacifists refused the call. In all the others, Dr. Jekyll took over. They obeyed. They must henceforth be known to history as former pacifists; they went home, took up arms, and fought in the ensuing carnage.

Our Mr. Hyde undoubtedly thinks of himself as peaceable and decent of spirit. When his country is at peace, so is he. He could not imagine stalking an enemy at the behest of military authorities. Alas, he knows nothing of the sinister Dr. Jekyll lurking in his shadow — or just under his skin.

Evelyn Underhill, the English mystic and peacemaker, wrote of the same astonishing but constant phenomenon, the numbers of what we might call "fair weather pacifists" who succumb to whatever call to arms. Gandhi said in the same regard that true peacemakers belong not in peaceable places, but where the peace is most endangered.

Another example, closer to our own times. Three months after the November revolution in Czechoslovakia, Vaclav Havel, former prisoner, now president of his country, visited the United States and addressed a joint session of Congress. He spoke of the mighty threats confronting humanity—greed, militarism, environmental destruction. And he went on, with an eloquence well worth quoting:

The salvation of this human world lies nowhere else than in the human heart, in the human power to reflect, in human meekness and in human responsibility. . . .

Without a global revolution in human consciousness, nothing will change for the better in the sphere of our being. . . .

*We are still incapable of understanding that the only genuine back-
bone of all our actions, if they are to be moral, is responsibility, responsibility to something higher than my family, my country, my company,
my success.*

The Congress was dazed or dazzled, or both, by such unaccustomed
spiritual acuity. When had our pedestrian politicos heard the like? They
offered Havel a standing ovation.

Mr. Hyde, you see, is also a social and political phenomenon. And so
is Dr. Jekyll. Less than a year later, the same Congress embraced the horrors Havel had indicted — militarism, greed, environmental destruction.
They approved a war in the Persian Gulf that destroyed and continues
to destroy, in the notorious sanctions and later in the second Gulf War.

This wartime loss of moral equilibrium and clarity affects all — Christians, authorities, and the citizenry at large. We have seen the domestic
desert storm of yellow ribbons and flags, heard the pealing of church
bells, and recently, the bishops' applause for our leader's "performance."

In New York City, a great cathedral welcomed the architect of the
first slaughter and his henchman warrior. We were assured that the
performance was an occasion to pray for the dead, nothing more. He
stood, in the presence of military serial murderers, unindicted and self-
assured, in the pulpit blessed years before by the presence of Dr. Martin
Luther King.

And this same edifice but a few months previously had dedicated its
Lenten sermons to the biblical denunciations of the war!

And yet, and yet again, Christians, we are told, are "brought forth by
a word of truth." More, as midwife and image of this extraordinary
second birth, the "Word of God dwelt among us."

Thus, twice born, we Christians — know it or not, care about it or not —
stand on a different footing than citizens who profess no faith.

Need it be said? Citizenship in this or that nation can never exhaust
the meaning of our vocation, or preempt the claim of Christ with its
own claim on our conscience. Beyond the beat of war drums, national
law, ideology and frenzy, beyond denial, even beyond our crimes and
betrayals, we are bound over to the Prince of Peace.

Our vocation takes us in other directions than the world opens before
us. Above all, given the violent times, such things as language, behavior,
debt of citizenship, and culture must be reckoned anew.

A war, let us say, is mounted. Immediately, choices are narrowed. The hand of Caesar is extended, index finger pointing; Uncle Sam wants you, your money, your son, at the least your silence.

The reckoning must be totted up, weighed to the jot, calculated again and again, as wars erupt and a blood debt comes due once more.

Language too gets inducted. In one way or another, we Christians (I limit the reflection to ourselves) suddenly have another book than our Bible thrust in our hands. It is a military manual. The commandment is clear: Kill your enemies.

That bizarre wartime anti-bible were perhaps best read standing on one's head. Or perhaps read backward, from last page to first. Or perhaps it should be read in the dark, or in some other improbable situation or setting. For the text stands our morality on its head. Ethically speaking, it is pure darkness.

According to the book, murder is now rewarded and honored, hunting licenses are issued against children, ecological ruin is taken for granted, a matter of small interest or none at all.

It becomes damnably difficult in such times to keep the Bible open as a guide to behavior. Confusion, anger, the siren song of patriotism, even preaching and "just war theology" obscure the plain sense of the Word of God. The armies line up, on the ready. The president's rhetoric is fiery. Do some dare stand back, think twice, object?

The warrior state offers its own version of the Beatitudes, of right and just. In such a frenzy of "patriotism," peacemakers can only be accounted troublemakers. War is the great emulsifier; everyone "for the duration" must behave alike, walk in lockstep, smartly zip up the flag.

Suppose someone speaks up in public against the war, saying something loud and clear like the mantra, "Hell no, I won't go"? Opposition greets this malefactor, legal jeopardy, sometimes even violence. He or she is told quickly and not always politely: "What are we to do? The president has declared this a just war! And who are you to say nay? Are we not urged to render unto Caesar?"

I counter with questions of my own: "Please tell me, who are the 'we' of your question? (To my soul I name this the emulsified "we.") Are we citizens only? Are we citizen-Christians? Are we Christians the war has reduced to former Christians? Do we have a message to others in wartime? Does our faith cast light on a dark time?"

Let it be said plainly: War cancels faith. For the duration. War is the great exercise in practical, lethal, (inevitably linguistic) atheism.

Brought forth by a word of truth? The Word dwelling in our midst? The confusion thickens; or even worse, a baleful clarity. The authorities commend a mad assurance in a just cause. Shortly the language of the led, the citizens and the captive media, matches syllable by word the language of those who lead. The ventriloquists lie and the puppets nod. And we are reduced, as Dietrich Bonhoeffer wrote, to the misleaders and the misled.

Consider the just war theory: myths, clichés, millennia old, dusted off by the churches, adroitly seized by the president to his own advantage in the slaughter of Iraqis.

Here we go again, one thinks wearily. Any war in history, pre-Christian era, Christian, post-Christian, has been defended as a just war. By either side. By the leaders and citizens of either side. By the churches of whatever side.

In almost any culture, any religion, the theory never fails its votaries. Among the great majority of Christians and their authorities and theologians, it has an unassailable status; it is a universal substitute, convenience. It is also a subterfuge, an evasion of the plain teaching of the Gospel. In wartime, for the sake of the Gospel, Christians are called to far different tasks than killing; called to undertake a thankless long haul of resistance, to summon patience, sacrifice, courage, to be prepared for persecution.

But the just war theory offers a better way—painless, a quick fix; the war, unwillingly undertaken, so they say, is a "lesser evil." So they say. Less evil, in casu, than Saddam Hussein, and before him, less evil than a Manuel Noriega, less evil than the authorities of Grenada, less evil than the teetering dominoes of Vietnam.

So far, not so good. The theory fails to take in account something crucial.

This "lesser evil" (for example, killing a multitude to save a few, causing "collateral damage" in order to remove a tyrant, smart-bombing and pulverizing the barrios of the poor, burying enemy soldiers alive to minimize one's own casualties), like the genie released from the small bottle, is evil indeed, lesser perhaps, but the evil shortly grows monstrous, devouring, genocidal, irreversible.

More, the theory sets in place, authenticates, a reality the Gospel had sought to declare null and void: the reality of enemy.

We heard much concerning the just war theory during the Vietnam years. Even the silence of the churches invoked it, justified it. Yet the theory was there, I thought, lurking in the shadows, clue to a decade and a half of "no comment" from the Catholic bishops.

The theory stopped the tongue. One had a sense that save for the sublime Cardinal Francis Spellman, the bishops were ashamed to apply it to so shameful a war. Vietnam a just war? The theory stank in the nostrils of Americans, who had caught a whiff, even from TV tubes, of the burning flesh of children.

The silence of the church nonetheless was infinitely eloquent. It was a code of sorts, for this: *in wartime, the Gospel is irrelevant.*

We could only conclude that the bishops had settled the matter of the war to their own satisfaction (if not to ours). To many of us, their prolonged official silence implied captivity to an anti-communism, contempt, racism that fueled and justified unspeakable cruelties. The war was "just" because communism was evil. Therefore, anything goes.

Christians should have learned something from that war; bishops too. The derisive laughter of Mars should have taught us something. It manifestly did not. War after war—Grenada, Panama, Afghanistan, the first and second Gulf wars—shunted the Gospel aside, held it to scorn, buried it, like the Iraqi soldiers, alive.

Love your enemies? The Word of God in our midst? But we were at war!

The moment the war was launched, we all became realists. The Word of God might apply elsewhere (or elsewhen) or to simpler times or to one-to-one conflict or to pacifists and religious (whoever these latter might be; for the most part they were mum as the others).

Love your enemies—a strange command, when you think of it. It is like the text of a drama, written with a mysterious ink. When the play is staged, the text disappears. It is in a sense self-canceling. You say it aloud, act it out and are struck by the tremendous, curt implication. The enemy disappears!

Love, and then *enemies.* The two cannot coexist, they are like fire and ice in the hand. The fire melts the ice, or the ice extinguishes the fire.

The fire wins out (at least in the Gospel text)! The verb *love* transforms the noun *enemies.* The enemy is reborn by the power of love.

Astonishing. Now the enemy is a former enemy, and a present friend, brother, sister, lover even. Talk about rebirth!

Love, you, the enemy, and lo, the enemy vanishes where he stood.

Also, it is not only the opponent who undergoes a dazzling transformation, but myself as well, who against all expectation has learned love in place of hatred, who had once been stuck in the same plight as my enemy. Together we made a frozen mirror image, awful, redundant, implacable. I was the enemy of my enemy. A sound definition of hell.

Break the mirror! Christ commends, and confers, a mutual rebirth. Now for the hard part. If, according to Christ, there can be no just war because enemies have been transformed by love, something else follows.

No humans, not even those armed and at war against my country, can be regarded as legitimate targets. Christians may not kill, period. Christians may not be complicit in killing, period. May not hurl napalm at children. May not bury alive in the desert the nameless soldiers. May not launch the smart bomb against women and children in the shelter.

Are women and children the enemy? No sane person would declare so. (But we are not all sane.) Are the soldiers the enemy? The just war theory says so. But Christ denies it. He has granted the soldiers, too, a kind of deferment, an exemption from killing and being killed.

We heard stories of former wars, stories that underscore the absurdity and pathos of bloodletting. On Christmas day during World War I, a cease fire was declared. The exhausted soldiers, Allied and German, issued from the trenches, exchanged cigarettes, chatted, traded photos of their families. A day later they squared off once more, one imagines with half a heart—back to bloody business as usual.

Another episode. During the same war, we were told of a platoon of young French draftees en route to the front. They marched through a town. Local citizens came out in force to honor them. But then something bizarre: a wave—was it of grief or rage?—gathered in the ranks of the soldiers. Marching along, they began a strange bleating—"Bah! bah! Bah!" Sheep being led to the slaughter! The horrid truth, alas, too late.

And what of ourselves, Americans, Christians? We soldiers, civilians, church members, women, children, are called to be—conscientious objectors against war. Against any war. Christian presidents are called too, and Christian generals—strange, bizarre, unlikely as it may seem.

Christians are called to be objectors against all and any war, against "just" war, invasive war, preemptive war, defensive war, conventional war (whose horrendous effects we have seen again and again).

The above declaration, admirably simple and to the point, would of course put many exalted authorities out of work. So be it; better unemployed than so employed.

Let us remind them, and ourselves, that we are called to other tasks than killing.

The ethic of Jesus is set down in some detail and embarrassing clarity, in the fifth chapter of Matthew's Gospel. "Blessed are you makers of peace." And immediately, since we are to know that such a title is not cheaply conferred or claimed: "Blessed are those persecuted for the sake of righteousness."

The "good works" that follow the ethic are indicated in the twenty-fifth chapter. Summoned to love the (former, transformed) enemy—and thereby transformed, reborn, ourselves—we are to undertake the works of justice and peace.

There is another implication of what I call the "just command" to love our enemies—that terms such as "combatants" and "noncombatants" no longer wash. The terms imply that some, because they took up arms, stood outside the love invoked by Christ. As though others, for being disarmed or unarmed, were thereby, and solely thereby, judged more valuable.

So reasoning, we remain stuck in the pernicious language of the just war, implying that the unjust soldiers, enemies, tyrants, drug lords lie beyond the pale; that such lives can be wasted with impunity. The language is outmoded, passé, morally regressive. It will not jibe with the Gospel and its vision of the human: just, peaceable, compassionate.

More, such language condemns us to a cycle of violence and guilt, in which we are whirled about, off kilter, shamed, celebrating crimes we should weep for. The guilt of the generals haunts us, the pale implacable face of the wartime president, the mass graves filled with the living and the newly dead. The guilt of those who launched the bestial slaughter, the guilt of those who know of it, who parade and rejoice. The guilt of those who have no objections to register.

The time is short. Reject the errant history, the pseudo tradition. There can be no just war. There never was one.

Even the Jesuits, no coven of raging radicals, have urged an ethical housecleaning of the just war theory. In their Rome publication, *Civiltà Cattolica,* they editorialized in the course of the first Gulf war: "War cannot be conducted according to the criteria required for a just war. The theory of the 'just war' is untenable and needs to be abandoned. Besides being immoral, modern war with its destructive force of conventional and nuclear weapons is useless and harmful."

And again, in the same editorial: "To declare that war is the last resort is often to attempt to justify the very desire to wage war. But an even more serious problem arises with the just war theory. The 'just cause' is invoked most of the time, to give a moral and juridical guise to a war one intends to wage, for purposes quite different from those officially stated."

Amen. One can only sigh, "Better late than never!"

Toss out, once and for all, the bombs and guns, the blessings and Te Deums, the myths of "sweet and befitting death," the lethal distinctions between lives expendable and lives precious.

No winners, only losers. The losers are slaughtered, the winners brutalized.

War, as anyone but a ninny or a general or a tyrant or a president must know by now, puts everyone in the gunsights of the gods.

Topple the idols. Disarm, Christian soldiers.

9

Jesus and
the Syrophoenician Woman

Jesus rose and went away to the region of Tyre and Sidon. He entered a house, and would not have anyone know it. Yet he could not be hid. Immediately a woman, whose little daughter was possessed by an unclean spirit, heard of him; she came and fell down at his feet. Now the woman was a Greek, a Syrophoenician by birth.

And she begged him to cast out the demon from her daughter.

He said to her, "Let the children first be fed, for it is not right to take the children's bread and cast it to the dogs."

But she answered him, "Yes, Lord; yet even the dogs under the table eat the children's crumbs that fall there."

And he responded, "For this saying you may go your way; the demon has left your daughter." And she went to her home, and found the child lying in bed, and the demon gone. —Mark 7:24–30

I COMMEND this text to you, and to my own soul. Many of us, we are informed, for different reasons, can lay small claim to the Bread of Life; which is to say, to Christ's attentiveness, His response, His healing. Certain claims are neither large nor persuasive. What, after all, is the worth of a canine claim, proceeding as it does, from a dog's life?

Indeed for certain among us to voice the claim, let alone to insist on it, is considered a joke of sorts. The joke is often told, in ways diverse but unmistakable, by those on the inside track. Some claims, if you follow the joke, are no larger than a crumb, no more persuasive than a hungry dog's whine. Such might be thought the claim on American compassion, of the Afghan children and refugees, the claim of Palestinians upon Israelis for a cessation of settlers' scorn and violence; and least persuasive of all perhaps, the claim in these days, of the children of Iraq, dying under American bombs.

Those securely in possession are given to glances, shrugs, slamming of doors in faces, such words as might improve things when a stray dog enters a banquet hall. Or the wrong person, an outsider.

I mean words and phrases like "collateral damage" and responses that pass into a kind of mordant immortality; such surely were the words of a former secretary of state, responding to questions as to the fate of Iraqi children under the American fist. She gave with this: "We believe it is worth the cost." Surely she is not to be thought a disinterested judge of the cost, and of its payment. She pays nothing, except perhaps the jettisoning of her own humanity.

Speaking of claims, the harshness of Christ toward this invasive mother is surprising, shocking. He seems bent, in contrast to other encounters with women, on humiliating her, making sport of her, and by implication, her daughter's outcast condition.

Outcast the mother surely is, on at least two scores. She is a woman, and a non-Jew. Were she a Jewish woman, her status would be humiliating enough, as we learn from Torah and Christian testament. She would periodically be rendered unclean, unfit for worship; she would have little or no right to legal recourse or redress of wrongs. Literally, as we are told by Luke's Gospel, one like her could be described as bent double under the burden of a humiliated legal and religious status.

But at the very least, in such a hideous arrangement, a Jewish woman had a claim of sorts on the apparatus of salvation. There survives in the Bible a tradition of women—Sarah, Hagar, Rebecca, Rachel, Deborah, Miriam, Judith, Anna, even Jezebel and Delilah, who surpassed, some gloriously, the destiny to which they were condemned. Such women spoke up loud and clear, liberated themselves and others, sweetly deceived men, murdered even, seized by whatever means a place in the history of their people.

But the woman who approaches Jesus is radically an outsider from every point of view. She and her daughter are Gentiles; in the awful words of the "chosen," they are no better than dogs, and to be treated no differently.

So a cruel word game is under way, hardly rare in the culture of the times. For once Jesus, it would seem, yields to it. He plays the game for only a sentence or two.

And what of the woman? She tolerates the abuse. She must, for she is a suppliant, a nobody, at the end of her rope. In the law, she has no claim on Him. For another reason too, she can be patient and attentive, and watch for an opening.

Her behavior, we think in admiration, is a window on her soul. She breathes deep; we sense that in her own eyes she is a being of worth. As such, she requires no instruction, from Jesus or anyone else, as to her place in the world.

And if that instruction is offered, and moreover, is deliberately cruel and abusive, she is skilled in letting such things come and go. She has heard the like before. And has let it go, and survived. This too will pass.

So she persists, she listens. Christ may invoke an image of defeat and even of degradation; she is a dog, she does not belong here, where humans gather. Given her chance, she will turn his words around, to her own advantage.

I commend her tactic, her dogged persistence. There are a few things in her favor; and by implication in our own. The One she approaches for help also knows something, and will know much more, of the status of outcast. There is a strange congruence here, which time will clarify, between the persistent woman and the reluctant Healer. One day, Christ will be accounted a criminal bound over for capital punishment, destined to be removed from this world. A malefactor, whose presence and provocations arouse the hatred of both temple and state.

It is unlikely in such times as we are enduring that we will win a hearing from the church or from civil authority for that matter; each so strangely resembling the other in reaction to such lives as we are called to live.

Today, my church remains adamant against the healing of the world which we name peacemaking. The famous bishops' letter on nuclear arms is widely disregarded; in places, it is entirely dismantled. And shortly after Mr. Bush announced open season against tormented Afghanistan, the bishops gave him carte blanche. They declared his war "just."

Their document was, in effect, a rehash of ancient canards, secular in origin and intent, designed to make a prima facie case for atrocious, indiscriminate violence. So doing, the bishops' letter ignored two resources: the Gospel and recent history.

Simply put, the bishops reduced the Sermon on the Mount to a dead letter. Other words and instructions of Christ — "Love your enemies," "Put up the sword," and the sublime legacy of the Eucharist, "My body given for you," "My blood, poured out for you" — these may well have never been spoken or enacted.

The bishops ignored as well a widely circulated conclusion dating from the end of the first Gulf war. At that time, the influential Italian monthly edited by the Jesuits, *Civiltà Cattolica,* concluded that the deployment of "weapons of indiscriminate killing and destruction show beyond doubt that modern wars cannot be or be called just."

In November 2001, the Catholic bishops spoke as the bombing erupted. A few months later, in a small Afghan village, in the space of one night, an entire wedding party of some fifty-five people was obliterated by a smart bomb gone astray. And I said to my soul, "The Catholic bishops have blood on their hands."

In these matters of peace and justice, each in its own way a matter of life and death, the church, in collusion with the warmaking state, is hardly speaking for Christ. It could even be said that the church speaks in contrariety to Christ.

The conduct of Christ may be thought instructive. The woman enters a male gathering. Male bonding is exclusively in progress. She is unannounced and uninvited. And Christ chooses the occasion to try her mettle. Where is faith found to be genuine, he implies, except in the testing of faith? How shall the quality of faith be known, except under duress? Will this woman fold her tent and go away, will her face fall, hearing a demeaning image laid on herself? Will she creep off like a very dog? Or will she stand her ground, rebut him, do him one better?

Obviously there is something at stake here, something more serious than verbal jousting. A Zen scene perhaps. The master launches a puzzle, a koan, even an insult; the disciple must solve it, unravel it, if necessary rebut it. The search is perplexing. It exacts great expense of time, effort, even of bearing contempt—and at times a whack on the shoulders with bamboo.

The woman of our story is no novice in this business. Her wits have been sharpened on the carborundum wheel of the world. She has heard the arguments before—who is to survive, who prosper, and who go under, arguments that do not invariably favor the powerless and the poor.

She reads faces and eyes. The same faith that sent her in search of a healer stands strong in her, though the quest seems futile as she, it would seem, is derided and dismissed.

But she refuses to pack up and go. Humiliated before others, regarded publicly as something less than human, an intruder, a dog fit only to be put to the chain or the door—she will not be cowed, she will turn the insult to her own advantage. She will crack the code.

"If I am a dog" (she grants the hideous premise for the moment—and her granting is a measure both of humility and unbreakable dignity)— "If in your eyes I am no more than a dog, you have not by that canceled my claim on your compassion. Can you not feel compassion, even for a dog? Then do so."

We think of the church, and the treatment accorded to peacemakers today, and we think of Christ and the woman. In one instance, two priests took part in a nonviolent action against nuclear installations near Philadelphia. They were apprehended, then freed as a trial date was set. Then the local cardinal intervened. Judging the priests guilty, he removed them from their parishes and sent them to a place of ecclesiastical detention. A chief priest of our millennium was showing himself more fiercely punitive than Herod or Pilate.

The church in effect often cuts short the encounter of Christ and the woman. It is as though the story ended with the insult; as though under its blow, the woman turned away.

But we insist on the whole story, and its actual outcome.

When we so insist, we are struck by a notable contrast. Authorities reject, ostracize, place certain people beyond the pale, sometimes on a lifelong basis. In one way or another, we have all undergone it.

With Christ, there is a far different outlook leading to a far different outcome. A less inhuman humanism, a more human humanism, one might say.

"It is not good," declares Christ, "to take the children's bread and cast it to the dogs." Thus the Zen master proposes an image that implies, as koans do, a tease, an insult, a puzzle, an obstacle, a test, an apparent rejection. And on the moment, the woman unlocks the koan, turns aside the insult, and passes the test brilliantly. "Even dogs may eat the crumbs that fall from the table!"

And at her riposte, as Matthew's Gospel tells, Jesus is lost in admiration. He gives in, heals the woman's child.

He is mastered by her sweetness and strength, the unbreakable spirit of a woman whose life had been a long eking of life from a sour root.

I love her spirit, and commend it to you. She is like a woman of Northern Ireland, or of South Africa, or of the South Bronx. A survivor, and how much more.

Regard her closely. A rotten culture, or a rotten religion (or both in conjunction of interest) have branded her: outsider, pariah, dog. Jesus echoes the insult. But as matters turn, he utters it only to declare it null and void. She has entered a new covenant "in my friendship." And the spirit of death is banished from her family.

What shall we name that quality of hers, a gift that makes her a kind of ideal outsider, soon to be drawn inside? Courage, persistence? She will accept the stigma (for the last time) and turn it around. She rejects rejection, and so wins the day. The outsider stands within. An ideal, a hope abiding.

I do not know whether some church authorities will renounce their sinfulness, will one day heal and bind up those they have wounded so grievously, those who suffer and die in war and under sanctions, in future Afghanistans and Iraqs. I do not know.

Of one thing I am certain: of our calling to holiness, to persistence, in season and out, in the work of healing even as we seek healing for ourselves.

Let me comment briefly on the conclusion of this Gospel episode. The mother declares that her child is afflicted with a demon, an "unclean spirit." A strange diagnosis indeed. But Jesus has no quarrel with her words; in effect he agrees with her. And it is of this spirit, which the mother knows has laid claim to her child, a spirit alien, dangerous, enervating, arrogant, lethal—of this the child is delivered.

Biblically speaking, such "spirits" are inevitably carriers of death, in all its analogues and metaphors. Indeed, if we are aware today of the spiritual plight of our culture, we North Americans would appear afflicted in a way parallel to the child. The spirit of death, of violence and racism and sexism and homophobia and consumerism and militarism, the obsessive vengefulness of the Bushites, these haunt our lives, our institutions, and yes, even our churches.

We note with dismay the purveying of death, domestically and in the world at large. We recall the Vietnam War, the Contra war, Grenada, Panama, Iraq, Afghanistan. We think not just of physical death, but of that "second death" of which the Bible speaks—a spirit of death that freezes the soul; death of the heart, numbing of the mind; death to compassion, of access to the truth, of a sense of one another. And worse; the "putting to death" or putting to the door, with malign intent and sour will, of human variety, of sexual and racial and religious kinship, all that "wet and wildness" celebrated by the poet, to the honor of the Creator.

Biblically speaking, it is worth recalling that the health we call reconciliation and community and peace are seldom attained by the powerful, by those in command. Indeed the Bible underscores the opposite—the wrong power, the spirit of control and domination, of greed and violence: These are the illnesses that run amok, that, but for the compassion of God, are terminal.

Like many of you, I have been at the side of the dying for over fifteen years; have stood by sisters and brothers afflicted with AIDS and cancer, relatives, friends, as they lived out, generally with nobility and good grace, their last days among us.

One cannot but note, in the midst of such atrocious suffering, a strange irony. Many of the dying are freed, some speedily, some gradually, of cultural entanglements, obsessions, fears, violence, greed, moral numbing. More, in their dying, many surpass themselves; they succeed in freeing others as well. Thus in the strange irony of grace, physical death brings with it a power, a sea change. The dying are freed of the spirit of death; they renounce the cultural illness that invades and possesses the living. Once healed, they become, at the end, healers.

So we take heart. We commend the woman who quietly, simply, with all her heart, on behalf of someone she loved, refused to give up. We might think of her act as a kind of "forgiving persistence" toward Christ. We might also wish to ponder a kind of "persistent forgiveness" toward the church. And we can be grateful.

The woman refuses the insult, persists in her crucial errand. And so prevails.

And so must we. And so shall we.

We must forgive, deepen our love, persist in our conviction that the church can be redeemed from sin.

In so fulfilling our vocation, we ourselves are healed.

10

You Shall Love

One of the scribes, when he came forward and heard them disputing and saw how well he had answered them, asked him, "Which is the first of all the commandments?"

Jesus replied, "The first is this: 'Hear, O Israel! The Lord our God is Lord alone! You shall love the Lord your God with all your heart, with all your soul, with all your mind, and with all your strength.' The second is this: 'You shall love your neighbor as yourself.' There is no other commandment greater than these."

The scribe said to him, "Well said, teacher. You are right in saying, 'God is One and there is no other. And 'to love God with all your heart, with all your understanding, with all your strength, and to love your neighbor as yourself' is worth more than all burnt offerings and sacrifices."

And when Jesus saw that he answered with understanding, he said to him, "You are not far from the reign of God." And no one dared to ask him any more questions. —Mark 12:28–34

EVIDENTLY our Lord's "credibility" is falling on hard times. He insists that the love of God and the love of neighbor are one. On the face of it, this seems quite simple; more, seems in accord with tradition. And yet, then and now, the word is not invariably well received.

Orthodoxy, he says in so many words, is not enough. In the current inspired jargon, he invokes something known as "orthopraxis"—invokes it standing as he does, face to face with men who are deliberately detached from a working faith, those in charge of the one true faith, the scribal class.

Our text is the climax of a series of debates with these wizened intellects. The setting is the Temple, their power center. The issue in debate is of course central to the religious understanding of both sides: the "greatest commandment."

Ours is also the only text in Mark that shows Jesus not altogether hostile toward the scribes. Indeed with this story, the controversy has reached a flash point. We are party to the very last confrontation; there remains only the arrest and prosecution of Jesus.

A scribe approaches Jesus, having witnessed the debate with his peers, and seen the outcome. Signals are given, "Well done, teacher, you have answered forthrightly" (v. 32). The speaker may well be a prospective disciple, one who may prove unlike his fellows, neither deaf nor blind.

Jesus is described as — impressed. Yet his sympathy is elusive; the subtleties of his discourse pave the way, not for an invitation to the scribe, to "come follow me," to join the band of friends for something horrendously final—a total condemnation of the scribal class.

"Beware the scribes," he warns somberly. They make a great show of religion, these pretenders. They demand the best seats, honors, salutations, and meantime "devour the houses of widows." Strong stuff indeed.

We picture this wavering scribe, a pretty good man who is not good enough, stuck in his system. The irony is delicious. Professionally, he is bound to love God. Professionally, he is hindered from loving his neighbor. What he ends up doing is a charade of the real thing. Which is to say, he is enamored of the "idea" of the love of God, the "idea" of the love of others.

Thus he makes the better the enemy of the good, or the idea the enemy of the deed. The question of the "first of all the commandments" becomes in his eyes a kind of deadly staple of rabbinic bickering.

What indeed is the greatest command? The answer of Jesus seems at first to be cautiously orthodox. He quotes from Deuteronomy, with minor changes.

Suddenly, however, the text spontaneously combusts. Jesus, a steady eye resting on his interrogator (might there be a seeker hidden under the robes of this official type?), puts the scribe to a test. It is no mere contest of wits he enters, something the scribe, like an academic on the make, would have reveled in. It is a radical revision of the law, a compassionate account of the ethical illness of the keeper of the law. Revision of law, for the sake of the keeper of the law!

Jesus, healer, physician of the spirit, relentless diagnostician of the illness of the powerful. We are little attentive to this aspect of his work in the world. Perhaps it strikes too close to home.

In any case, his conduct here, the skill and subtlety of his protocol, reminds us of another scene in Mark: his alteration of the Decalogue in favor of—which is to say, in contest with—the rich landholder (Mark 10:17–32). The latter had approached, evidently seeking a kind of frivolous tradeoff of compliments. That gentleman too got more than he bargained for. His ego suddenly stalled when the Lord calmly revised the Decalogue with his own coinage, a command extemporized, "Thou shall not defraud."

The addition was breathtakingly to the point, for fraud was exactly the game this spurious believer was playing. He was an oligarch, according to Mark, a member of the most oppressive ruling group in Palestine.

So here, confronted by yet another stand-in for a wicked system, Jesus, straight-faced, adds to the command of love of God, recorded in Leviticus; adds, as though through spiritual hyphenation, another citation, this one from Leviticus (19:18) concerning obligations to the neighbor.

Thus he joins in one, conscientious realities the scribes, at all costs, would keep singular and separate. "There is no other command greater than THESE." Love of God, love of neighbor. (Plural. Period.) His answer is startling, unsettling in the extreme, to those who considered religious matters settled, by themselves, once for all.

As one commentator writes, "Jesus brings together two widely separated commandments. While each is warmly commended by the rabbis, so far as is known, no one except Jesus had brought them together, as the two regulative principles which sum up the human duty."

The point Mark is making by this bold marriage of mandates is entirely consistent with his vision of the vocation of Jesus. In Jesus, heaven has come to earth; therefore, the love of God resides, flourishes, or dies, in love of neighbor.

I recall a story in this regard. It concerns the remark of a young Jesuit working in the slums of Cartagena, Colombia. In the course of working on the film *The Mission,* it occurred to us that it would be important for the actors to visit a parish, to gain some notion of the common life of the poor. We did so.

With a kind of sadness, the priest remarked to me later in the day, "I sometimes wonder if we folks here are Catholics at all." Noting my bewilderment (I thought he was a rare instance of that endangered species), he added laconically, "We seem to be too little interested in people."

He was pointing exactly to the scribal illness, an infection that threatens our right sense of Christ, of one another, of vocation.

I have had cause to reflect, more times than I care to recount, how this same illness in our midst poisons the wellsprings of healthy instinct, cools the ardors of passion for peace and justice, renders good people uneasy about the quality of their faith, substitutes ecclesiastical gerrymandering for observance of the Beatitudes, plays whore to the powerful, exacts loyalty oaths in place of risk and fidelity, lauds a barren orthodoxy even as it castigates fruitful imaginative orthopraxy.

We live, alas, in a scribal generation. Many of us have suffered at its hands. Prior to our trial in the courts of Norristown, Pennsylvania, in 1981 for damaging three unarmed nuclear warheads at the nearby General Electric nuclear factory, a group of our friends went about the area, seeking the help of local congregations in providing hospitality for those who would come from afar to support us. The response of the churches was an ecumenical moment of some note. From Quakers to Catholics, one heard the slamming of church doors for miles. It was brought home to us yet once more, slow learners as we are, that nuclear weapons and the large prospect of nuclear war were by no means scandalous to Christian congregations. Nor was the iniquitous law scandalous, though it was obviously geared to protect high crime and persecute those Christians who objected to the arrangement.

Simply put, we were the scandal — nonviolence is the scandal. Violence, even such violence as beggars description, was normal. Nuclear weapons, which in unbridled scribal fashion, even short of their detonation, "devour widows' houses" — these were normal.

A curious scribal analogy, so close as to be astonishing. One could all but hear the coins, bearing Caesar's idolatrous image, striking the temple coffers. General Electric, of course, is the largest employer of the region, and through its employees, the largest beneficiary of the churches.

We need not summon images of Armageddon in order to understand the crime in progress here, the command violated. The weapons of General Electric are mingled with the rain of horror that has already fallen on the poor of our country, of the world. The Second Vatican Council called the international arms race a "monstrous larceny against the poor." The homeless of New York are visible testimony of the crime.

The Levitical tradition is cited boldly and altogether unexpectedly by Christ. Quite a healer he was, shifting the terms of argument, fresh and firm in tone, reminding the mindless powerful, bringing them back bodily to their own despised and neglected tradition, harping distressingly not on the minutiae of good conduct, fine manners, punctilious observance, jots and tittles — but on the bone and marrow of godlike reality.

The verse of Leviticus he cites, "You shall love your neighbor as yourself," comes as the culmination of a very litany of commands, regulating public and personal conduct, prohibiting vehemently the exploitation of the weak and poor. The commands are worthy of a long and lingering look.

"Leave your field for the sojourner to glean" (v. 9).

"Do not steal or deal falsely" (v. 11).

"Do not oppress the neighbor, exploit employees, or discriminate against the disabled" (v. 13).

According to Mark, the citation and its accompanying detailed commands would have been as well known to the scribes as they were ignored in practice, ignored and despised by the dominant social group, the fraternity of the fruitless and faithless, one of whom stood before him.

This questioner too got more than he bargained for. Still, we have a sense that he swallows hard, and even agrees—in principle, as they say.

Whether the agreement includes practice is left hanging. Jesus recognizes that the scribe is "thoughtful" —*nounechos,* the only time this word appears in the Greek Bible. A curious word, and beyond doubt a deliberately limited approbation. The scribe has grasped the text, in the manner of many academics and others, only intellectually. His life is thus a vast desert, a terrain of the missed point.

Jesus issues to him no invitation to follow into discipleship. However aware the scribe may be of the imperatives of love, he belongs to a system that is simply killing others (killing as well, one might add, its own apologists). To repudiate that would be to stop being a scribe.

And yet there is hope, the hope that must be strictly circumscribed, doled out, one might say, in small measure. The hope is a kind of placebo, for the scribe has a mere child's capacity. He is "not far from the realm of God."

He lingers there, in the suburbs of hope—better, malingers. He cannot dare enter, he cannot quite walk away. He merely hangs around. Imagine the man's plight, so perilously like our own. His religion has forbidden him to fall in love!

Let us pray for this morally slack, verbally skilled literalist, who so resembles ourselves, that someday he meet and marry the truth—the truth which his professionalized, acculturated, deadly moralistic life keeps at distance.

11

John the Baptist Sends Inquirers

When John the Baptist heard in prison of the works of the Messiah, he sent his disciples to him with this question, "Are you the one who is to come, or should we look for another?"

Jesus said to them in reply, "Go and tell John what you hear and see: the blind regain their sight, the lame walk, lepers are cleansed, the deaf hear, the dead are raised, and the poor have the good news proclaimed to them. And blessed is the one who takes no offense at me."

As they were going off, Jesus began to speak to the crowds about John, "What did you go out to the desert to see? A reed swayed by the wind? Then what did you go out to see? Someone dressed in fine clothing? Those who wear fine clothing are in royal palaces. Then why did you go out? To see a prophet? Yes, I tell you, and more than a prophet. This is the one about whom it is written: 'Behold, I am sending my messenger ahead of you; he will prepare your way before you.' Amen, I say to you, among those born of women, there has been none greater than John the Baptist; yet the least in the reign of heaven is greater than he."

—Matthew 11:2–11

MY REFLECTION centers about different versions of time, and about an altogether special friendship. There are two pivotal figures in the scene. I imagine them coming forth in darkness to announce (for our sake, be it said), the "right time," the time proper to advent.

First John emerges. He strikes the gong twelve times; it is midnight.

An hour later, Jesus emerges; it is still dark. He strikes the gong—once. Against odds, a new day has begun, obscurely.

This is quite daring, unprecedented, that two unknown Galileans literally take the time into their own hands. How dare they?

More, this telling of the time aright was done, we are told, at the furthest geographical point from the headquarters of the twin powers—the Temple and the imperial Roman authorities in Jerusalem. The new time starts in the desert of the lower Jordan valley.

But the supposition of Temple and Roman occupier was alike: we alone know the right time, and tell it. It is the time of the law, proclaim the Temple authorities. The books of the Pentateuch are intact; the Sabbath is widely, meticulously observed; the commerce of Temple sacrifice is teeming; Temple taxes and levies are satisfactory; lepers and women keep a needful distance from the clean; the occupying goys are respected and obeyed (even if secretly despised); Samaritans keep to their place. People in effect have drummed into them correct notions of right and wrong, and follow through. For the most part.

No, it is the task of the empire to tell the time, proclaimed the occupying power. It always had been, was, and would be, in saecula saeculorum. In times past, Babylon, Assyria, and Egypt had told the time right. Now Roman time rules the world.

It is the time of armed force, of a collaborating religious establishment, a time of the ascendancy of a Pilate, of the advantageous services of a half Jew named Herod. It is an apt time to hire Jewish collectors of Roman taxes, as a way of drawing the populace into the orbit of advantage. It is time to foster the prospering of wealthy landowners, and (regrettably) the eviction of small farmers when the harvest fails. Time also for a judicious application of terror, furtive use of spies, and the threat to execute of capital punishment against troublemakers.

These tactics, this ideology, meant that a great world power was reading the times aright, that the imperial venture rejoiced in good times rightly told.

We who know the outcome, as death overtook both John and Jesus, realize of course that the Temple and empire were correct. Both troublemakers were destroyed by the twin powers. Once more, law and order reigned.

Still, we have that troublesome, conflicting sense of the times. First John, sounding a midnight hour. Did he know that an era is coming to an end, that closure was at hand? The last of the prophets, he is called. The greatest ever born, Jesus calls him, an Elijah. A man of working faith, I call him.

An ascetic also, a desert solitary in the line of the Nazarites, long haired and lean, sparing of food and spurning drink, denouncing the powerful, name-calling, down-putting, all no and seldom yes in face of the uses and users of a soiled world.

Finally, know it or not, John dramatizes an ending, a midnight hour, a closing of a scroll. Dramatizes it in his own fate, locked up as he is, and facing execution. In his ethos also.

And Jesus, an hour after John, also tells the time. He sounds a dawn, delayed but sure to come. Something unknown, a new eon, a new way of being in the world and before God, something of this is near birth. We shall have to wait and see.

But shall we? Already we sense, though dimly perhaps, the lineaments of the new kairos. They are in utter contrast to the style of John the Baptist. Jesus comes neither fasting nor ritually cleansed; shockingly, He comports rather continually with the types abominated by His seemly cousin.

More, Jesus declares such criteria of justification as John approves, to be null and void.

The observance of the law is of hardly any avail. Where it applies to the searching spirit, it admits of a great variety of ways and styles—including no fasting, no purifications, and a rather noticeable consorting with prostitutes and tax gougers.

Indeed where the law is useful at all, it is in areas where love of God and of the neighbor make common cause.

The implications surrounding the "new time" are enormously broad and searching. They are also dangerous to the timekeeper.

To this point: If the love of God and neighbor are the sum total of the law, what then of—everything else? What of the vast liturgical apparatus of the Temple priesthood, the minutiae of sacrifice, the infinite convolutions, debates, rabbinical refinements which whirl like a wind about the scrolls? What of ego and money and pride of place?

Granted all this is passing away—questions, questions.

Who then is to be in charge of human life, who mediates, who dispenses merit and punishment, who blesses and condemns, declares clean and unclean?

And Jesus in effect answers (a nonanswer to be sure). The questions as put are wide of the mark. They are questions raised in ghostly voices by an old regime. They are drawn from stuck minds and methods and structures and authorities, here declared stripped of their power, canceled.

Further, another angle, this too from Jesus. If there is a question befitting the new times, it would go like this: Are we responding to the love of God for us, concretely, consistently, in our love for one another?

In this and nothing else are summed up the law and the prophets.

To turn more closely to our text of the day, there is something intriguing and affectionate in the exchange between Jesus and His cousin. Strength meets strength, each of its own kind. Each is taking the measure of the other, not by way of competitiveness, rather in a love that that seeks further understanding. In John, the old and outdone is sounding its tocsin. Nonetheless his exit is unselfish and insightful; Jesus is to grow great, I am to diminish. And in Jesus, the new announces itself, in stark contrast with the old, but for all of that, companionable and grateful and warm of heart.

I believe Jesus loved John, and that His love was greatly reciprocated. I celebrate this friendship as an advent gift, a cause for Gaudete.

Such love as Jesus bears toward His cousin sums up the greatness of His friend. Let the disciples and messengers take note. None in this world is greater than John.

Then a surprising turnabout, a kind of koan: the least in the realm of God is to be accounted greater than John. What are we to make of this edifice of honor, built high and then summarily set rocking?

We live with the koan, until the advent of a clap of enlightenment. Until then, let us simply offer this: Jesus talks to those disciples of a John whose situation is strikingly like our own.

They and we are assailed with criteria of greatness, with cultural icons drawn from the genetic pool of church and state. We too have our Pilates and Herods and high priests. We are urged to venerate them, mime their behavior, approve their version of the human — generals, tycoons, politicos, to bow before the infallible pronunciamento of a cardinal, to approve the greed and inhumanity of televangelists, to join the lockstep of good consumers and subservient taxpayers and hairspring warriors. It is precisely among these that a spirit like John the Baptist towers, a Himalaya among foothills.

Jesus is here applying the world's criteria to the question: What is a human being, or more precisely, what is human greatness? The criterion comes down entirely in John's favor, to the world's disadvantage and down-putting. The culture's anthropology, Jesus implies, is recessive. With a double command, it invites us backward — imprison John, enthrone Herod.

Then, an about face. Let us apply another measure of the human than the world allows. Indeed this measure exceeds the imperial imagination and at every point surpasses all worldly power and genius.

Jesus has put it plain; so, before His birth, had His mother. According to this measure, the last shall be first, the poor fed, the mighty are toppled, the meek possess the earth, the peacemakers are named anew ("the sons and daughters of God"), and the rich are sent away empty.

Now it is in accord with this new measure, and keeping in mind the criteria of the world, that John lags behind "the least in the realm of God."

The awful truth of John's fate invites the "deconstruction" of the koan. In this way, because he is considered and dealt with as a capital criminal, the least and lowest, the off-scouring among humans—it is for this reason that he (we dare paraphrase) "shall be first in the realm of God."

I have a poem to offer. According to its fiction, John has already perished by the sword. He is reflecting on his death, and the contrasting death of Jesus by crucifixion. I hope you will agree that the poem concerns friendship:

> A sword
> forbade me to grow old; it cut
> time like a parasite from eternity.
>
> Could death have eyed and pierced my body, could I
> have stood upon the nails an hour,
> would He take warning from His murdered shade
>
> casting His fate in smoky runes
> with points of light
> like lips where death had fastened?
>
> I follow from sad limbo,
> till death unfasten, till His rising
>
> unwind and wear me
> aureole choir crown

12

Christ before Pilate, Witnessing to the Truth

Pilate went back into the praetorium and summoned Jesus and said to Him, "Are you the King of the Jews?" Jesus answered, "Do you say this on your own or have others told you about Me?" Pilate answered, "I am not a Jew, am I? Your own nation and the chief priests handed You over to me. What have You done?" Jesus answered, "My reign does not belong to this world. If My reign did belong to this world, My attendants would be fighting to keep Me from being handed over to the Judeans. But as it is, My reign is not here." So Pilate said to Him, "Then You are a king?" Jesus answered, "You say I am a king. For this I was born and for this I came into the world, to bear witness to the truth. Everyone who belongs to the truth listens to My voice."   —John 18:33–37

ONE THINKS of the images that have been created through the ages to portray this "kingship" or rule of Christ. First came those borrowed from the Constantinian era, the grand mosaics of Ravenna and Rome and Sicily. They are overpowering, larger than life. They convey the absolute juridical power of the Pantocrator Christ. The new images celebrate the new status of the church, advancing from a persecuted minority to the "official religion" of the empire.

Christ, it goes without saying, is no longer shown as the accused and abused suffering Servant hailed before Pilate. Now He is the friend and advocate and beneficiary of Pilate.

The change hardly stops with the later images, the God of "power and might." Images always go far beyond themselves; they urge new attitudes and behavior, celebrate new social structures. Icons became signs of immense social change, celebrating a new and prosperous status of the Holy vis-à-vis secular power.

Now The Holy One is also powerful. This powerful Christ would also be secular, which is to say, He would purportedly bless that most secular of instruments, the sword.

For centuries, Christians were forbidden the sword; now they would wield the sword. The emperor would summon and preside over church councils. We are told how at one such council, the bishops passed under the raised swords of the emperor, into an imperial banquet. They were celebrating a council of the now "universal church." Their decrees, it goes without saying, were entirely satisfactory to both powers.

We are still paying for that dinner, more often than not, in blood.

With celerity, the theory of the "just war" as a "lesser evil" was elaborated.

For many centuries, a manifest absurdity will hold firm. From each party of a given conflict, a schizoid church will declare that justice is on *its* side of the bloodletting, injustice on the adversary's side. It will demonize the "enemy" and confer a blessing on the arms and exploits of its favorite. Meantime, as the game proceeds in the distorted mirror, the one declared accursed will be domestically absolved and urged on by *its* church.

And for the duration of the conflict, the Gospel will be a closed book, the Sermon on the Mount will be irrelevant, the command to love our enemies will be of no practical consequence.

Everything comes undone. Christ, the endangered One, no longer witnesses to the truth before Pilate. He is shortly to be condemned to capital punishment.

Done with all that. Constantine has "rehabilitated" Him. He is exonerated, a success in the world, inoffensive to the powers.

Thus the images of Christ go forward toward the high Renaissance. The austere sovereignty of the great iconic mosaics is changed in two directions. There emerges the personal piety of the Madonna school, and its opposite, the superhuman gymnastics of Michelangelo.

In the latter, no Christ stands before Pilate, but still, judgments are painted aplenty. The court is assembled in high heaven; the scene is extratemporal and extraterrestrial. The End Time is out of this world and indefinitely distant in time.

In location and guise, Christ the judge is not greatly different from Jupiter. He is regnant, he judges. In such art, the great ones of earth stand outside judgment; after all, they are the patrons and benefactors of the church. They commission the paintings, and win plenary indulgence for their bountifulness.

But where in such divagations is Christ allowed to take His stand where once He stood—in the dock, the accused One, shortly to be convicted and punished? Just for a moment in the history of art, in the frescoes of the Dominican convent in Florence, He speaks aloud, words concerning His crime, words that rebuke His imperial tormenter: "You say I am a king. For this I was born, for this I came into the world, to bear witness to the truth."

We take note, and we are set off balance. Christ has come, he avers, not just to speak the truth, but to "bear witness to the truth," a difference of some note.

Could uttering the truth before the powers evade consequence? According to the Accused, to speak the truth is to bear witness to the truth. The truth is thus defined and refined for our sakes. The truth is hardly neutral, facile, abstract, cheap, easygoing. How then can the truth be acceptable to the Pilates of this world? The truth is consequential. Pilate and his kind will have blood.

But Christ will not shed the blood of another; He will only allow His own blood to be shed. Christ will not be complicit in murder. He will die, but He will not kill. And so the summons: We are not permitted to kill, or to be complicit in killing. The prohibition stands firm: no matter the cause at issue, no matter the provocation, no matter the flags or polls, no matter the president, no matter the generals, the heavy triumphant faces and desert fatigues and flashpan victory. Every gun must fall from Christian hands, every missile must be transformed to a plowshare, every heart and structure must be disarmed. The attendants of the nonviolent Christ do not fight, kill or wage war.

We sense the drama which closes the scene. "Everyone who is of the truth hears My voice." It is very nearly the last word of the Accused before the scaffold. And it is hardly to be thought a plea for mercy or mitigation of sentence.

It is rather a last-ditch appeal to Pilate, a reaching out of the merciful One toward the merciless:

"Hear my voice, hear the truth. Salvage your humanity. Renounce your illegitimate power. Join those whose noblest credential is that they 'bear witness to the truth.'"

III

Prophets and Peacemakers

Sisters and brothers dwell in peace
What joy, what an omen!
Hand in hand, heart in heart
a double strength

A waterfall pausing, various, ever moving,
roses, surprising strawberries
a closed circled, an enclosed garden, a universe—

There
war's hoarse throat is silenced
and praise goes up night and day
and the stanchions of slaves in the hills
gather dust, spring ivy.

13

The Long Loneliness
of Dorothy Day

Tradition refuses to submit to the small and arrogant oligarchy of those who merely happen to be walking about. All democrats object to people being disqualified by the accident of birth; tradition objects to their being disqualified by the accident of death. —G. K. Chesterton

Her ultimate position on pacifism, and maybe on the whole modus operandi of the Catholic Worker movement—its steadfast opposition to national governments, to the state as the decisive instrument of social and economic justice—is neither one of certainty nor of doubt, but one of insistent self-scrutiny. —Robert Coles

I AM PROUD to write of Dorothy Day, an extraordinary woman, a friend to me and my family for many years. How vividly I remember her death, the wake at Mary House in Manhattan, the undercurrent of grief and joy and homecoming. Then the funeral.

The plain box was borne to the neighborhood church. There, for years, until age and weakness held her down, she had worshiped each morning at Mass, sometimes alone.

But on this morning, a congregation crowded the chancel, most of them Catholic Workers who were drawn to her work and vision. There they bade her farewell, praying that she might join the company of the saints.

The end of an era, we murmured. Indeed we were right.

I think of her first of all as a teacher. This was the service she did me and many others. As seminarians and young priests, first in our seminaries, then scattered in the world, we were little more than lapsarian sprouts—ignorant, eager, and innocent beyond belief.

The world of the 1930s was mobilizing for yet another war. And we went toward its bristling phalanx as though the horrid weapons facing us were designed to plow fields instead of annihilate the living.

Alas, know it or not, the main business of that world was the forging of swords. Plowshares, here and there turning the earth to sound use, even these were inducted; they were part of something called the "war effort," a horrid euphemism. They were in fact, in service to the Sons of the Sword, readying the earth for a sowing of dragons' teeth, and its harvest of armed and arrogant warriors.

In a moral grotesquerie, the world powers were seizing on the image of Isaiah to their own advantage, turning the image on its head. Plowshares were not to be thought secondary to the main purpose; anything useful to peace could be turned around to war. Let plowshares too be converted to the uses of death — broken, melted down, beaten into swords. A world of some trace of right order was flipping its mind.

Dorothy was born into a different world, from the point of view of metaphor and method, almost a different planet. The world of her childhood was unconvulsed with war. But she was to live on in a world of two universal wars; swords were set whirling in an ever wider and bloodier arc.

The great wars wrought another horror. It was less visibly lethal, but spiritually it was catastrophic. The wars robbed the human heart of its accumulated riches, its tradition, its self-understanding, its store of compassion. The wars ravaged our wisdom, uprooted it, burned it like a debris.

Up in smoke went a vision which formerly, if it did not prevail, at least was available, a minority vision to be sure, but genuine, irreplaceable. "Thou shalt not kill. Love your enemies. Walk a further mile."

By 1945 (to be arbitrary), such words were regarded in practice as irrelevant, apolitical, impractical, not for real, sabbatarian but hardly hebdomadal, applicable to personal decencies only, an unrealizable social ethic, and so on. Wars would continue, presumably to the end of time. In the meantime (a truly Dantesque crepuscule), we were offered something known as an "interim ethic."

Which is to say, as far as I can understand this flight of casuistry, we were to adjust our consciences to the practices and ploys of whatever warmaking nations we were assigned to by accident of birth.

I read this nonsense as a kind of practical, (barely) functional ethical despair. In accord with it, Christians were to give up on the plain words of the Gospel. The Gospel be damned or becalmed, we are stuck in "the nations," the "dwellers on earth." Let us make the best of a bad deal of cards, and be reasonably content there.

"For the duration" the words of Jesus all but vanished on the winds of fire that arose from Dresden and Hiroshima. The famous Mount of the Sermon, and the Sermon itself, had been, so to speak, nuked and firebombed out of existence.

It was this loss of ours, this lost tradition and wholeness and humanity, that the teaching of Dorothy, in measure, would heal.

But that long loneliness of hers did not begin with her adult Christian choices. These only continued a dark process which, under far more sinister auspices, had begun in her early adulthood.

It is important to remember that for many years, she was bereft of the faith. She wandered afar on a road leading to a dead end. The loneliness started here; she tasted for years the illness whose modern names are alienation, anxiety, dread, a sense of being askew, off center, lost in a void. A modern woman, in a destructive sense.

The world of her youth (and of mine too) came on strong, with a new jargon, new credentials and claims and a fast draw, a "new sensibility," a "unity of technique and self understanding." It was all hokum, a great lie. The modern world was a void. She grew to adulthood breathing its fetid air.

Then, as she wrote in chastened pride and gratitude, by an act of God she was lifted out of the pit.

To be ill is no vocation; to be healed is a glory beyond measure. Dorothy's wisdom, in the Pauline sense, was learned in a harsh school. Her passage went from the illness named sin to grace, from a curse to a mystery, from a killing loneliness to (what proved eventually to be, and hardly for herself alone) a most fruitful one.

She was a journalist born, a chronicler with one eye on the public storm, the other focused within. She grew, in a large sense, responsible. The word, its follies and furies, drew her, to critique and combat.

And she recounted her own life as well, in her column in the *Catholic Worker*, "On Pilgrimage," explicitly in her autobiography, *The Long*

Loneliness. She refined and enlarged on her ethic, with wry wit, concretely, personally, tracing the emergence of her conscience out of the wasting loneliness of her youth, the taste of death which anointed her tongue with bitter aloes. A taste that lingered on into age, a warning.

But meantime, redeemed.

That wisdom of hers! In early life she ignored or despised it. Then grace brought it passionately to the fore, until it transfigured her face.

Let me not call that wisdom something so jejune as "How to Succeed," as though life's best secrets lay in the pages of a mechanic's handbook. Not a "how to"—but an interior sense, access to symbols, esteem, celebration, ready payment of the price of—life itself.

It was a complex rhythm, and her elegant and eloquent hands played all the stops.

There was a tragic undertone too.

Steadfast to some, inflexible and stubborn to many, her stance against war all but brought the skies down. Houses of hospitality closed, readers of her paper canceled. Some stalwarts who had stood with her for years saw in European soil the cloven hoof of despotism, and departed to enlist in the war.

A lonely woman, alone in the church, in the culture, in the acculturated church.

Her conversion did not read, "religious at last," "safe at last," "selfish at last." If it was granted her to taste a different life, to taste the Author of Life on her tongue; and if that new taste cleansed her of the ashes and aloes of death—she also understood that her momentous gift changed little of the world around her, little of her beloved church.

She was blessed or cursed (or both) to live on in America, where life is cheap as dirt, and death fits the scene like a greased glove.

With eyes open, she embraced the church. For reasons too complex to dwell on here, her new community, long before, had made its peace with war.

A generation later, one can speculate that the church needed her almost as desperately as she needed the faith it held out.

She came with questions. Her church was hardly prepared to answer them. How were the humiliation and moral splendor of Christ, His cry of desolation, the transfigured dawn of Easter, to be manifest in such a world—short of resistance against mass murder?

This was her question, and it went to the heart of things—to the writing, the jailings, the (so-to-speak) detoxifying of academe, the spurning (usually with gentleness) of camp followers and the merely curious, and the task and sorrow and burden she carried—and then her death; these raised the question, again and again.

Know it or not, she must supply an answer, live the answer, live as though there were an answer. She offered, as she conceded, only a measure of light on the question.

And that, as matters turned, was enough. If even a few would submit to live in the eye of consequence, would take the punishment for living, would live as though death had no dominion, as though they were denying to death the last word—ah, then what might not be hoped for?

A long loneliness linked her to an ancient Easter pageant and hymn. Women had stood at the cross; a day later they made their way to the tomb; along the way they wonder aloud—"What will we find here? What is the meaning of it all, the death, the awful outcome?" They sing: "Mors et vita duello conflixere mirando" (Life and death are locked in mortal struggle).

The words and music might have been the swan song of the ascension of Dorothy, as they had been the overture of her surrender to Christ, her characteristic and crowning chord.

I do not want to forget Dorothy Day, or to forget that vocation, which drew her strongly in opposite directions, to the needy — and just as strongly to solitude.

Her work on behalf of the needy is a matter of record. Far less taken in account was a solitude of spirit that in key moments of her life drifted into something far more painful, until "long loneliness" became a synonym for life itself.

Losses aplenty; a sense of being unacceptable, of living too close to the bone, too close to the Gospel text, of having one's work judged as a kind of gaffe, a sorry mistake, or worse.

She renounced the love of her life, her common-law spouse Forster, father of her child Tamar. To her, the loss was the price of her conversion, since he, with considerable heat, cast off any part with the God and church she was turning to.

Loneliness and loss. Of solitude she knew little, that was the irony—and of loneliness so much.

One thinks—the equation ought to be just the opposite. One ought to be skilled and desirous of the good uses of solitude, and flee like a plague that dark bane of the solitudinous, known to the medieval moralists as "acedia."

Did she know that darkness? Beyond doubt she did. I mean a sense, both perverse and permeating, that literally nothing makes sense, whether within the soul or in the world without, and that one's own existence, one's hope, one's work, make least sense of all.

And all the while, her courage, perseverance, compassion, were admired by all (or nearly all) as ably and amply hers.

These seemed to herself either lacking, or if acknowledged, of no weight to counter the mood.

I remember her face, the eyes looked equably, or as required, angrily on the world. Her tongue was resourceful and witty, her mind headlong in intelligence and inward in repose, a mind that guarded and gave her store of deep waters. The hands were elegant and workaday, the frame tall and commanding. She was easeful and attentive with this one or that, street person or celebrity, the deranged, the obsessive, the would-be saints and the all too actual sinners. With all of us.

I must not forget her. I hear it as a command. A command that might also be called a vocation — hers, mine, any Christian's, anyone who would claim the word "human." Do not forget. Do not forget the poor, do not forget the forgotten.

And do not forget the wars, nor the warmakers, nor the victims.

She heard the command and obeyed, and the Gospel broke her life apart. Given the world, and her times, the violence raging across the world, she must pay the cost of the blessing she sought, "Blessed are the peacemakers, they will be called daughters and sons of God."

How long a time, I reflect, how perversely and foolishly long it was, until I grasped her simple skill — a skill better named a grace — her skill of remembering.

I knew of Dorothy from my earliest years. Her *Catholic Worker* newspaper with its plain unchurchy images by Ade Bethune, came to our home from almost the first issue. With its uncompromising squads of close print in columns, the paper languished there on the table, next to the livid hagiography of the *Messenger of the Sacred Heart.* My father read the *Worker,* and my mother.

I entered the Jesuits. I was teaching in New York, and came with students to Catholic Worker events, the Friday night meetings legislated by her close friend and mentor, Peter Maurin.

Older Jesuits, some among them secure in this or that competence, were an interesting barometer of attitudes toward Dorothy and her movement. As long as she stuck close to (what they defined as) her proper turf, they applauded. How could they not? Her life cut too close to the bone of the body of Christ to be scanted.

But then she grew outrageous, and the long loneliness was under way. Many Jesuits, among others, recoiled. Here was the rub: She began to trace the pathology of the wounds she was tending. She inquired publicly who or what had inflicted these wounds. And she went further: She undertook a diagnosis. For the times, for the church, her analysis was daring, unheard of.

Why, in a sane world, she asked, why should a wounded human lie in a ditch untended? She began so to speak, literally to re-member that body. The crime, the neglect, were universal, she cried. All over the world, on an "average" day, the unemployed and unemployable, the victimized and vacuous, the homeless and feckless, the alcoholics and druggies, the flaky and furious — in great numbers these were struck down, and fell into ditches.

And the world went its amnesiac blank-eyed way, the way named "money and routine and ego and academe and religion." The way named, on the largest signpost of all, lettered in blood—war.

The Levites passed by, and the priests, and many others.

Before the pope spoke up, long before the bishops and priests, Dorothy cried into the contrary wings: *"No more war, war never again! No just wars, no such thing!"*

At this point, many took scandal. I was warned, many a finger wagging. A young Jesuit, I heard a chorus of renowned brethren raise its voice. "What a pity!" they declaimed. "She really was capable of good work, she had charism and talent; now she's gone wacky, this pacifism bit."

Pacifism, world poverty. Connections. That was the fault; she was making connections.

I was hooked. (A day would arrive when I too could be called irreformable.) The attacks of the high and mighty served only to buttress my resolve. I was all the more eager to learn from her.

I want to remember those times, when Dorothy's spirit entered my young life. To savor that time, to make it my own, to draw a measure of her strength from it.

It started like this, I think. She took seriously a parable of Jesus. She entered the story. (Ironically she was following the method of St. Ignatius: be present to the scene, find your place there, live within it.) She stood by the wounded one in the ditch. The shadow of those who passed by, passed her by. Her spirit entered the abandonment, the loneliness of the lorn and violated and wretched of the earth. She made the parable of the Good Samaritan true.

She felt the full force of the forgetting, the amnesia, the loss of humanity—those who were bound elsewhere, were intent on their own affairs, who were engrossed (literally rendered gross) by concerns which did not admit of trouble or delay.

Not for them the interrupted life of the wandering Rabbi. In the story of the Samaritan, in effect, He tells His own story.

Dorothy paused and knelt. She lifted up the battered head; in exemplary fashion she performed the four or five steps of healing commended by Jesus.

It was an epiphany, a moment of recognition, a spasm of conscience and compassion. That was the beginning.

Then, the act of mercy was extended and transformed. It lengthened out, became a life, a vocation.

Thereafter, Dorothy Day was permanently interrupted. Interruption became the form and soul of life. And she discovered that the victim lying helpless in the ditch was there by no accident, was not to be thought an exception in a game whose rules were to be accounted fair and square.

No, some deep fault lay along the world, a wound in creation itself. She walked the fault, a tremor shook her. She walked and walked, she tore her heart open by main force, she began to pray, to cry out. She succored one victim, and was led further.

And she came on hundreds, thousands of victims.

And ah! this was it, the revelation, the one the Jesuit critics had missed, or perhaps had come on and ignored, or examined and found wanting and put to one side. (Had "passed by"?)

It was too simple — and after all, she was a woman, and they were male, clerics, highly if conventionally educated, with a strong bias toward their kind.

What had she seen? The tragedy of the victim was by no means accidental, nor was it in any way to be equated with the will of God for humans.

Something else was at work, something eminently sinful. Choices against, overwhelmingly against, multitudes of the living. Caught in the gun sights of war and cut down; war being a simple and appalling synonym for the modern world, its main horrific work and business-for-profit.

Multitudes were simply declared expendable. They were victims of a cruel triage whose calculus made of the cities of the world, battlefields strewn with the homeless, the dysfunctional and dying.

She learned a new name for war. It was a kind of mad "peace time" murder, murder by proxy — by winter weathers, hunger, despair, neglect, injustice, economic rapine. Her realization was so simple that to dwell on it only serves to complicate beyond measure. Let us say, she lived with her eyes open. She made moral connections.

This was her genius, seeing the nexus, following through. She succored the victims, and she dared to look up. And she saw what Paul saw, "the spiritual forces of wickedness in regions above," a portent, a horror, a hell coming to earth. It was Mars on rampage.

She could have said "Sin!" and let it go at that. She could have invoked the Famous Fatalist of religious do-nothings, the darlings of frigid will, and said with a sigh, an exhalation of bad faith, "Yes, after all, the poor you will always have around," and let it go at that. "Let us be resigned." Or said to the poor, "You will always be around. So. Be resigned."

She had learned something, and would not turn back. She spoke of modern war, its larcenies and murders, its insatiable appetites. In the 1950s, she repeatedly resisted the absurd nuclear air raid "shelter drills" in New York, went to jail, and won advocates. And eventually the willful nonsense stopped.

By now she was a scandal. A Catholic scandal. A scandal to the cardinal of New York. She was resisting war. All war, any war. Call it what one will — necessary war, virtuous war, inevitable war, Christian war, war on war, present war, envisioned war. (In every case, the absolutely last war, the war that would end war, would bring on the realm of God, would eliminate the implacable enemy and vindicate the virtuous.)

She said no. With each and every war, she repeated the no. She wrote in her paper in June 1940:

> *Many of our readers ask, "What is the stand of the Catholic Worker in regard to the present war?" They are thinking, as they ask the question, of the stand we took during the Spanish civil war. We repeat, that, as in the Ethiopian war, the Spanish war, the Japanese and Chinese war, the Russian-Finnish war — so in the present war, we stand unalterably opposed to the use of war as a means of saving "Christianity," "civiliza-tion," "democracy." We have inherited the Beatitudes. Our duty is clear. The Sermon on the Mount is our Christian manifesto.*

She was a practical visionary. Christ offered the vision; the works of mercy were her task. The earth and its resources need not be wasted; there were better uses for human talent than the devising of better ways of killing. In the same issue, she offered alternatives:

> *Instead of gearing ourselves . . . for a gigantic production of death-dealing bombers and men trained to kill, we should be producing food, medical supplies, ambulances, doctors and nurses for the works of mercy, to heal and rebuild a shattered world. . . . We do not take care of our own unemployed and hungry millions in city and country, let alone those beyond the seas.*

And in the same editorial, she sums up her position;

> *We are urging a seeming impossibility — a training of the use of non-violent means of opposing injustice, servitude and a deprivation of the means of holding fast to the Faith. It is again, the folly of the cross. But how else is the word of God to be kept alive in the world? The word is love, and we are bidden to love God and to love one another. It is the whole law, it is all of life.*

To her way of thinking, no war, actual or intended, could qualify as acceptable to Christians. Every war was an unmitigated horror and sin. No war could conceivably be just or serve a whit toward a better future or an improved conscience. Not one but guaranteed, in a covenant sealed in blood, that another and worse would follow.

What a lonely — dare one call it eminence? — where she stood. Better call it a pit, like the dry well into which Jeremiah was cast.

Could she not understand, this neo-convert with set jaw, that she had entered the veritable church of the just war, the church of Augustine and Thomas Aquinas and the eight (or ten, or was it twelve?) "conditions for a just conflict," each of them raked over by casuists of every nation and every war in history? And by consensus of this or that warring party, invariably shoring up the justice of any war of history?

Why, it was as plain as it was absurd. Every war was just. Every competing party, every church of every nation at war said so, a moral cacophony to deafen the angels. The Second World War was manifestly just. The war in Vietnam was just. The cardinal of New York said so, and who was she to say nay?

Talk about loneliness, talk about scandal. Wars came, wars were won and lost. She too lost. She lost friends, her paper was lashed with every contempt.

And she withstood, and suffered it through. Her no stood firm.

She was an affront to the atomized academics, the hair splitters, the just war chess players (your king for my queen, my castle for your rook) — to those whose Gospel was quietly closed and shelved, at the latest war cry of this or that khaki-clad cardinal.

What a lonely business, this Gospel peacemaking. And it must be understood as the simple consequence of a choice. You chose to live in such a way, you prayed, received the sacraments, submitted to a spiritual, daily discipline. And it always led somewhere, into deep waters, and dark. Friends walked away, become former friends.

Then lo! new friends arrived on the scene. For awhile one's family said nay; then a new family stood at hand.

You might call it predetermined, but the term would occur only to an observer, at second hand, or third. To the one who underwent it, the loneliness following on the shock of reality apprehended was perpetually shocking, and wounding as well.

That sense of being an outsider in a culture of yea-sayers never left her. Ironically, she turned it around, lifted the shame on high, held it before God, a matter of faith.

Must she, time and again, go it alone? She must, so it seemed. She practiced what she preached. She counseled resistance, and she resisted. She went to jail, and she urged others to do likewise.

Thus for a half century her life ran against a headlong current. She plugged away steadily, the sublime and elegant worker, on cross-country buses, at her typewriter, in soup lines and clothing rooms. She served and was served, she fasted and feasted, rejoiced and mourned, she went into court and lockup and came out on her feet. In writings and speeches and travels, she refined her beliefs, without ever cutting loose from life and work, or from the communities that through Peter Maurin and herself came into being.

Eighty-three years, and now a memory, infinitely precious, an irreplaceable resource.

I wish to remember her, in the active, even passionate and partisan sense of the word—to keep her life before me, to make that life available to those I love, to feel its moral tug and urgency, to explore her way.

The day she died, I took down her photo from the wall, placed it on a table with a candle and a few flowers, and prayed there awhile. I did not want to forget her; more to the point, I did not want her to forget me.

What might it mean, "to keep her life before me"?

I think of my lifetime and hers, of the wars upon wars that threaten to make of fair earth a monstrous death camp, of the misuse of talent and money and resources—of the waste. How we long for peace, how peace evades us! And what to be done?

A change of heart, for a beginning. A wrenching conversion of heart, a new understanding of peacemaking (the peacemaking that is always in the teeth of war)—as simply the life Christ summons us to.

Dorothy, I think, came on a quite simple, paradoxical insight, something like this: in the Gospel, peace is a verb. You make the peace. You do not inherit it, or hoard it, or borrow it, or sit on it. You make it.

And this: You make peace in a (somewhat) parallel way to the making of war. Which is to say, you pay up. Peace must be paid for, as war is paid for.

I do not write such words lightly. They strike me with dread, even as I set them down.

I first read of that price in the utterly fearless eyes of Dorothy, the eyes of a friend. With an imperious sweeping arm, she pushed aside the spurious, deadly, conventional "golden mean" of paganized Christianity.

Peace, she teaches, implies the making of peace. It is never done with. It implies resistance against the "filthy rotten system" (her words) that makes of us drudges and cowards and war tax–paying chattels, that adroitly adjusts our will and conscience, like the sinister clockwork of a time bomb—adjusts us to a world of injustice and cruelty and death.

She and her like may yet salvage us, our endangered humanity.

Let me suggest a few forms of resistance in accord with her spirit:

- Let American Christians renounce all complicity with war preparation, research, development of weaponry. Let them quit such jobs. Let them and their families be supported in such principled decisions, financially and morally, by their Christian communities.

- Let Christian households review before Christ their due of federal war taxes, and resolve on ways to discontinue this blood tribute to Mars.

- Let the American bishops urge the above as serious matters of conscience. Let them also counsel young men and women to resist military registration and draft. And let the bishops begin to take seriously the implications of their own vocation to civil disobedience.

- Let all rites and pomps implying necrophilia and idolatry of the flag be banned from Christian premises. Instead, let Christian communities, especially on days of war celebration, Memorial Day, Veterans' Day, and the like, undertake processions to local laboratories, weapons' factories, think tanks, air bases, nuclear bunkers, naval bases—those plague spots where in secrecy, the epitaph of humanity is being composed. In such places, let the believers vigil, pray, distribute leaflets, sit in, be arrested.

Hope springs eternal. Those I love are repeatedly locked in jails across the land, for acts of nonviolent resistance. On December 6, 2002, my brother Philip died after spending nearly eleven years of his life in prison for nonviolent resistance against war.

Thus the long loneliness is bequeathed, verified, honored in practice, as many keep green the memory of Dorothy Day.

14

Martin Luther King Jr.
and the Arm of Justice

*Notes for a talk at Columbia University
on the first Martin Luther King Jr. holiday,
January 20, 1986*

~

THE STICKING POINT at which the great man met society and was gunned down is still the same. We see it again and again in the public spectacles that inevitably include the lockstep military and the guns. We hear it in the so-called tributes, in what the politicians and tycoons and academics have to say as well as what they refuse to say; in their cant and newspeak and hypocrisy. Official America cannot stomach nonviolent Dr. King, alive or dead. He must be buried twice.

Thus King — too much to stomach. Most of the others remembered in the rotunda of the Capitol and honored by national holidays are cultural cliches. They fitted America, hand in glove. But inevitably the hand of the typical American hero, carefully gloved, held a sword. Which is to say only that America loves those who love America and emulate American violence and illustrate its usefulness in the world — rather than those who passionately seek to turn America around.

Martin King did not fit America. I hereby indulge in the understatement of the century. He was a species of unassimilable misfit. He was never really loved in this country, except among his own people and, more or less grudgingly and gingerly, by a certain minority of others — religious whites, northern liberals, the young. Bobby Kennedy bugged him fervently. Johnson detested and feared him and set FBI hounds on his trail. After King's speech at Riverside Church denouncing the Vietnam War, Johnson withdrew all federal protection, and shortly thereafter, Dr. King was murdered.

98

It is said that America loves heroes, but makes sandwiches of them. Dr. King was safer dead than alive. Now he could be honored by highly placed hypocrites who detest what he stands for and stand for what he detested. Now Dr. King could also be honored at places like Columbia University, the granddaddy liberal institution of the North—the begetter of those liberals on whom Dr. King could least depend when the racist chips were down. Precisely because the liberal chips were placed on the same bets as the racist—but undercover, liberals are artful dodgers indeed.

What would Columbia look like if Dr. King's dream were embodied here? The question is a serious one. If it were idly put, or not posed at all, as is usual on such occasions, we had best spare our breath and go on with the business of Columbia, which is hand in glove with the business of America.

Let us at the same time not waste the occasion by flogging a horse already over the hill. The fault is nearer home. The business of Columbia, the business of America, is the business of most of us. It is too easy, and too foreign to the austere style of Dr. King, to let ourselves off, in favor of excoriating Big Business or Big Military, or for that matter, Big Learnery. The appetites and ambitions that fuel all of these burn away in ourselves. The rip-off of real estate in the neighborhood, the control of rents and rates, the mauling and eviction of tenants, the vast portfolios, the millions flowing in from grateful tycoons who were taught their game here, the CIA present on campus, both recruiting and indoctrinating—these speak not only of the voracious appetite of Columbia, they speak of ourselves.

There was once, like a vagrant day of spring, brief and poignant, another spirit abroad at Columbia, and far different longings in the air. It was as though the entire university had breathed deep of unpolluted air. At least for a time, a certain number of students, even a few faculty, were differently driven.

There followed something astonishing, a unique surge of life, unexpected as a drawn breath in a corpse. It was a revolt against death, an ultimatum of the spirit, issued not only against the owners, but more importantly, against being owned. This for a brief and brilliant and clumsy and contentious few days.

After which law and order (the normal institutional disorder and moral lawlessness) again won out. The briefcases won out, and the trustees and the endowments and the CIA and its School of International Affairs and the military and the enormous real estate holdings.

There are few at Columbia today who could look on those days without disdain or nostalgia or the kind of dread that attends the presence of a stalking ghost. The mainline students and faculty, if they know about the uprising of '68, tend to distrust such untidy, unclassifiable events. The defeated liberals look back on them as a kind of jailhouse dream. Very few regard such days, shot through as they were with the example and words of Dr. King, as a kind of week of creation, instructive as they were, and visionary and offering light on national darkness.

Can those days tell us anything — about America, about education, about divestiture, about other ways of being human? Possession, which is nine points of lawlessness, closes the issue like a tycoon's briefcase. Columbia once more seized its larcenous goodies, which the students briefly threatened — O horrors! — to redistribute more equably. The briefcases snap shut like a jaw. We are a long way from Selma, Birmingham, the jails and sheriffs and dogs and fire hoses. A long way from the songs and Freedom Rides and sit-ins. A long way also from the valiant and solitary spirit who sang and walked and wrote and shouted like an archangel and combated the demons with his great heart, and so perished.

I wonder today about many things. I wonder if our memories cannot be marked by some better spirit than dead regret or guilt. I wonder if the big buck and the big bang can be eliminated as hideous derisive symbols, dancing and grimacing on the graves of Vietnamese and Americans alike. I wonder if compassion can be resurrected in us, and selfishness disarmed. I wonder if our own spirits can long survive the violence we unleash in the world. I wonder if we can deflect the gun, with the good right arm of Dr. King, the arm of justice.

Hear again the words of Dr. King, at Riverside Church (April 4, 1967):

I am convinced that if we are to get on the right side of the world revolution, we as a nation must undergo a radical revolution of values. We must rapidly begin the shift from a "thing-oriented" society to a "person-oriented" society. When machines and computers, profit motives and property rights are considered more important than people, the giant triplets of racism, materialism, and militarism are incapable of being conquered. . . . A nation that continues year after year to spend more money on military defense than on programs of social uplift is approaching spiritual death. America, the richest and most powerful nation in the world, can well lead the way in this revolution of values.

There is nothing, except a tragic death wish, to prevent us from reordering our priorities, so that the pursuit of peace will take precedence over the pursuit of war. There is nothing to keep us from molding a recalcitrant status quo with bruised hands until we have fashioned it into a brotherhood and sisterhood. We still have a choice today: nonviolent coexistence or violent co-annihilation.

15

Thomas Merton,
Friend and Monk

I NAMED IT "The Year of Everything Awful."

On second thought, not entirely. The year was 1968, up and down, to and fro, the pendulum swung. I was as though fastened to it. First, a cross-world voyage to Hanoi in January, to bring home three captive U.S. pilots. Spring brought the murders of Dr. King and Robert Kennedy. May brought a momentary clearing of skies — Catonsville and the fiery disposal of pollutive draft files.

October came, and nine of us were tried in Baltimore and were speedily found wanting, thumbs-down by Dame Justice and a three-year sentence. We were released on appeal, and I returned to Cornell, not a whit chastened.

Then December, and the blank snows of the upstate countryside signaled that an awful year at long last was giving up the ghost. December 10, 1968, brought a late meeting on campus with leaders of the Students for a Democratic Society. Momentous (as matters turned, ominous) changes were under way. The students were not so subtly shedding a nonviolent ethos; throughout the evening a disturbing rumble was just barely audible, as though of an underground quake of impatience and ill feeling.

Cold, cold. That night seemed as I trekked somberly home, to be (in more senses than one) the bitterest weather of the year. Arrived, I turned to the television, curious to learn the local temperature. A fragment of a news band crossed the tube: " . . . famous Trappist monk, today in Bangkok." That was all.

Now what event was crowning the terrible year, yet another plait of thorns? I began calling TV stations. It was after midnight, the world had shut down. Finally, a New York voice confirmed the worst. The operative word was "died."

Thomas Merton was dead. No question of sleep, I trudged about all night in the snow. From that night, the quote from Ezekiel was verified again. For a decade I could not utter a public word about my friend.

Even now, thirty-five years later, as I take up a splendid biography by Jim Forest (*Living with Wisdom: A Life of Thomas Merton,* Orbis Books, 1991), an old pang strikes. So much of memory leaps from the pages, texts, and photos. Friendship, indefinable, unmistakable, showing its sharp, sweet, mournful features. And gone beyond recovering.

But of course not altogether so. In gratitude is recovery.

Gratitude also for Jim Forest, and a book that gives pain and pleasure at once. I had wished at one point, as Mertonmania gathered force and PhDs proliferated and the lode of Merton's life was mined to exhaustion—wished that my poor friend might be allowed to rest in peace at last. Ashes to ashes my dream, Tom Merton going with the current of some Kentucky river, a Gandhian dying fall.

Relief from all that. Jim's prose is sprightly, robust, even numinous when occasion warrants. The text befits the monk, the writer, the gyrovague, the curious, far-ranging, *penetrating* mind that arrived among us, mined lode after lode of scripture, of ancient church writers and modern, that dug further and further into Zen and Gandhi, into the hieroglyphs of postmodern poetry, that crossed the safe parameter of monastery, church, whiteness, America, all those handrails and posted warnings that promise safe footing and a sodden heart.

He taught novices and welcomed friends and raged against the dark—of the times, of his order, of God. He put on among other guises, always consciously and mostly with good humor, the robe of a monastic Job. Then with an abruptness that stopped the heart in its tracks, he was summoned elsewhere, in lightning. We are still wondering, half appalled.

Quite an achievement on Jim Forest's part, to tell such a story with no hint of burbling, and a large measure of admiration (as is befitting, since he too was a friend, and his subject so admirable).

Over the years I forgot much, but now, with the help of *Living with Wisdom,* I recall: "(Merton) moved to a one-room apartment with a wrought-iron balcony at 35 Perry Street in Greenwich Village." I pass the house each week, en route to an AIDS patient dwelling further along on the same street. The iron balcony is vanished. Memo: kiss a hand to number 35.

1940. "He took a job teaching English at St. Bonaventure's (University) in Olean, New York." Recall: several years ago, I'm invited to speak at the same campus. Proudly they show me the Merton collection of letters and manuscripts.

Impressed no end, I am shortly to be depressed. On this campus of the Friars Minor of St. Francis, past the library, past the relics, march the squads of ROTC. Do the Merton papers rustle in a wind of incoherence and dismay? Would they, if the will were the way, self-destruct?

He wrote at the time, which is to say, wartime: "The valley is full of oil storage tanks, and oil is for feeding bombers, and once they are fed they have to bomb something." O prophetic soul!

Merton enters the Trappists, pronounces vows, is ordained to the priesthood. Writes Jim Forest: "He was troubled by the toxic fertilizers being used on the fields, the noise of machinery, and the sense that the monastery was imitating corporate America. There were dead birds in the fields and sick monks in the infirmary with illnesses Merton didn't think had visited the monastery in the days before crop dusting."

Thomas Merton is long dead, the time is the late 1980s. I visit another monastery of Merton's order. A group has gathered for a day of prayer preparing for civil disobedience. The courteous Trappist community welcomes us to worship in their chapel. Later the abbot will join us for a picnic lunch.

But throughout the morning, our prayer is interrupted. Time and again a small plane veers south to north overhead, back, forth. Toil and trouble! They are dusting the wheat fields with chemicals. The wheat is to be ground and baked in Monks' Bread, the financial mainstay of the community.

When questions arise with Father Abbot, he brooks no discussion. "This is a safe and sound procedure." Period.

To revert. The year is 1965. Writes Forest: "Merton received a group of pacifists . . . for a retreat on 'the spiritual roots of protest.'" How could one know at the time? The retreat proved a watershed for many who took part. Most went to prison, some died. No one walked away untouched.

Something funny happened too. The abbot had given strict orders (to be transmitted by Merton) that no Protestant in attendance at Mass during the retreat was to be offered communion. With considerable chagrin, Tom transmitted the order. Friends of the quality of A. J. Muste and Mennonite theologian John Howard Yoder were present—each beyond doubt for the first time at a monastery and at Mass.

Still, such things tend to right themselves. My brother Philip and a friend careened in late, from New Orleans, having driven all night. The

Eucharist was well under way. Philip had, of course, heard nothing of the stern abbatial pronunciamento. So, when communion was passed, he passed it on, to everyone present. *Sic solvitur,* and then some.

Jim Forest again: "Lorenzo Barbato, a Venetian architect . . . brought Thomas Merton a gift, a liturgical vestment, a stole which had been used by Pope John XXIII during his installation." Sometime in the early 1980s, friends gathered in Louisville for a two-day conference on Merton. The Gethsemani community invited us to pass an afternoon at the monastery. Among other events of that day, a Mass was offered in the novitiate chapel. I was invited to offer the homily.

Someone suggested that I don the above-mentioned stole, extremely and splendidly baroque in character, enlaced with jewels and gold and whatnot. Placed weightily on my shoulders, the marvel offered quite a contrast with my attire of jeans and a denim shirt. I arose, disquisitioned with merciful brevity on the Gospel of the day for the feast of St. Francis of Assisi. And all during the homily, I could hear behind me, where a clerical circle was assembled in the sanctuary, the drumming of a shoe on the stone floor, insistent and plainly audible to all.

I learned later that the foot in question had as owner a former Jesuit. He was thus conveying in a peculiar Morse code his annoyance, whether at my words or attire or both remains to this day uncertain.

But no matter. The delicious wackiness of the scene, the splendid tatterdemalion, won a gargantuan belly laugh from most of us.

All thanks to the great friend and monk, thanks too to his scribe, faithful and skilled. The latter quotes the former; let the words serve as an epitaph:

"No matter what mistakes and delusions have marked my life, most of it I think has been happiness and, as far as I can tell, truth."

Prosit, dear lucky man. You live.

16

Archbishop Romero, the Four Churchwomen, and the Jesuit Martyrs of El Salvador

WE DO WELL to look to the martyrs for a measure of light, for the vision they offer—a way of being human in an inhuman time.

One aspect of an inhuman time is the fervor with which good and great things are held in derision, things as noble as martyrdom even. This fear and dread of the heroic is peculiar to the times, one might almost say pandemic. It is a time much resembling the time of Kierkegaard. He termed it simply "the era of leveling."

Somewhat like this: In our country and elsewhere, one can hardly conceive of anyone or anything, any truth or person or ideal, worth dying for.

The notion is greeted with a kind of amused puzzlement; it violates the dogma of the "deadly average." The idea of true heroism strikes anger; it violates the canon of the achiever, the self-made, the selfish, the "devil taking the hindmost."

In our country despite all this, we can take heart—a genuine goodness flourishes in those who "stand somewhere and pay up," to use Camus's phrase. These reject macho images, tenderly care for others, do good work modestly, have an eye to the down and out, harbor persecuted aliens, pray at nuclear missile sites, tell the truth in court, survive long terms in jail, serve the AIDS ill and the multitudes of poor and homeless, the victimized, the mental patients, the abandoned and expendable. In so doing, they cope with backbreaking needs that seem ever to multiply, never to be assuaged. All honor to them!

Among others in New York, one thinks of the Catholic Worker community, Emmaus House, The Upper Room, The Coalition for the Homeless, Part of the Solution, and a multitude of others. They are redeeming the evil times.

Such activity, it goes without saying, is not widely honored. Perseverance, goodness, improvisation, prayer, hope—such qualities win no kudos. The culture looks elsewhere for its icons; on its heroes it paints a far different face.

The image of the cultural icons is the face of the anti-martyrs. These are the big spenders, the big bullies, the "leaders" who are the "misleaders." Their mark is a violent, often sanctimonious savvy. They know the score, the culture, and play its game to the hilt. They ride herd on the backs of the defenseless and vulnerable. They would rather shoot than talk, much prefer the big stick to the velvet glove. Witness the rattling of weaponry, the threats, the sanctions, the bombings of defenseless children and the aged, the refugees, the wanton deadly adventuring in the Persian Gulf.

However diverse, the methods come to one thing. Our cultural icons have a marked preference for death in all its works and pomps, its metaphors and analogies, as the prime way of dealing with conflict and human differences. They are obsessed with propagating fears and dreads, colluding with death squads and contras, weapons and wars, police and guns. They know something, these leaders, and act on it. Death is indeed the big stick that beats all into submission, the social method that solves all intricacies, levels all differences.

Thus "death as solution" becomes quite simply the acceptable norm of conventional politics, from Salvador to Afghanistan to Iraq. The same spirit decreed the death of Archbishop Oscar Romero and his noble companions. (The successor of Romero, reproached for not showing a like courage, is quoted as asking, "Do you want me dead also?")

Domestically we are no longer shocked at the awesome power of the spirit of death, as it lays claim to ourselves. We take the spirit quite for granted. Cops patrol schools, armed guards protect merchandise, dogs and private goons patrol affluent neighborhoods. On the public scene, abortion centers flourish, death rows deliver bodies legally disposed of.

Abroad, Salvadoran, Nicaraguan, Honduran, Guatemalan peasants have perished day after day in great numbers, for no understandable reason, to no one's demonstrated benefit. So perish the children of Iraq and the peasants of Afghanistan. The deaths, the weapons, indeed the ethos are our own, "made in the USA."

Here and elsewhere, people get in the way. They get in the way of oligarchs and corporate moguls and juntas and Husseins and presidents. They get in the way of oil, in the way of world markets, of nuclear missiles, in the way of subs and warships. People fleeing death in Central America get in the way of immigration officials, jobs, neighborhoods.

In sum, many get in the way of a certain "way of life." All such must therefore be removed, by one means or another. It is simple as that.

Sometimes the spirit of death, according to exigency or occasion or even whim, announces its immediate, passionate, stark presence. It fools not around, it cracks like a discharged bullet. Such is the story of Archbishop Romero; of the murdered churchwomen, Ita Ford, Maura Clarke, Dorothy Kazel, and Jean Donovan; and of the martyred Jesuits and their coworkers Celina and Elba Ramos, as well as of countless troublesome spirits across the world. They got in the way, so they were removed. That is their obituary.

It mattered not a whit that one victim was an honored and saintly archbishop, others were devoted priests or nuns, a hundred or thousands of others were nameless and poor. The contract went out, the guns leveled them, each and all.

Each and all. No matter their dignity, consecration, the love and respect that attended them.

Here is an estimate, quite modest it would seem, of the work of the Salvador Jesuits. It was written by one of them, Ignacio Ellacuría, president of the Jesuit University in El Salvador, who was assassinated on November 16, 1989, by twenty-six soldiers, nineteen of them trained at the "School of the Americas," in Fort Benning, Georgia. (Ellacuría was responding to an attack on his Jesuit community, printed in the *Boston Globe*):

> *The description that we are utopian comes close to being accurate....*
> *It is true that we aren't politicians and that, in that sense, we are more utopian than pragmatic. We are people of the gospel, a gospel that proclaims the realm of God and calls on us to try to transform this earth into as close a likeness of that realm as possible.*
>
> *Within such a system it is difficult to accept unbridled capitalism, because the evils it has produced in history outweigh the good. As the bishops of Latin America stated in Puebla in 1979, "We see the continuing operation of economic systems that do not regard the human being as the center of society, and are not carrying out the profound changes needed to move toward a just society."*
>
> *It would be better to accept systems that better confronted the problems of the poor, and gave them the special place bestowed on them in*

a gospel vision. Such a vision emphasizes the common good; it calls for liberation, not just liberalization.

In the case of El Salvador, the Jesuits here have condemned institutionalized and repressive violence, and we have done all that we could, including calling again and again for dialogue—to avoid and diminish revolutionary violence.

We have endured a good deal during these recent years. One of us, Rutilio Grande, was murdered, and the rest of us received an ultimatum: "Get out of the country, or be killed." We decided to stay. Since then our home and our university have been bombed fourteen times.

First, the threat of death, then death.

Or the spirit of death chooses another method. It conceals its hand in the jargon of "civilized discourse," diplomatic double-speak, or (in the case of the NATO church) in frivolous worship. In such wise this spirit conceals its addiction to real estate or family unity or doctrinal orthodoxy or something grotesquely known as "national security."

No matter the guise, the advice offered to fractious spirits is the same: "Don't rock the boat, Stand nowhere, Pay nothing as you go, Ask no questions." And if such good sense is spurned, there are other, so to speak, "peacekeepers" at hand. . . .

In scripture the spirit of death is revealed as an epiphany of darkness, in what Paul calls "the upper air," which is to say, in the higher echelons of power. Shored up by xenophobic myths, moral unaccountability, military force, multicorporate greed, there the spirit of death concludes its bargains, out of sight or mind of the citizenry, ourselves. Consider the gang around George W. Bush. A Faustian agreement indeed!

The barter is concluded in exchange for a promise: "All this will I hand over to you, if you fall down and worship me" (Matt. 4:9).

The Gospel story is no empty tale. Such authority as decreed the death of our martyrs demands a pact with the spirit of death.

Indeed it must be said as directly as possible: Those who lust after high office in the superstate must be willing to consummate a bargain with the spirit of death. Brzezinski spoke of it quite openly, Kissinger was more covert. It comes to the same thing: The power thus conferred will be awesome and many will die. Somewhere a hecatomb will be raised in celebration of the pact (or as the *New York Times* recently described it, the "rite of passage" of the president in the sands of Arabia).

From "the upper air," the same spirit filters down and down. It lays claim on us all, afflicting and stifling areas of decent striving. It argues in favor of false peace, moral compromise, and complicity. It stifles, mitigates, urges moral adjustment. "Things could be worse," it suggests. "Silence is golden."

Antipathy, dread, fear and trembling, floating anxiety, numbing, all afflict us. In time we become accepting of such conditions, events, crimes as by any civilized standard are morally abhorrent. And the citizens, numbed and obeisant, summon for response not rage, but a feeble whimper.

The spirit of death freezes spontaneous movements of the heart. A vicious dualism emerges—winners and losers, us and them, some favored and others cursed, some beloved of God and others abominated, a few in charge and many under the heel, one condemned (as a new Hitler), another in possession of Realm of God.

Eventually, the "spirit of the upper air" becomes our only atmosphere. In compromise and cowardice, we bend the knee before the high crime of the ruling spirits. We distance ourselves, or psychologize, or liturgize, but in any case trivialize, our vocation. In such wise we lose the ability to utter a simple no in face of illegitimate authority and its claim on ourselves, our lives, our children, our income—finally, our conscience, our humanity.

The spirit of death creates its own world: a loony zone, a culture of unaccountability, fear, mind control, bitterness, suspicion, dread of human variety.

The same spirit makes of violent death and human expendability two sides of the common coin of the realm. The currency is, to say the least, debased. At home and abroad, according to the American arrangement, more and more people are judged as of little or no value.

Examples abound. Of the lethal folly of the Panamanian invasion, we have been told little or nothing to this day. (Indeed, we know more of the deaths of Romanians than of Panamanians; a conservative estimate puts the number of the nameless dead of Panama at some two thousand. This is the price paid for the capture of Noriega, who for years had been an American hired gun.)

Under the "system," here and elsewhere, more and more people live in misery and die out of due time. Until the ultimate cosmic absurdity is touched, all the living are expendable before the nuclear arsenals of the world. Thus despair reaches its obscene dead end.

The Bible has a name for all this; so did Archbishop Romero. The name is idolatry. The idols, according to these noble sources, wage war against the martyrs, against their holy and faithful choice — to shed their blood rather than the blood of others.

Idolatry. We come on the word again and again, in the Bible, in the writings of Romero and Jon Sobrino and Ignacio Ellacuría. The military, the courts, politics of a certain kind, property, ritual purity—these are an apt terrain for the activity of idols.

Naming these, exposing them, is the work of deliverance wrought by the martyrs. More, the martyrs urge that such is the vocation of the faithful, the poor, the prisoners, the disappeared: Name the idols!

Naming and exposing the forces of death, and enduring the combat that follows, these can hardly occur unless the martyrs had first invoked another Name.

Romero, the churchwomen, the Jesuits, all were enabled to name the idols because they first named, invoked, adored, served, stood with, the one, true God. They knew God; they therefore knew the demons. They adored the God of life; therefore they refused obeisance to the gods of death—to national security, private property, to honors or the credit of a great name.

These are the words of Romero, naming the idol of "national security" in his own tormented country. His analysis, I believe, is entirely apt to our own culture and its behavior:

> By virtue of this ideology (of national security), the individual is placed at the total service of the state. His or her political participation is suppressed. . . . People are put into the hands of . . . elites, and are subjected to policies that oppress and repress all who oppose them, in the name of what is alleged to be total war. The armed forces are put in charge of social and economic structures under the pretext of the interests of national security. Everyone not at one with the state is declared a national enemy. . . .
>
> The interests and advantages of the few are thus turned into an absolute. This absolutization becomes a mystique. It is as if the national security regime, which attempts to give itself a good public image by a subjective profession of Christian faith, were the only, or the best, defender of the Christian civilization of the West.
>
> The omnipotence of these national security regimes, the total disregard they show toward individuals and their rights . . . turn national security into an idol, which like the god Moloch, demands the daily sacrifice of many victims in its name.

The legitimate security that the state ought to seek for its members is cruelly perverted, for in the name of national security, the insecurity of the individual becomes institutionalized.

For the idols to do their worst, anonymity, disguises, respectability, duplicity—all are invoked. The idols, be it noted, also welcome a certain kind of religious practice—abstract, formal gestures, creed by rote, gifts and bribes, faith without works, obsession with pride of place.

The idols are passionate beings. They will kill the one, the few, or the many who interfere, challenge, unveil, speak honestly, unmask the lies. Those who dare stand for something, or stand in the way, are cut down. Those who speak concretely about political malfeasance, military violence, corporate greed, who in sum confess to an aversion against murder, however legally sanctioned, are dealt with, and not gently.

A dangerous business indeed, this naming of the idols. Romero dared it and was removed. So with the churchwomen, so with the Jesuits and the innocent women at their side. In the inelegant phrase, they blew the cover of the idols.

Let us not hesitate to invoke the martyrs. They preferred living acts to dead symbols. For this we honor them.

They risked death at the hands of the violent, rather than compromising and pussyfooting. For this we honor them.

They refused to live as functionaries of superchurch or superstate. For this we honor them.

They named God, and stood by that name, and withstood for God's sake. For this we honor them.

They named the idols, for our sake also. For this we honor them.

They endured in a tranquil spirit obloquy and contempt, from Christians and others, oligarchs, bishops, politicians. For this we honor them.

They refused to separate peace from justice. For this we honor them.

They died for others; and in the words of Romero, they arise from death in the Salvadoran people. For this we honor them.

17

The Colors of Corita Kent

SHE WAS ALREADY FAMOUS in the early 1950s. The joy in her work, its riotous color, was her gift to a good gray world. It seemed as though in her art the juices of the world were running over, inundating the world, bursting the rotten wineskins of semblance, rote and rot.

It should in plain justice be set down, all she was offering at the time (and continued to offer, despite all) on behalf of the church.

One emotion seemed denied to Catholics; the lack might be thought of as biological, environmental, genetic, a matter of deficient diet or dour instruction, unrelieved by lively season or good sense. Alas, how plumb the heart of that plodding virtuous set-jawed lockstepping be-mitred leadership, and the flock that doddered and tottered behind? They needed joy, joy, joy!

Corita Kent had it in abundance. She gave it, pressed down, flowing over. Her art poured out; she was a very witch of invention, holding aloft her cornucopia. The serigraphs hung on the clotheslines drying, in the little back shed where she worked, across the street from the campus of Immaculate Heart College near Los Angeles, where she talked things through, planned, sketched with her students. It was like the mixing room of the hues of creation, colors in combat, contrast, harmony; enough and more for a century of sunrises. Or the room was like the wardrobe of a master clown, if God were a clown—a heresy she seemed secretly, bemusedly, more than lightly inclined toward. Confounding thereby colorless cardinals.

At that time, many of the nuns discarded the old garb. The new costumes were instructive as to personality, dreams, bemusements of the wearers. Corita began to array herself in outrageous nonfashions. She took her lead, by all evidence, from nature, a formerly forbidden ground. Orange boots, wild orange, yellow, plum, cerise gowns.

Was there a message? The gowns were another form of art, celebrational. They were an assault on horizontality, dead weight, dogmatics, liturgy stuck in *Dies Irae,* the world (the church) as Haceldema. Oh, she was dangerous, that one!

As to her fame, it grew, and yet never seemed to matter. What was she to do with it, this unwieldy baggage of repute? she asked, looking at one with utter insouciance, an innocent in the garden of experience. Fame? The look gave the answer. Why, exactly nothing.

For a period, there was much soul searching in her community, the Sisters of the Immaculate Heart. Nothing like the church militantly in pursuit, one thought, to engender introspection in the hardiest spirits.

They brought in a psychologist for a plenary session. I was ferried westward to join in; on what basis was blessedly unclear. In any case, the meeting of the minds, with the Pacific beating outside the old beach house where we foregathered — the meeting went, in the opinion of a few, from burdensome to nigh intolerable.

My sense, obscurely arrived at, was that such dissection, such autopsical pursuits, ought decently to wait on one's decease. One day I fled the premises as quietly as might be, and began walking along the shore. And there, walking toward me, was Corita, likewise fleeing.

Something here, I thought, of the brooding, cherishing, mothering even, of the nest of mystery. We laughed, and let it go at that.

You wouldn't believe it, at first sight. All that savvy and subtlety, the way she absorbed, as though through pores of the soul, the skill of self-concealment. ("She's so NATURAL!" they'd cry.)

She knew more than a few things, and told infinitely less than she knew; what art was, what the art of living was. She made it all look easy. And in a sense, when you thought about it, it was, the art and the living, and the living art she made of it.

You might have thought, if you were not a close friend, there was no struggle in her life. No contrary winds, no exhaustion from teaching, travel, work, work. No sense of humiliation, no "woman bent double (under the law, that killer) for many years; and doctors hopeless to help." You might have thought, How easily she does it! And how wrong you'd be.

I arrived one Holy Week at the Santa Barbara house to "conduct a retreat." It was that time of century when priests commended to women certain matters of the spirit, more or less evangelically related — (more or less) — matters, which, moreover, the preacher might or might not be thought to exemplify.

Preaching aside, example aside, it was a week that remains green and sunlit in memory. I arrived, to be shown my quarters. And lo, hands, presences, imaginations, had gone before. The walls of my dwelling were inundated, floor to ceiling, in a blaze of Corita serigraphs.

Did they have something in mind, those women? Would the preacher perhaps be enabled, in such a setting, to say something of a Love that bears even with our world, even with the Los Angeles Catholic church?

File under "our world," the news of that week: Holy Week, and the unholy bombing of North Vietnam.

The sisters were preparing the chapel for Holy Thursday, and after that, for the Great Leap of Easter. Whole buckets of orchids began arriving from the neighbors' bounty. One of the sisters asked, "Does your mother like orchids?"

Now in our straitened circumstance of Ol' Clay Farm, where the appearance of a turnip's pate above ground was in the nature of a major breakthrough, what might be called the California Question had not frequently risen.

I swallowed, "I expect she does."

Thus there arrived at my mother's door in Syracuse, New York, on Easter morning, a long elegant box containing, not one or another orchid bloom, but entire sprays of mauve, purple, and white. There were sights not often seen in our northern Appalachian setting.

The day I departed Santa Barbara for New York, the same hands, or others, came to my room, removed the serigraphs with care, packed them up, and presented the bundle. Happy Easter!

But first, as to Good Friday. As in the first instance, Year One, trouble was brewing.

And yet, as the First Instance might have ruefully reflected under Pilate's lash or Herod's scorn—how innocently it all began!

The sisters and I planned a ceremony of reconciliation. It seemed no great matter. Prayers were composed, hymns sung, silence ensued. A sense was conveyed, and more than a sense, that the Lord's death had commended to us what we now commended to one another—the grace of God that renders us gracious.

There were, of course, older, more traditional forms of the sacrament. The sisters, for the most part, preferred the public ceremony of reconciliation. For those who did not, private "confession" was available.

However. Evidently, the group was not entirely composed of pioneers. On my return to New York, I was summoned to Jesuit headquarters. The message concerned a smoke signal from the chancery of Los Angeles. Yours truly had dared conduct a verboten form of the sacrament of penance. A wrist was slapped, dire warnings issued. O Corita!

Her work in the mid- and late 1950s was still playfully devotional. "Devotional" was considered befitting. She was after all a nun; her turf was prayer, the saints, Jesus and Mary, the Bible. Nonetheless, it was that persistent playfulness that stuck in gravelly throats. How dare she?

There was the Case of the Notorious Serigraph. It depicted an indubitable, large, rotund — yes, even piggish — tomato. It was overweening in its pop presence; so much had seldom been made of the commonplace. It was as though a whole bushel of tomatoes had incontinently converged in one. Or as if Corita's elbow had toppled her pot of crimson paint over the paper; as then she decided to make sport of the mishap, rounding things off to a nicety, to a joke.

And then, and then — straight-faced, she scrawled words along the bottom edge, something to the effect of, "Mary, the Juiciest Tomato of All"!

In a manner of speaking, all hell broke loose.

There were, after all, traditional images of Mary. These had the iconic character of the sacred, out of time, out of place — out of (most of all) youthful hands, playful hands.

There were questions and implications aplenty here, not all of them esthetic.

Questions like: Who owned the images, anyway?

It was clear, at least it was becoming clearer, especially to women, that the purported owners of the images also placed a heavy hand, a claim, on those who approached the images, those who believed in the presences, those who sought in the icons ways and means of coping, rhythms and beckonings of the human.

Was it to be borne that the human achieve a breakaway, escape custody, scrutiny, no one laying commands, warnings, declaring limits?

There were authorities all over the place (all over the church) raising just such dire possibilities, raising such questions. It was quite simple. They owned the icons, so they defined the human. *In casu,* they said who Mary was, and who she was not.

More to the point, they decreed what metaphors, images, forms, tropes, poems, hymns, dances, sculptures — they did the sorting out, sober as a final judgment—which of these befitted and which did not.

This way of proceeding, a favorite tactic in church and state, was inviolate, sanctified (as was decreed by the authorities). Various weighty names were invoked; such and such was "God's will," or indubitably was not. Such and such honored, or dishonored, the saints. The pronouncements had the mordant quality of magic, incantations; they were beyond cavil or reproach, certainly beyond discussion.

Thus in controlling the icons, a powerful aura was created around a certain conception of the human. And this operated with particular force, when the feminine-as-holy was invoked, sculpted, painted, praised, celebrated. Touchy! Who owned the Blessed Virgin?

Well, one thing was clear: Women didn't.

A second thing was clear, clearly a heavenly mandate (to the owners): Men did.

The consequence was weighty indeed. If men owned the icons of the Blessed Virgin, it followed that men had a large say on the subject of women—who were they, how they were to conduct themselves, where and when they fitted or exceeded something known in certain circles as "their place."

Would it be intolerable to state the following bit of logic? If men owned the icons of women, men owned women.

Beyond doubt dynamite dwelt in the images. And to speak of the nefarious Sacred Tomato, it was as though this innocent, Corita, had wantonly planted a charge of dynamite in the fruity heart of things, the ecological original. And then hung around, while a (male) foot (whose else?), provoked beyond bearing, gave the image, so to speak, a vigorous kick— and thereby set off the charge.

I often thought of it. The best weapon was a light touch. The best revenge was an unswipable smile.

She had claimed the icon; reclaimed it, better.

Why get lathered up about such things? A smile of recognition and relief comes to one's face, at thought of her. How guileless she was, and yet how stunningly wise. Tomato indeed!

She broke the claim, writ on tablets of stone, with the light stave of her innocence. What's the problem? What's your difficulty? They fumed away, impossible to ignore her, equally impossible to control her.

It was as if the images, noble and precious and under triple lockup, suddenly had been sprung. The doors opened, the holy ones walked free; out of the stale sacristies, away from "close custody."

Corita and I were invited to a Chicago panel. The subject was "religion and the arts." Also summoned was a liberal East Coast bishop, a Bishop Wright, considered at the time a kind of public advocate for lively minds.

The bishop, as became apparent, was leaning toward larger honors. He issued portentous pronunciamentos concerning, well, not much. He would in a season of due ripening, turn red, or rather purple, in visage and raiment.

Corita, nothing daunted, referred to his Eminence mischievously and publicly as "Bishop Wrong." We also discovered a prop which we placed surreptitiously on stage, just before the bishop was to speak. It was a ridiculously elaborate Louis Quinze throne; on it, a mannequin, legs crossed idiotically.

The jest was not well received. Corita predictably took the worst of the riposte. The bishop referred to Lady Bird Johnson's effort to "clean up the billboards that deface public highways." "Alas," he said, "Corita has brought the billboards indoors; she obviously considers them art."

She was diminutive, and in the latter years, frail.

I never saw her angry or out of sorts, though I frequently beheld her in physical and psychic pain. She seemed constitutionally unable to harbor a grievance.

This is what her friends remember, and mourn — her capacity for friendship, for them.

She knew that the times were a very breaker of bones. Often, friendships tore apart. No point in dwelling on a tragic truism. (Except to dwell on her, and her struggle to remain faithful to her community and those beyond.)

"Those beyond," including myself, never considered ourselves (never were considered) at the periphery of her affection. Did her love for us allow of such an image—periphery, center? We all felt ourselves at center. She made certain we did. She beckoned us there. The gesture was irresistible.

In the 1970s, she accepted work for the great corporations, and a few of us were set back, wondering what this might mean. Her designs appeared in the pages of *Newsweek* and *Time*, sometimes double spreads.

Was she being taken in? We wondered if anyone was advising her of the activities of these corporate sharks, always anxious to "front" as patrons of the arts, latter-day Maecenases, scattering largesse even as they milked and bilked the world.

At the same time, during those same years, twenty or more, she could be counted on to devote her talents to this or that cause. Thus the posters on behalf of peace, the women's movement, anti-hunger events, ecology. The work was invariably donated.

Images, images. The image maker herself exists in the public image. They "know who she is," it goes without saying. And all wrong, it goes without saying. Nevertheless, she is dealt with mercilessly, arbitrarily, is turned and hefted and tossed about according to the vagaries of public appetite, socialized greed, the preening and scheming.

Who gave a damn about her sense of herself, her dignity, privacy? She must give a damn, and then some; she and a few friends. If they don't persistently, no one will. She (and they, which is to say, we) bid fair to become mere grist for the mills of the demigods, provender of the consumer clutch.

Tread easy. Many have perished without a cry.

Every artist, in a sense, asks for it. The packaging and huckstering of the product includes the image on the wrapping. You, Corita.

By and large, she dealt skillfully with a punishing life. There was something unkillable in her, untouchable even, reserved to a few. *Noli me tangere.* Some tried to own her, and were rebuffed. Her implacable courtesy could turn an assault to a standoff, or better.

Her art followed the course of life, as a shadow follows a form. At the start, she concentrated on images and words drawn from nature and the Bible. (It was a principle she never abandoned that words and images belong together. Sometimes, not often, the principle got too industrious, plying both sides of the street, so to speak. Then the work reached a point of illegibility.)

In the early fifties, she quickly endeared herself to liturgico-literary-middle-professional-Catholics. Her serigraphs illustrated the psalms and prophets and prayers of the church. Her naive eye caught resonances and reflections and hints of the natural world, translated them in a tender wash, just short of sentimental.

And that calligraphy! She drew words rather than wrote them; her brush danced across the page in a lively farandole. The writing was worlds apart from the impersonal ersatz "excellence" of that truly awful "Palmer Method," a form of torture in my childhood. (It occurred to me later that the handwriting corresponded exactly with the theology of *extra ecclesiam nulla salus.*)

Corita's script was backhanded, informal, flowing. It was pleasantly offbeat, sophisticated; the scrawl, intermittently legible, of a child who wrote for the fun of it, and was apt to abandon words, as fancy caught, in favor of doodles, stick drawings, or plain daydreaming.

That was her knack: writing that looked improvised, a second thought hurrying after the first. And yet there was seriousness too. In the first years, a word or phrase of scripture set the tone. Later, mockery was often the message. She held up to gentle derision — consumerism, glowing ads for second-rate products, the volatile appetite of the marketplace. And then on to the women's movement, the antiwar movement, billboards, even on a huge gas storage tank in Boston. All grist for the golden mill.

She was neither an art historian nor a philosopher. Her comments on her own work invariably took the form of a gentle nudge toward freedom. Freedom now! The medium was the message.

She saw life as redemptive, rewarding. To her, original sin was, so to speak, a recessive gene. It showed up only in the shadows; its forms were negation, cowardice, self-distrust.

This was where her art came in. Subtly, not so subtly, she kept offering forms of the joy that finally prevails, keeps going. In the face of the sin that says dourly nothing can be done. Or says (the same thing) the church is hopeless, life is a drag, don't bother me, time on my hands.

In 1968, Corita was invited to Cornell. A commune in downtown Ithaca, peopled by student activists, decided to host Corita for supper.

The intractable house canine was in attendance. This portent had been yclept "Hershey," in honor of the general in charge of rounding up youthful fodder bound for the Vietnam War.

Hershey was a warlike spirit; like his prototype, he was apt to display remarkable molars in a sudden snarl, bust out of civilized confines, spoiling for a fight. Woe to the newcomer, human or canine!

We sat cross-legged on the floor, eating Japanese style. Hershey stalked about, in and out, bound for trouble. Corita, as I recall, kept her equanimity, though at one point the dog, snarling for bait, grabbed at her skirt and tore it. Order was restored with difficulty.

Later in the evening she presented a "light show" in Annabel Taylor Hall. Images ricocheted off walls and ceiling. The time was the late 1960s. Redundant to add, the air was redolent with spicy smoke.

She was in and out of bouts of serious illness for many years. She underwent a wearisome series of operations; she survived, went on with her work. To inquiries about her health, she would say ruefully, things like, "Some of me that was inside me is now outside me."

She would urge me to visit her gallery in New York, near the United Nations, and "choose what you want."

Once in 1981 she gathered her unsold works, made a great roll of them, sizzling with her colors, and shipped them on. "To make use of as you want. Sell them, give them away."

In the early 1980s, we arranged an exhibit on the Lower East Side of Manhattan, in a place known rather amorphously as a "movement gallery." The day of the opening, the Bread and Puppet Theatre performed all afternoon, in and out of three theaters, in and out of the street, with mime, song, marvelous symbolic staging; then a street procession of clowns and monstrous puppets.

Inside the gallery, I read poetry, and we opened the Corita exhibit. All sales to favor the Plowshares Eight defendants, at the time facing trial.

Months later, most of the art had disappeared; one presumed into the hands of purchasers. And no report on sales or profits was ever made. To this day, no art has been returned, no proceeds accounted for. I told her of this. "Oh, that's nothing new," she said with a laugh. "They do it all the time."

It was typical of those we love. Some live long, under sentence of death even. And we forget the sentence, the death. We think of them as perpetually in the world, at our side. Fiction? Coping? Something of these.

So in summer of 1986, a friend called. Corita was back in the hospital, surgery again, it looks grim. And I thought, *When hasn't it?*

It was so grim this time, as to be final. I thought, *I must get to Boston.*

She had survived the surgery, lost considerable weight, even from that destitute little frame. I found her in a tiny room of an old wing of the hospital. When I came in unannounced, bearing a flowering plant, she broke out weeping. "You make me cry," she said through tears. (She had said to a friend sometime before, "Oh, if I could only weep.")

I said, "I hope you won't have that put on my tombstone, 'I make my friends cry!'" Then she laughed.

We had a good hour together. She was weak as the newborn, but perked up wonderfully for the occasion, very much herself, propped there on pillows, with her own art on the walls, undoubtedly the most cheerful thing her friends could come upon.

We talked and reminisced and wandered far afield in time, calling up friends, occasions, the dreadful years of war when our only recourse, it seemed, was to "have a party," and the only reason to announce one was to plan another.

That was the last visit. A day or two later, she signed herself out of the hospital, and friends took her into their home where she died ever so gently. She left instructions—no funeral. Her friends, she wrote, might decide to gather for a party, that would be just fine.

East Coast and West, they did.

18

The Promised Land
of Rabbi Abraham Heschel

$\mathbf{H}$OW DOES ONE, especially at a thirty-year remove, convey the flavor of a friendship? It seems impossible on the face of it, a perilous undertaking. For friendship demands the reciprocity and mutual presence which, in this instance, death has so brutally canceled.

Then a second thought occurs. Does friendship so demand, does death so prevail? Perhaps until the story is fully told, the book stands open and the spirit lingers and awaits the telling, awaits a friend to proffer a due threnody, memories that fly in face of death.

I remember Abraham—a man of prayer, and a man on the line.

He walked vectors of insight and moral effort, gracefully and at great cost. I passed and paused, and we met. For me it was a providential moment. I had much to learn, and he an immense store to offer.

I recall the first occasion. Three of us came together: a minister, the rabbi, and myself. The time was 1965; Johnson's war in Vietnam raged. We called a press conference to express the revulsion of (at least a minority among) the religious community. The press arrived, we delivered our word.

Then, the task of the moment done with, two of us prepared to depart. (Knowing as we did that we had done what little lay in our power. Knowing in our bones that, by no means available to us, the war would be ended.)

As we rose in our places, a hand was laid firmly on the arm of the minister and myself. And the voice of Heschel was in our ears, a word uttered with great urgency. "Are we then finished, we depart content, and the war goes on?"

We should have known. The question was quintessential Heschel. Which is to say, it contained its own answer. And awaited ours.

We did not go home. We sat again, we three, and of that gesture of the rabbi, both simple and crucial, an organization was born. It came to be known as "Clergy Concerned About the War."

It perhaps goes without saying that in the beginning we were hardly inundated with proffers, contributions, new members. As Abraham would say ruefully, "We should have called ourselves Clergy Unconcerned. Then you would see them flock to us!"

My own fortunes worsened. The cardinal of New York, Francis Spellman, was an inveterate hawk. I was apparently disturbing his complaisant flock—and his powerful self. So. Under mysterious ecclesiastical marching orders, I was ordered out of the country in the fall of 1965, bound for Latin America, a one-way airline ticket in hand.

Meantime, Clergy Concerned had mounted a New York meeting against the war. I was told later that in a solemn liturgical gesture initiated by Heschel, an empty chair was set on stage that night, signifying my enforced absence. When someone attempted to occupy it, Heschel gravely gestured him elsewhere.

On my return to New York some months later, Heschel joined in the general rejoicing.

The war worsened, as wars inevitably do. By now it carried its own momentum, rolling relentlessly downward, a snowball nearing hell. But meantime, what lives and fortunes were not borne under and consumed!

Another era, another war. For a time, during the thirty days' Israeli-Egyptian conflict of 1967, it was as though a shadow fell across our friendship. I asked myself, would Heschel object to this war, as he had objected to the Vietnam War? Away from New York that summer and heartsick with thought of my friend, I wrote him a questioning letter.

Then second thoughts intruded. His health had declined drastically. I had no heart to raise an issue bound to be so painful. I tore up the letter.

In the spring of 1968, I traveled to Hanoi to recover American prisoners of war. There, like any Vietnamese peasant or worker, I cowered under the savage bombardment of, so to speak, my own air force. It was a momentous education, I learned my lesson. On return, within a few months, I joined eight hardy spirits in the burning of draft files in Catonsville, Maryland.

Those terrible years! Heschel too was learning, and quickly. He moved from civil rights to antiwar work, which grew more and more demanding of time and emotion. He aged visibly. By 1972 when I returned to New York after a stint in prison, it was dolorously clear to friends and family, he was ill indeed.

I referred to Abraham earlier as a man of prayer. Is the insistence, I ask myself, redundant, discipline being one with religious faith in all traditions?

Perhaps, perhaps not. In those days of fervent war and perfervid antiwar, public acknowledgment of one's faith, even among friends, was by no means usual. One's politics were public property, sometimes in a crass sense; faith was another matter, almost a matter of embarrassment. One marched abroad; but one believed in a corner. The dichotomy was, for the most part, distressingly adolescent.

In this matter of an unashamed faith, publicly acknowledged, Heschel was as usual at odds; with him, tradition stood strong against fashion. One knew where he stood, as for example, one knew where Martin Luther King stood. Their faith was consistent, lucid, intense, political. They and their like announced God's word in the world, God suffering and rejoicing amid people, the people acknowledging God's sovereignty in a passionate quest for justice and peace, in prayer and worship.

Faith and life in the world, it was all one, it was to be proclaimed, in the image of the prophets, from the housetops, in season and out.

And war, what of that horror — and what of the warmakers? Were these attending, mending their ways? Or was the world rushing, pell mell and ignorant on its course, paying no heed, contemning the prophetic word?

To Heschel, no matter the outcome, one simply went on. Faith was its own credential, the faithful ones stood there, spoke up and paid up — sometimes dearly.

This was the faith of Heschel and, I dare say, of the community that gathered around him, to pray, to strive and strain for peace in a bad time. The winds of misfortune that scattered so many, destroyed so many — those same winds, chancy and violent, also brought unlikely people to one's side. This was our great good fortune, amid such tragedy. We discovered new friends even as others shucked off. So discovering and walking together, we "doubled the heart's might."

At that time I was given a great privilege: to assist at the seder ceremony in the Heschel apartment. I was so warmly received! The food was excellent; the prayers of intercession—for an end to war, for the peace that passes understanding, for the victims of the war (the American dead were our chief import in those horrid days; and who could calculate the numbers of Vietnamese, Cambodian, Laotian dead?). We prayed for the victims everywhere; these were Heschel's fervent prayers—and mine also.

This, I thought exultantly, *was an ecumenical spirit I could take seriously.*

Vividly I see him at table, bearded head bowing and rising in prayer. It was as though he was rapt into the "shekinah, the mysterium tremendum." I know no better way of putting it; he knew how to pray.

In a gathering of family and friends, or in attendance at the majestic assembly of the Second Vatican Council, it made little difference. He lived before God.

Great suffering attended his last days. With what reluctance I recall this! And for better or worse, I was there. (Indeed, it might be adduced, and was at the time, that I became an element of his suffering.)

The war, the war that bled our youth, our innocence, our religion, our freedom! The war was an albatross which Kennedy bore until it bore him under. Then, a stench in the nostrils, a weight dead and beyond bearing, the war was lowered like a rotting carcass on the shoulders of Johnson. By then, the war had become both emblem and legacy, no president could die intestate, each must inherit it, bear it. The war rotted and clung, festered and stank to high heaven. It became Nixon's war.

Nixon's war — interminably. The war, those dead in war dead became a haunt, a pursuing chorus of Furies. The war rounded on him, as it had on his predecessors. It would bring him down—as it had his predecessors.

There was an election to be won, and Nixon narrowed those famous calculating eyes like a gimlet or a gun sight. Purpose set, gun cocked; to win as they say, by hook or by crook.

His genius was notoriously opportunistic. He concocted a species of devotion (to a degree only, and tactically only) — to the prospering of Israel.

Were his emotions aroused? Was his devotion a matter of principle? It is inordinately difficult to attach such words, implying moral alertness and compassion, to such a phenomenon. In any case, Nixon won the prize upon which he had staked everything, including what rags of integrity clung to his frame.

And what could the future hold, for those who saw on the political landscape only disaster and humiliation? I sought out my friend more frequently, in his closet of an office, cluttered to the ceiling with tomes, at Jewish Theological Seminary. Any port in a storm! Or more exactly, this port above all.

I was an ex-prisoner (of war, so to speak). I was also, as was my friend Abraham, more and more isolated in America.

It could not be denied that Nixon was a genius of sorts; master of the bloody tradeoff, he contrived divisions among people of common cause, and so in effect, won them over. Israel or Vietnam? The question cut across boundaries, divisions, religious traditions; it cut to the bone of our humanity, what remained of it. Continued support of Israel, continued assault on Vietnam? Could we choose one at the price of the other? What were my friend and I to do?

I proposed a newspaper ad, stating a united religious opposition, Jewish and Christian, against Nixon's war. Heschel agreed to the project, and we went about New York, seeking financial help from the Jewish community. (It perhaps goes without saying, no such help was forthcoming from Catholics.)

We came on no help, there would be no ad. The Jewish community among many others had made its decision. So had the majority of Jewish Seminary faculty and students—among many others.

The decisions of New Yorkers coincided nicely with the electorate at large—Jews, Catholics, everyone. It was Nixon all the way: Nixon's war, Nixon's economics, Nixon's chicanery to come. We, a few Catholics and Protestants and Jews, wore a kind of albatross about our necks. Nixon bound it tight.

Thus the last days of Heschel stood tragic and solitary, in the prophetic line he had so honored and celebrated.

And I reflect ruefully that he resembles us lesser mortals at least in this: Never in his (or our) darkest hour did he imagine the tragic days that lay ahead. How literally he (and we) would be required to live out and stand by the hurtful truth of God's word.

There remains a species of cold comfort which I have frequently reflected on. Abraham Heschel stood in opposition to the crimes of his lifetime. First, as the Nazis rampaged through Poland, he then departed Europe with the hope that he had left such crimes behind.

Alas, innocence had fled the world. The gods of war flew faster than his passage. It was Mars, no other, who horridly greeted the distinguished foreigner to our shores.

In his years in America, Heschel entered the old age of the patriarch whose name he bore; burden upon burden upon burden laid on him. There were the civil rights years and the war. And finally the opposition of his own people.

Immensely revered in some circles (in every circle, one thinks, except his own), he was denied the dubious honor known among Catholics as premature canonization.

Thus too he entered the larger human family, an exemplar of our common plight and hope. He was scorned and rejected, even as he was loved beyond measure.

"In honor and dishonor," he fulfilled his vocation. Which is to say, his name. Like Abraham, summoned again and again, to "come forth, into a land which I will show you."

By what means come forth, bearing what necessities of food and clothing and lodging? What can be taken along, what must be left behind or jettisoned on the way? Who is to chart the direction, who to tell right from wrong road? And that other "land, I will show you" — what is its name, how far distant does it lie, what welcome awaits? No matter: "I will show you."

No matter, no moment? But this is of the greatest moment, for You have reversed all logic, have turned the world on its head. Which is to say, I, Abraham, know with the knowledge implied in love and custom, every detail of my homeland, the land I am ordered to depart.

You know it too, and with a kind of surgical cruelty You, Jawe, speak of what must be abandoned: "the land of your kinsfolk, and your father's house."

And of that other land I know nothing, not even its name. Is its name Mirage?

To whom could one go, for surcease, for strength, in those terrible Nixon years? One autumn, friends came together to celebrate the Feast of Tabernacles, held incongruously at Heschel's seminary amid the New York stalagmites. There under an immense bower of green, we pronounced our muted alleluia. The reign of God, the reign of justice and peace! Across the crowd, our eyes met, we raised a glass. To a harvest he would never see. Nor I.

It was Christmas 1972. Nixon, we were told, had worked out a deal involving the fate of two notorious prisoners. A simple solution, innocent of any moral content. Both prisoners were to be freed simultaneously: Jimmy Hoffa and my brother Philip. Thus would various constituencies be placated, from antiwar people to the Mafia.

The news came of Philip's imminent freeing. Abraham approached me. Could he be included in the group of friends who would voyage to Danbury, Connecticut, to welcome Philip out of prison?

There were complications, he explained. He must perform his devotions en route. Would this be objected to?

Far from it. It would be, I averred, our privilege to pray with him along the way. So he prayed his psalms, and we joined his prayer as best we might.

Of that memorable day, there remain two photos in my possession. One was taken in the car en route. The lighting is bright and cold, perhaps the sun was just coming up. Heschel sits, his leonine profile, grave, recollected, is lit with the aura of dawn. Just out of the photo, his book of devotions lies open.

The second photo was taken that same morning, just after Philip's release. A crowd presses close around. The two stand face to face, tall man and short. Heschel grasps Philip by his lapels and engages him fervently, even fiercely, eye to eye, head aloft, beard wild in the wind. The figures are frozen and speechless in time. One can imagine, if one cannot reconstruct (indeed my memory reconstructs) the passionate welcome and gratitude that welled from Heschel's tongue.

All unknowing, and mercifully so, we were nearing the end. Heschel was to live only a few days more.

That same joyful day, on the return trip to New York, Philip and I were invited to tea a day or two hence with the Heschel family.

The afternoon arrived. Minutes before we set out across Manhattan, a frantic call reached us. Abraham had been found dead. Would we come quickly?

We hurried over. The truth was terrible. Our friend had left this world. Having himself become, according to the promise, the father of a multitude. Of blessed memory, father—and more: friend.

I told my soul in gratitude and grief, how blessed I was, that one named Abraham had stood with me in fair weather and foul.

And if foul days far outnumbered fair, and the dreadful imbalance in nature and nation might well perdure—might worsen, might indeed tip us into chaos—still one consolation was at hand. One life might redeem all. Our world had known a Heschel.

The weight of one such life, or of a few, is of such vast import in God's sight as to restore, to recoup, to adjust the scales of moral creation into balance once more. So I thought then, and so I trust.

19

William Stringfellow
and the Eschaton

THE SCENE IS Block Island, Rhode Island, in the late 1960s. A spread of some fourteen peerless acres slopes gently down and down like the domain of a land god, to the magnificent beetling cliffs. Below, another domain, the sea god's empery.

And crowning all, like a coronet on a puzzled brow, stands a strange suburban transplant of a house, maybe second-rate California cottage-cum-pretension. A transplant that, so to speak, hadn't quite taken, the main house.

Bill couldn't be held responsible for the diuertic architecture. He and Anthony had been won to the view, the hill, the quiet. The times were apt for buying; such places were not yet off limits to modest lower-middle-class folk.

The setting was graced, so to speak, and if one could credit his eyes, within sight and sound of the ocean, by — a swimming pool, the only such anomalous marvel to be found on the entire island.

The previous owners had attained in Bill's mind the status of a myth. The couple were a species of alcoholic owls. They covered the large window in the living room with heavy drapes, drawn close all day. And the most prominent feature of the room was a bar, stocked to the hilt. The loving pair, arising toward noon, would proceed to refresh themselves liquidly during the ensuing hours, in semi-darkness. Toward sunset the drapes would be drawn back. And when night fell, the partying would be transported outdoors, to poolside.

The tenor of their days seemed an accurate if somewhat peculiar (and perhaps presumptuous and certainly uninterrupted) celebration of "the End Time."

Thus it seemed inevitable. With his flair for locating a vision (even one with so dubious a prelude), in the here and now, Bill consecrated the property as "Eschaton" (the biblical word for the "End Time" or the "End of the World").

The acres, in more notorious days to come, would be named in the media the "Stringfellow Estate." Little did the pundits know, and little was said on the subject, but as years passed and his health declined, Bill was wrung dry financially. It was as though the land were falling into the sea. To pay ruinous medical bills, the splendid meadows were sold off, acre after acre.

I was sprung from durance vile in 1972, and shortly voyaged to the island. As may be imagined, my arrival was a warm reunion of hearts and minds. Bill, with his usual finesse, instructed a cab driver who met my flight to waste not a moment in transporting me to Eschaton; no delaying for media or curiosity hounds.

In the ensuing days we would hear now and again a cab commissioned by tourists, stopping at the front gate. The voice of the driver would intone something like "up yonder's the house where that there priest fellow was fin'ly taken by the law." Hilarious.

One day Bill said in his laconic fashion, "You've got to have your own place here." There was talk of an apartment-wing on the main house, or a cottage on the grounds, anywhere I chose. In due time, the latter was decided on. I wandered the fields alone, summoning the daemon of the place, and it spoke, "Close to the cliffs, come."

Anthony and Bill are long gone. So is the California Concoction uphill, sold off to a succession of moneyed folk from somewhere else. That main house has been gussied up and added to. Gone once for all is the semi-shabby lived-in look that only dogs and cats, and the humans they grant rights of cohabitation, lend to a house. By invitation of a new owner, I toured the place at one point. I came out weak-kneed. It was immaculate, sterile, and lifeless.

But ah! the cottage. It stands there at land's end like an angelic sentinel. What was the cry of the ancients, landlocked and lost, as an epiphany opened before them? "The sea, the sea!"

It's as though you've never before seen a sunrise or sunset or a first star or a new moon. You stand there like Adam or Eve toward the end of the Big Week. Big Anthony used to say, peering eastward, pacing the deck for his evening smoke, "Next stop, Portugal!"

Anthony died, then Bill. There in the lower meadow just above the cliffs, we planted a splendid pine grove and buried the ashes side by side, two small neat boxes fashioned by a friend. In the house a simple plaque on the wall is inscribed, "Near this cottage the ashes of William Stringfellow and Anthony Towne await the resurrection. Amen, Alleluia."

It is a place where the elixir of memory spills over. People who visit say it all the time, in all sorts of ways. They write poetry, leave ecstatic notes, find something enhancing or helpful to do. Mostly they love the solitude, find themselves rapt into sunrise, sunset, evening star. They shuck off an overwrought urban shell, are renewed, awakened, once more know themselves beloved.

Stringfellow, friendship, that astonishing, unrepeatable gift. It seems as though at this remove, death does little except to isolate and enhance the gift, to offer it anew.

Understood in this way, resurrection makes great sense to me. The friend lives on, in ways I can only stutter over. As a great ancestor also was at near loss for words, thinking of what is to come, "Eye has not seen, nor ear heard. . . . "

In the early 1960s I was living on the east side of Manhattan. Anthony and Bill, I discovered, pitched their tent a stone's throw away, across Central Park.

I had read Bill's book *My People Is the Enemy.* And one day, an inspiration of sorts. Why not send a note to the famous author, thanking him? And by the way—would he consider writing a page or two introducing my new manuscript?

In no time at all, a response arrived from Bill, in effect, "Of course, why not, and how about coming over for dinner?"

Over I went. The two dwelt in a penthouse atop a run-down building a short distance from Central Park. One entered the building and, with sound dubiety, ventured into an ancestral elevator. One's throat tightened as the clanking marvel shunted and lurched unsteadily upward.

The ample rooms of the penthouse bore a lived-in, doggy look. An outsize terrace faced east and south. Out there, I was to learn, country matters flourished; not only corn and tomatoes, but for a brief time, until dismayed neighbors summoned the health department, rabbits as well.

Heady years, people forever coming and going. Among church folk of migratory proclivities, there arose an unspoken dogma; the Stringfellonian menage was to be accounted among the prime sights and sounds of the city. Not to be missed!

The gyrovague Christians arrived, hot on the spoor of the famous author, theologian, Harlem lawyer. They came and came. Bill was, alas, constitutionally unable to say nay.

The future, Socratic, generous to a fault, recondite, valiant of spirit, was under way.

Like it or not (I think he liked it indeed; it tickled his sense of the absurd), Bill was becoming, harrumph! a national figure.

The apartment seemed never to be empty — friends, clergy, drinking companions, the merely curious, this or that troubled or evicted or otherwise needy soul.

I remember someone decked out in Texan sombrero and boots. Bill and Anthony departed on an assignment and the gent stayed on, house sitting. On their return his corpse was discovered; a suicide.

Domestic partying was frequent. There was a hilarious all-night auction of art, a fund-raiser for SNCC or CORE. Corita Kent donated several of her incomparable serigraphs.

But the nonstop pace was taking a steep toll. Bill was losing weight and vitality, was failing alarmingly.

The medical decision came down. It was chilling. There must be, and immediately, an unprecedented surgical protocol, the removal of his pancreas.

Into hospital and under the knife, and a medical marathon followed. We sweated the awful day through, as Bill hovered between worlds.

He survived, barely. The plump young theologian-lawyer, face unlined, eyes cool and confident, achievement bound, lauded and stroked by the elders — he aged overnight; from then on he was a radical diabetic.

In the Harlem and post-Harlem years the ingredients of greatness, elegance of mind, and generous spirit were held in a kind of suspension. Among the poor he was on perpetual call as arbiter and advocate.

Uncommon goodness to be sure. But something was wanting. And according to our Bible, the greatness in question is not an achievement, cannot be; it is granted, or it is not.

What occurred in his last decade seemed to me a kind of transfiguration. To those who loved him, his appearance all but stopped the heart. His face grew seamed and scored, and so noble. He was vulnerable, frail, astonishingly patient.

When the Catonsville Nine went on trial in October 1968 for destruction of draft records, Bill was in attendance. He persuaded his friend

Bishop Pike to come along, the only prelate of whatever denomination to touch with a long crosier such miscreants as ourselves.

Bill was haggard and drawn, an elegantly turned-out skeleton. Few will forget the scene in the parish hall of St. Ignatius in Baltimore, where a teach-in was mounted each evening during the trial.

Bill's turn came at the podium. He stumped forward with great effort on his cane, turned to the audience and shouted a single sentence, "Death shall have no dominion!" That was all.

He kept going, we scarcely could imagine how, with travel and public appearances and uncertain accommodations and nourishment at all hours to stave off insulin shock. And the threat never distant of incarceration in hospitals, which he tagged with precise biblical passion, as among the most awful of principalities.

The changes showed, in his face, in his writing. He passed, somewhat like Bonhoeffer, from acclaim and good repute and competence and the beginnings (and more) of theological eminence to—stature, tragedy.

He passed from the company of Job's friends, talking about God, to a Job—enduring God.

20

The Faithful Witness
of Philip Berrigan

IT IS WEIRDLY INSTRUCTIVE, in view of later unforeseen (and yet somehow foreseen) developments, to review a few of the press comments at the time of the Catonsville trial and sentencing in 1968.

Something strikes one, the decline and fall, since that time, of most things. Including media quality and media responsibility.

In that year of tumult and hope, a modicum of press comment appeared, concerning the severity of the sentences handed down to my brother Philip and Tom Lewis. Even the *New York Times* (whose current ideology would reduce the angels to fruitless tears) blew off a bit of steam:

> *When a United States judge sentenced two of the pacifists to six years in federal prison . . . he clearly ignored sound discretion. The powers of the bench include the power to fix sentences on those found guilty, but they do not include the right to impose punishment out of all proportion to the crime.*

The *Times,* moreover, had covered the trial in its somewhat avuncular way. So had *Time, Newsweek,* the Associated Press, and the local and national media. I mention such matters, despite the legitimate question of why press "coverage" (or "noncoverage") is in question. Of course, so goes the supposition, the media, being responsible agents of public information, as a matter of course, cover legal events of import!

Well, maybe. And then again, in the late 1980s, maybe not.

Let it be said two cents plain. The national media, in many matters of import, have ceased even the pretense of mediating. By and large, except for a few local exceptions, the media are derelict in reporting the actions of peacemakers. One thinks especially of the arrests, trials, and sentencing of nearly a hundred Plowshares anti-nuclear folk since 1980.

The studied ignoring of the peace movement holds true also regarding other, more massive events, some of which have included large numbers of arrests. Newsworthy? Hardly.

And then the Plowshares. Could it be imagined, for instance, that the *New York Times* would raise even a mild outcry as Helen Woodson was sentenced to eighteen years for a nonviolent anti-nuclear action?

It could not be imagined. We are, God help us, in another century, all but another eon. And so to speak, strictly on our own.

Let us strive to locate ourselves, in the omniscient eye of the cameras. We stand somewhere between those who walk lockstep in the track of the latest clone president, and those who, declared of no particular moment or worth, fall between the cracks.

Somewhere between. Even the homeless are reported on, from time to time. And the uglyfiers, yuppies, developers, corporate pirates, are positively celebrated.

I reflect that no old-time anathema can equal, in its impact, the studied silence of those who purportedly exist to inform the public. Some other analogy is required; something, God forbid, of the impact of being declared a nonperson, something of being a disappeared person.

In a sense, an altogether new, altogether American sense, Helen and the other Plowshares prisoners lie under a kind of cultural double jeopardy. They are twice sentenced. They are locked away for years and years, their sentences without doubt meant to freeze the resolve of similar venturesome souls. (In legal as in military skulls, deterrence is considered a quite useful tactic.)

At the same time as those convicted and so sentenced are declared nonpersons, their actions are declared by the media—non-acts.

Do they exist, do such defendants merit notice? They do not.

I dwell, perhaps overlong, upon these lamentable facts of life today. My brother Philip, along with over one hundred other Plowshares people, along with the actions they perform to draw attention to the plight of our children, our world, and in the crepuscular moral climate, our very humanity — these have been declared irrelevant. The defendants have disappeared in America, from public life, from public attention.

Indeed the analogy with the "disappeared" of Latin America is instructive.

Another example of this curious business. A recent issue of *The Critic* magazine in a fit of whimsy included my brother's name in a list of the formerly famous: "What's become of Philip Berrigan?"

Thus was a question, implying a certain media responsibility, both raised and evaded.

A phone call or two might of course have supplied an answer to the inquiry. But the question was not placed in view of an answer; it was frivolously posed, a fun question, part of a "Catholic trivia" game.

No matter the thirty years of nonviolent resistance by Philip's community, Jonah House in inner-city Baltimore, Maryland. No matter the moral persistence, the arrests and trials and jailings of its members and friends. No matter the example thus offered in season and out, of sticking by one's convictions.

Alas, Philip stands surrogate for the disappearance of others of like mind, including his family and friends, largely ignored by the cultural mouthpieces and their icons. Icons, together with their worshipers, have other affairs to hand. They are alike hot on the spoor of the dying culture, the pursuit of porcine politics, deception, triviality, big (invariably tainted) money, saber rattling.

What indeed had become of Philip? Let us grant it. Proudly. He, Elizabeth, their three children, the Jonah House community—all in a manner of speaking have indeed disappeared—into the heart of things.

Dignum et justum. The deepest reality is one with "the things which are not seen." A practical as well as a visionary insight. Those who touch on, insist on, the spiritual implication of these dreadful years become invisible to the one-eyed giant, whose range of vision, trivial, grandiose and appetitive as it is, can encompass only "the things which are seen."

The community of Jonah House has gone its way, against all odds, unrepentantly opposed to nuclear violence and its lethal spin-offs—the decrepitude of political life, domestic violence on a spiraling scale, sexism, racism, executions, and the vile social triage being worked against the poor.

For more than thirty years the community has kept to such issues, when almost every element of the culture, including the media, was urging the folly and uselessness of such effort, through a contemptuous (and contemptible) silence.

No matter, the work must go on, foul weather or fair. Jonah House has become a publishing center, a place of worship and prayer, a distributor of food for the poor, a workplace whose members earn their living by house-painting, carpentry, and like tasks. And foremost, a community of nonviolent resistance that in Camus's phrase, "keeps paying up."

What has become of Philip?

At this writing, yet another disappearing act. In jail yet once more. Having been tried and convicted, yet once more. Just before Christmas, on December 19, 1999, along with three other intemperate souls, he entered a National Guard airfield in Middle River, Maryland, near Baltimore, poured a vial of his blood on a so-called A-10 "Warthog" bomber, fresh from U.S. provocation and derring-do in the Persian Gulf where it scattered depleted uranium-tipped missiles. It was the sixty-eighth Plowshares action since 1980.

Philip and myself reflect ruefully that nothing is more apt than the present situation to clear the air, illustrate one's intention, and tot up the cost of making peace today. One is clear above all, as to motive — glory, notoriety, glamour, and the rest, having long fled.

E.g. and to wit, "What ever happened to — ?"

For his part, Philip carries on, in prison or out, no great matter. As does his family, and a multitude of friends, like him, un-housebroken in America.

In the day of the toad and the night of the long swords, Philip wears his humanity like a Buddha, a jewel in the forehead. He and others like him light up the national darkness. And the darkness, to borrow a phrase, does not comprehend.

Meantime, this poem. It was written in 1968, after we burned the draft files at Catonsville, Maryland. Whatever the merits of the verse, its sentiment holds true today, truer than ever.

> Compassionate, casual as a good face
> (A good heart goes without saying)
> someone seen in the street; or
> infinitely rare, once, twice in a lifetime
> that conjunction we call brother or friend.
> Biology, mythology cast up clues.
> We grew together, stars made men
> by cold design; instructed
> sternly (no variance, not by a hair's
> breadth) in course and recourse. In the heavens
> in our mother's body, by moon and month were whole
> men made. We obeyed then, and were born.

21

Poems for Philip in Prison

A Birthday Poem for Philip in Prison
(October 5, 1992)

Not a day passes
I'm not caught up short
with the awe of it, the mastery too—

as though, manacles sprung
hands steady, in prayer—
and you, protagonist, world navigator
showing the way.

It's not fame, I know
you look toward, but soul.
You gleam like a Greek urn
incised with scenes
from a broken life,
its Easter aftermath.

I stammer and celebrate, both,
the grief, the glory.

~

For Philip in Prison, 2001

This is dignum et justum, the exact
address of the just.
This fits like a skin a frame
the tegument of noble souls, your soul.

Over hill and dale of nightmare, barbed wire,
miles of it, arresting the sun,
betraying pure light for a Judas shekel,

woven on hell's loom, bristling with ironies
hell knows nothing of;

in this thorny next
the future broods precious eggs unborn.

O my brother, ten, only ten
and the times are redeemed.
You, Susan, Greg, Steve—God keeps count,
wills the total

like a priest's cup passed, full, unfailing
breathing
sacrament.

~

MY BROTHER, PRISONER IN TRANSIT
(MARCH 17, 2001)

What logic cannot do, and mourning might
or might not (chancy, you're stuck on a trestle,
a train galloping behind, that's the world)
—a poem will.

   Give it time, give it
mind entire.
   I did. An hour, two. A lamp lit,
and my brother's face stood,
emblem of courage unvanquished,
of faithful faith.
Brother, where you are I would be, your gift and mine
acknowledged or not (but who of us greatly cares?)

   Four brute walls hem us in,
bars forbid the season,
unblinking Cyclops sting the eye blind.
   And loneliness, a ghastly
guardian mastiff, baying, You're mine, mine!

Christ confers it, this harsh salvation, this plucking
by hair of head away, far from the crooked age.

Cruelties bless, disguised.
    Lockup. And you look up
in prayer, the open sesame of mystics, hermits.

We live
a drama of End Time, of time and scoundrel world
surpassed.
    What comes of it, this submission?

Time cannot tell, eternity is mum.
But
sure to be, a promissory note
steeped, signed in Christ's blood.

                        ~

ON BLOCK ISLAND, THINKING OF PHILIP IN PRISON

Walking by the sea
I put on
like glasses
on a squinting
shortsighted soul—

your second sight

and I see
washed ashore
the last hour of the world—

the murdered clock of Hiroshima.

22

Homily for My Brother,
Philip Berrigan

Philip Berrigan died on December 6, 2002, after suffering with cancer for only two months. His family and friends kept vigil and prayed with him nonstop during his last week. He had spent nearly eleven years of his life in prison for antiwar and anti-nuclear action. His son Jerry made a wooden coffin. Hundreds of people walked in procession with the coffin to the Church of St. Peter Claver in Baltimore, where this homily was preached during the Mass of Resurrection, on December 9, 2002.

~

DEAR FAMILY and friends from near and far, I begin with a poem called "My brother's battered Bible carried into prison repeatedly":

> That book
> lived with thumbprints
> underscorings, lashes—
> I see you carry it into the storms,
> past the storms
> I see you underscore
> like the score of music,
> all that travail
> that furious unexplained joy
> contraband! the guards shake it out
> the apostles wail
> Herod screams in his stews
> like a souped-up record
> the women wail like camaeun sybils
> they toss it back—harmless!
> the bars slam shut
> now, seated on the cell bunk

you play the pages slowly, slowly
a lifeline humming with the song
of the jeweled fish, all but taken.

The story of Lazarus (John 11), we are told, is the most extended in John's Gospel, except for the Passion account. Evidently much is implied here. Let us linger over a few themes.

These notes were set down while Philip lay dying surrounded to the last by loving care, tears, and an altogether obscure hope.

And I thought in these days of the gradually diminishing hope of Mary and Martha as the days also passed for them. Their brother was sinking toward death, while Jesus played St. Elsewhere. Then Lazarus died and was buried and the stone sank in its socket. The hope of healing vanished like a smoke.

Jesus, so the reasoning of the sisters went, might well have brought relief to illness. But death intervened, and before death, who could prevail? Four days passed. Now in their hearts it was hope against hope to the fourth power, against hope, against hope.

A letter to the poet Milosz by Thomas Merton isolates with a kind of merciless mercy, the genuine article, hope, in contrast to its counterfeits: "You and I must not allow any palliatives, huckstered as 'just as good.' To disguise the near despair in which we are called to make our way, a near despair named hope. Hope which is constantly being delayed and betrayed in such a world. Hope which does not lean upon contrived utopias or money or ego, or a religion which has no argument with the iron bound rule: things as they are."

Philip was diagnosed, and in slightly over two months, died. Cancer pummeled him under like the horsemen of apocalypse. The speed, the near frenzy of death, were terrifying; no slowing it down, no bargaining with it, no give and take.

A question remains to this hour: "What intervention did we hope for? Were we cheated? Were we chasing moonbeams while the horsemen plunged on, dragging Philip for their quarry?"

I think we were not cheated as we gathered to keep vigil those many days and nights. I think the Jesus of Lazarus came to us, mysterious and disguised. I think Jesus came in the coworkers, the sister and fellow prisoners, former and current, including Sisters Jackie, Ardeth, and Carol in prison for beating swords into plowshares. I think Jesus came in our own family, in the skilled medical people who arrived by night or day as need required. I think Jesus arrived in the great tides of prayer that surrounded us with light, and thus we were enabled, to give Philip up, not to death, but to resurrection.

Dear Ones, I have a second text equally beloved on which I invite reflection.

In Revelation, chapter 6, verses 9 and following, the fifth seal is opened. In previous episodes, the horsemen have wreaked their worst, leaving behind a welter of sanctioned murder, famine, and ecological ruin. Among their victims are the martyrs. The image is stark. They are crowded in a mysterious space under an altar of sacrifice, in a kind of holding cell. This is no Eden, no paradiso, no beatific vision. Women, men, and children have given their lives—yet they are strangely shaken by a sense of their unfinished lives. While time lasts, and the unborn wait in the wings of the world stage, the martyrs are told they must wait. Their voices are clamorous. They cry out for blood. "How long will it be, holy and true Master, before you sit in judgment and avenge our blood on the inhabitants of the earth?" It is a cry wrung from the psalms of vengeance and the curses of the prophets. Their cry is also in stark contrast to the last words of Christ on the cross. "Forgive them, they know not what they do."

The victims of the fifth seal are martyrs, yet they need more time. Time to learn forgiveness, time in another sphere than mere time. "They were told to be patient, until the number of their sisters and fellow servants who were to be killed as they had been, was complete." They received no direct answer to their plea, "How long?"

Cold comfort from on high, to be sure. They received a white garment, the sign of a costly victory. And the sole response to their impassioned plea is a generalized call to patience, which might well seem a strange sort of virtue to commend to the noblest of the saints.

Patience, impatience. The two seem complementary, a kind of high-wire balancing act of the spirit. From 1967 to the day of his death, Philip must learn patience, a harsh, grating unattractive so-called virtue. He learned patience through bolts and bars, through stop clocks and time served, at the icy hands of judges and guards and wardens; he must learn it through the warmaking state and a complicit church, through long sacrifice and small return, through thirty-five years of American wars and scarcely a week of genuine peace.

So he learned patience from many unpromising teachers. It was like an iron yoke placed on his shoulder.

And Oh, he was impatient. Let me recall one instance. A conspiracy trial opened in 1972 against Philip and seven others. Philip was already behind bars. The government carefully constructed its house of stacked cards. The trial was removed from New York and Philadelphia, the purported sites of felonious acts. It was moved far inland to Harrisburg, with its few Catholics and conservative politics.

More, the prosecuting team was chosen with malicious care. Catholics, that was the clue! Pit hand-chosen functionaries against discredited priests and thus vindicate the cause.

So there arrived on the scene the prosecutor, a rabid, florid, Catholic acolyte of the state. He affirmed publicly, and on occasion loudly, his contempt for the Second Vatican Council, for Pope John, and above all, for lawbreaking priests. Clearly, this entity was awaiting a great moment. He hoped to place Philip on the stand, under a barrage of questions regarding his antiwar activities since Catonsville. If Philip could only be trapped, it was altogether likely that a life sentence would follow. Of the Harrisburg Eight, all but Philip voted against his taking the stand. Of course he would welcome cross-examination, "Let the truth be told, no matter the price." He was icon of impatience at white heat.

Finally, he yielded to the others at the strong urging of defense attorneys. Ramsey Clark arose in court. "Your Honor, the prosecution has offered no case worth rebutting. The defense rests." The prosecutor was livid, the jury deadlocked. And the splenetic judge was forced to concede a mistrial.

If Philip's patience was marmoreal, his impatience was a lifted hammer. The blow struck marble, repeatedly. What we had at the end was a masterwork of grace, of human sweetness. We gazed on him with a kind of awe.

Dying, Philip won the face he had earned at such cost.

IV

Sermons and Homilies

then showed me he
in right hand held
everything that is

the hand was a woman's
creation   all lusty
a meek bird's egg

nesting there   waiting
her word   and I heard it

newborn   I make you
nestling   I love you
homing   I keep you

23

Keeping the Flame Alive

Maccabees and the Fire of Peace

These reflections were offered at a Festival of Hope on May 4, 1997, the night before the trial of the Prince of Peace Plowshares, including Philip Berrigan, who had hammered on a warship at the Bath Iron Works in Portland, Maine. The six defendants were found guilty. The long quote below comes from the Second Book of Maccabees 1:18–36 and 2:1–6, which includes the story of the miraculous preservation of the sacred fire.

~

As we shall be celebrating the purification of the Temple on the 25th of Chislev, we consider it proper to notify you, so that you may celebrate the feast of Tabernacles, of the fire that appeared when Nehemiah, the builder of the Temple and the altar, offered sacrifice. For when our ancestors were being deported to Persia, the devout priests of the time took some of the fire from the altar and hid it secretly in the hollow of a dry well, where they concealed it in such a way that the place was unknown to anyone.

When some years had elapsed, in God's good time, Nehemiah, commissioned by the king of Persia, sent the descendants of the priests who had hidden the fire to recover it; but they notified us that they had found not fire but a thick liquid. Nehemiah ordered them to draw some out and bring it back. When the materials for the sacrifice had been set out, Nehemiah ordered the priests to pour liquid over the wood and what lay on it. When this had been done, and when in due course the sun, which had previously been clouded over, shone out, a great fire flared up, to the astonishment of all.

While the sacrifice was being burned, the priests and all those present with the priests offered prayer; Jonathan intoning and the rest responding with Nehemiah. The prayer took this form: "Lord, Lord God, Creator of all things . . . accept this sacrifice on behalf of all your people Israel, and protect your heritage and consecrate it. Bring together those of us who are dispersed, set free those in slavery among the heathen, look favorably on those held in contempt or abhorrence, and let the nations know that you are our God."

149

In Second Maccabees 1:19ff., we have an event long past, a midrash upon it, and a metaphor. An original event becomes legendary, is passed on and on, embellished. Thus it becomes the pith and marrow of hope in dark times.

Thus the story: by order of the Prophet Jeremiah, priests sentenced to exile took a portion of fire from the altar in the Temple in Jerusalem. En route to Persia, they hid the sacred flame somewhere in a cave along the way. They keep the place secret. Years go by, a generation or even two.

The current king of Persia (Artaxerxes I, so the apocrypha goes) proves benevolent. He hears the story of the hidden fire; he commands the priestly descendants to seek out the place of the flame.

They do so. And find, alas, no fire alive; but, at the depths of the cave, a "thick water." Which they bring back.

A sacrifice is prepared (even in Babylon), and the "water" is poured over the victim.

It is sun-up. A great fire spontaneously combusts on the altar and consumes the entire offering.

The priests pray, in essence: "Keep your heritage intact and sanctify it (which is, today, ourselves). Gather together our scattered people, deliver those in slavery, look mercifully on the despised and abhorred—all this so the nations may know that you are God."

Quite a prayer, and what a response! The petitions are like elements that, despite all so-called laws of nature, combust.

And here the metaphor fails: How could a flame perdure in a cave for years and years, with no material to feed on? Let it be suggested that the image was meant to fall short. No flame lit by mortals survives for generations of itself.

And yet, this flame did not die. It was transformed, rather, to a "thick water."

And this liquid, on recovery (and the right moment and elements coming together; the hour of sacrifice; the priest-exiles at the altar, their faith still afire, with so little evidence to feed the flame; the people who also hope against hope) — despite all, the water turned to fire, flared up, consumed the sacrifice. All sorts of impossibilities, as it were, come together here.

The impossible comes to pass. We are right, then, to formulate a law, an all but absurd law: Unless these incompatibles were brought together, nothing would change, nothing.

This is the plight of the Maccabean Jews: the iron fist of empire descending on the victims, contempt for their faith, slavery, mass executions, the appalling exaltation of the inhuman, the humiliation of the human. Death in charge, no way out—a common presumption of tyrants.

Water and fire are incompatible. So are hope and empire.

Watery fire could not be, and yet it was. Against all odds, against all "laws of nature."

Beyond the physical metaphor, the midrash expressed in its daring: (1) the limits of "what we can do." But do something. Go seek the place of the fire. And even should you find nothing there of fire. And even should you find nothing there of fire, but quite the opposite, do not lose heart. Bring back what you find—something.

(2) Look, you, to the old intrusive act of Gods; where you were powerless, may not God make water fiery?

The priests who hid the fire did not live to see the resurrection of fire. They did what they could do, then they trudged on into exile with their people. Then they retired from the text—and from life, nameless.

Their service was austere, anonymous, crucial. They cherished and passed on the legend of the Kept Flame.

And what of those who sought the fire, and came upon nearly nothing—impossible, useless, a puddle of water in the cave?

What various directions, aspects, new understandings the midrash invites us to!

First of all, a sense of our being in exile, in our own Babylon — America.

Ours is a place, a time, a culture in which everything signified by the secret flame is most endangered, most apt to be quenched.

The large enticement is to amnesia, to forget the homeland, forget the tradition (the Torah, the holy Temple), sacrament, prayer, discipline— one another.

Forget, because, in forgetting is a kind of peace, and, in remembrance, only bitterness.

Keeping alive a sense of exile, we learn to translate, too, a sense of the homeland.

This is a deep, often ill-defined truth of our emotional life: homesickness for a country we have never put foot on.

Only we know such a homeland must exist; we know in the deep fiber of our mind, in our jealously guarded, always endangered sense of the human—we do not belong in Babylon.

What then? We work at other ways than those of greed and violence, other behaviors, in view of another citizenship. We work at decency, civility, affection. In this way, we work toward mutual survival; we lift one another up, out of despair.

Only the community can resist Babylon and survive. Only resistance keeps alive the flame.

Alive, the flame? Not likely. As we discover: Long before we found the cave again and entered, the flame had died and stagnant waters gathered.

The quest could hardly end more lamentably.

No fire, only water—and that smelling of naphtha, unfit for drinking.

Nonetheless, gather it up, bring it back. Something.

And prepare a sacrifice, an act of worship; gather the community. Do it; do it in exile.

Every action is done against odds. Odds of time and place and elements and public understanding.

What can come of this? Folly.

Do it. In these unlikely years of discontent, when high crime proceeds in secret and the vast majority of people are distracted or indifferent, do it.

Board the hellish "nuclear-capable vessel," pour your blood, breathe new life into Isaiah's word: swords into plowshares.

We keep the flame or we die together.

24

Three Youths and
the Fiery Furnace

*A homily offered at Trinity Church, Wall Street, New York City,
during Lent 1989, based on the book of Daniel, chapter 3.*

∼

SUCH BIBLICAL STORIES as these, one notes regretfully, are commonly relegated to Sunday schools, to the story hour of good children. This I suggest is a lamentable error. The relegating of such stories to edifying the young allows us to ignore their dead seriousness, their composition on our adult behalf, their long history of sustaining heroes of the faith.

Our present story for instance raises the crucial question of monotheism and its cost, and the temptations offered by the powerful to yield to a practical polytheism. Such questions, may one add, are notoriously to the point today. They are illustrated not only by the conduct of ancient tyrants and their subjects, but by our own leaders—and ourselves.

Perhaps the stories strike too close for comfort. Were those ancients in fact more idolatrous than ourselves? Are golden images dedicated to "strange gods," never raised in our cities or countryside?

And enlarging the contemporary point, were those who triggered the first atomic explosion named "Trinity" celebrating faith in the true God, or in a "strange god"? Was the Bomb a fitting symbol of the faith given over by Christ to His church, or was it an audacious idolatry, attempting to seize on the reign of Christ for its own?

Further, is the "fiery furnace" to be thought of as no more than a mad construct, the lucubration of a primitive despot? Or in our lifetime, is not the furnace constructed again and again, madly stoked, its heat amplified to the millionth degree, in Hiroshima, Auschwitz, and elsewhere? More and more, does not the nuclear multiplication of weapons make of our world, by intent and ideology and prospect, one vast fiery furnace?

Indeed, the questioning never ends, if true faith is not to be subverted. In the light (or darkness) of such questions, it is at considerable risk, it would seem, that we dare congratulate ourselves on a civilized leadership—or for that matter, an enlightened church.

Preparation of great crime, one beyond unaccountablility, is under way. We are told in the story, on the face of it, the first step is quite simple: a statue is constructed. A statue of the king, mandated by the king.

The implications are momentous, then and now.

A superhuman image of a leader is required, a myth is enjoined, in order that—against all promises and cajoling and stroking of citizens—something simple and final may proceed—enormous crimes, murder on a grand scale.

The specifications of the statue are joined closely to its purpose. The height and girth of the image must suggest, and more than suggest, the triumph, the conquest, the empery of this god. Nebuchadnezzar was literally the conqueror of the world.

The statue is designed to tower above mere mortals, to dwarf and deflate, to rebuke those among them devoted to other, lesser gods.

More, in creating the image of invincibility, a truly Olympian image, not just any material can be thought suitable. Its material must convey an unchallenged superiority. The statue must be of — gold. Only thus will the matter be worthy of the form.

The bowels of the world must be harrowed for their elusive residue, gold. Then will quality and scope be one, and the image stand — menacing, immortal, daunting!

Our story proceeds. The image is raised, the worship proceeds. Blasphemous indeed, if only in the appalled, few faithful ones.

These three youths, we are told, assess the scene, the image, the imperial summons. They are three. Against them stands the world conqueror and his minions. They decide to resist, unto death. Thereby they narrow, first of all for themselves, the seemingly boundless choices open to the worshipers of the golden image.

"Monotheists," someone has written, "have but one choice, and one only. And having made it, they leave themselves with no other god to deploy against the One they have chosen or been chosen by. The attraction of polytheism, on the other hand, is this: it widens every choice; it imposes no limitation."

Concerning our story and its three lonely protagonists, a commentator concludes with a kind of irony, "To embrace the image of the 'other gods' would of course have saved the lives of the three youths."

This feeble trinity of resisters are summoned, to a purpose, it goes without saying, beyond that of the king. For the beleaguered faithful of later and hardly better times, who told and retold the story, the summons of the king has the character of a vocation, a revelation, and this issuing from polluted lips.

Other kings will summon other believers. The story never ends. Therefore it must be told and told again, lest the community lose its moorings, and fall to an idolatrous obeisance.

But as to our youths. They are alone, this trio, they face the king. His visage, we learn from other episodes of the book of Daniel, is apt to darken, to turn sturdy knees to water.

They are young, and no one stands with them.

It is one thing, as we knew, to assert a principle, say, in a crowd, and sotto voce; even, if one so chooses, stridently. The crowd supplies a cover; one need fear no reprisal for speaking up when a large cacophony serves to drown out a solitary conscience.

But here we have something else — a courtroom, an immediate confrontation, three youths and this fearsome eminence. The king presumably has a sovereign interest, apt to turn irascible, in the liturgy proceeding on schedule.

What to make, then, of this inexplicable refusal? They refuse to bow to the great golden image. (It is not just any image of any god; it is his own ego enthroned, hungering for adulation.)

The story, in the inelegant phrase of Camus, is about "paying up." Our three protagonists must be prepared to face the panoply of an enormous, seemingly irresistible power. (Who was it who boasted in the flush of military crime, "The Third Reich will endure for a thousand years!"?)

Some few of us have had a rather ample experience in these matters of serving the idols. We eight of the first Plowshares group were summoned to present ourselves before a kind of latter-day (dare one say) nuclear Nebuchadnezzar. Our crime was this. In 1980, we entered a General Electric factory in Pennsylvania, symbolically transformed a nuclear sword into a plowshare, and refused to worship at the nuclear shrine which authorities were pleased to raise, not just in that awful place, but all about the planet. At that time and since, we were unable to persuade our souls to bow down, even with that implicit, invisible gesture whose name is—silence, complicity.

In our story, the king himself repeats the earlier edict—worship the image, or die by fire. More, he utters a scornful taunt: "What conceivable god would rescue you from the fires of the divine N.?" The words sound horrific, omnipotent. "What deity would enter the lists on your behalf, against such a world-class hellion as myself, a proven god?"

Like all such assertions, the words mask a great weakness, fragility. According to this newly crowned deity, the pantheon is understood as an unending contest or competition. The gods circle one another warily, in a kind of bear pit. And in this eternal contest, the most violent gods commonly prevail (as do the most violent humans).

Thus the king epitomizes and brings to scarcely bearable tension the forces that rack us humans—greed, pride of place, the proving ground where would-be gods strive mightily for their place in the American pantheon. In that place, in many places, a great golden idol has been raised. Nebuchadnezzar lives. In us.

The three youths venture an answer to the king's taunt. Their words are chastening, abrupt. I read them, I am put to shame by such moral clarity, by a faith that risks the furnace. They speak the language of the either-or, of Kierkegaard. In effect, "Do your worst. You may kill us or not, as you choose. And if by chance you spare us, know that we will still not worship your gods."

I am reminded of the multiple choices (the temptations really) presented by tyrants throughout history, choices subtle or fierce, designed to draw the teeth of resisters, to make a peace of sorts with an intolerable situation.

Franz Jaegerstaetter endured such a gauntlet of choices. In 1939, when the Nazis took over Austria, this devout young farmer refused military induction. Immediately a veritable squadron of churchmen, including his own bishop, descended on him, in jail. They excoriated him for his decision, assured him that if he were morally correct in refusing induction, surely the church authorities would have so instructed him. (They were in fact, one and all, collaborators.)

A further phase followed, another temptation. It was a proffer. This curious Christian resister, a husband and father, need not bear arms. He could act as a member of a medical crew, succoring the wounds of combatants.

It was all the same to Jaegerstaetter. What difference did it make, this bearing arms or not? If he yielded, he would be forced into the uniform, he would sustain his family with blood money, he would serve vile ends. He refused. And he paid up.

On August 9, 1943, Franz was beheaded by Hitler's forces.

I commend this Christian to you, and to my own soul. He is one of those few who stop in its tracks the train of logic that leads to death of the spirit, a ruinous adjustment to official crime. In such adjustments, the first victim is of course ourselves. We trade our souls, our human sense, our compassion, our love for one another, our verve of spirit.

Wall Street, nuclear installations, mighty towers of trade, vast luxury installations — these might well stand as contemporary superhuman, golden, probably idolatrous, images — of what? Of the superhuman claim of the god Mammon?

Something else may be occurring, something other than the universal idolatrous adoration of the pseudo-god. There may be a few who will refuse.

I hope there are. Let us hope so, together.

We are told finally that after the three youths were thrown into the fiery furnace for refusing to worship the false god, a mysterious fourth Being walked the furnace with them. The king looking into the furnace saw this figure dimly. It brought him consternation of spirit. What intervention might this be?

An angel trod the furnace, guarding the well-being of the intended victims. The three issued unharmed, the angel vanished on the moment.

We may be certain that this venerable tale, so often told and retold in mitigation of the fury of tyrants, reaffirmed the faith of the suffering servants of God.

Faith be it noted, not only that God is mindful and caring for Her own, but that God cares even for the benighted, beleaguered victims of their own idolatries, those who, in the final instance, have no other access to truth, except through their victims.

The resisters prevail, not only on their own behalf, but also on his.

The astonishing outcome of the story includes not only the miraculous emergence of the three youths. We must ponder also the emergence of the king, a changed man. There is hope, even for him, the story says.

Let us add in our hearts—hope even for us.

25

Learn a Lesson from the Fig Tree

*Learn a lesson from the fig tree. When its branch becomes tender and
sprouts leaves, you know that summer is near. In the same way, when
you see all these things, know that he is near, at the gates. Amen, I say to
you, this generation will not pass away until all these things have taken
place.* —Matthew 24:32–34

IMAGINE JESUS inviting grown women and men to go and stand in front
of a fig tree, and wait, until the burgeoning leaves speak to them. They
were to learn—from a tree. The tree had something to say, something
they could learn nowhere else, not even from Him. He could help, but
then He sent them away for the complete lesson. Had He learned it first,
what He had to say to them—from a tree? Was He offering an ecological understanding, the connection between nature and learning and
ourselves? Had He perhaps been appointed mysteriously to speak, by
the tree?

My friend the Buddhist monk, Thich Nhat Hanh, says he has never
encountered a more peaceable being than the little tree in his backyard.
He believes it should be honored with the Nobel Peace Prize.

The parable of our Lord has something of that tone. Surely we have
here a Zen moment, a long pause, an urging to slow down the busy
rhythm of our lives. Stand there, listen, learn.

Well. People heard what Christ had to say, and perhaps some of them
went to the fig tree and listened. Then they went home; and took their
lives up again. Or they stayed with Him, as they chose, and He chose.

But that tree! It was a parable of a lesson partly offered, of the heart
half-apprehending. He told them part of it, they must go to the tree to
learn the rest.

I remember an episode in my life along these lines. It concerns my dear
friend William Stringfellow. Only rarely, as I recall, did this cool friend
grow close and confiding. One evening in some mysterious way, I took

158

half a lesson from him; half he learned from me. Thus we came to some new depth of that precious wholeness we call "one another."

The scene is his home on Block Island; the time, the early seventies. I have been in and out of prison, and was visiting him. One evening I sensed there was a memory gnawing at him. I had gone to prison; he, in chronic ill health, clinging to a thread of survival for years and years, was simply unable to join me in jail. His anguish burst out.

Then he said this. "I take comfort from a story you told me some years ago, about a visit to Ireland, and the ancient round towers. How the monks, when a barbarian invasion was imminent, fled to the towers, taking with them for comfort only the book and the cup.

"And you said," continued Stringfellow, "I think we have a clue here as to faithful conduct today. Go to the tower. Take with you the Bible and the Eucharist. The savage tide will pass, you will emerge, a tradition will survive—biblical literacy and living symbols."

Dear friends, I am not sure about the translation of this memory of mine, but I suspect the main lines of the tale will reward scrutiny. Fleeing to the towers with the book and the cup is akin to that other puzzling non-activity; it is like going to a tree in search of wisdom.

The image of the tower brings together matters of great import. On the one hand there is the contraction of high resolve which the times impose on us. There is the duty to accept this, and not give up. We might once have dreamed great things in the world, accomplishments of note. We are forced to settle for—shall we be kind to ourselves and say—not much. We live with a sense that the best efforts we put out change very little of a vast apparatus of destruction and despair. The times are like a hand that closes on our throat.

Not many choices, we sense, are left to us. Often the best, most courageous choices we can come on only serve to limit our scope further. Talk about limited scope! Many of our most valiant friends in the peace community have had the prison key turned on them, for years and years. Neither church nor state, in contradiction to Peter Maurin, make it easy to be good. Anguish, ambiguity, rejection, scorn, punishment, are often our portion at the hands of both entities.

Not many in America can tell their own soul where we are, who we are, whither bound. Most people are ignorant even as to how few choices remain, how many choices have been seized from us—by the omnivorous media, by the wicked weapons we create and huckster in the world, by contempt for the poor and suffering in our midst, by abuse of the sweet world of creation. The power of choosing is endangered, vanishing. Indeed, choice itself becomes an endangered species — to those who endanger the species.

All of this seems overly gloomy. But there is another side to the image of going to the tree or going to the tower. The monks certainly were not seeking mere survival, a safe house, a life exempt from life. Life in the tower offered something of a different order entirely — a more patient perspective on the bad times. Occasions not merely to endure, but to celebrate. A community of intercession, succoring, compassion.

And they were not alone there, nor idle. For the book was open, they were literate in God's word, skilled in reading the signs of the times. And on occasion, they did what we do today, they summoned the living Christ upon the altar.

In consequence, the monks would never say to my soul or yours, "We have no choices left." Admittedly the choices then and now are few, and often wring the heart, bearing as they do loss and pain and that unsteady, un-American word, sacrifice. But how else, how else, we ask our soul, shall our humanity not go under, in the barbaric stampede of the times?

One choice occurs — that we take stock of our spiritual discipline, that we agree as to the crucial nature of the Bible and the cup. And that bearing these, we enter some lofty inner room, which I shall call the darkness of our soul or the darkness of our world. That we accept the pain of that, the consequence. And the reward, which certainly includes a longer patience, a more humane understanding, a skill in reading the signs of the times and as they say inelegantly, "in calling the shots right." So that we are no longer tempted to call darkness "light," or injustice "law and order," or wars "necessary" or "just."

Something like that. Meantime, let us rejoice in the meantime. How good to be alive, how splendid to be together. Thank you with all my heart.

See you at the tree.

See you in the tower.

26

The World as Machine,
the World as Vine

For the wedding of George and Annie,
July 16, 1988

∿

I am the true vine, and My Father is the vine grower. He takes away
every branch in Me that does not bear fruit, and every one that does,
He prunes so that it bears more fruit. You are already pruned because
of the word that I spoke to you. Remain in Me, as I remain in you. Just
as a branch cannot bear fruit on its own unless it remains on the vine,
so neither can you unless you remain in Me. I am the vine, you are the
branches. Whoever remains in Me and I in them will bear much fruit.
If you remain in Me and My words remain in you, ask for whatever you
want and it will be done for you. By this is My Father glorified, that you
bear much fruit and become My disciples. —John 15:1–8

THE WORLD is essentially a war machine. War on the poor, the under-
dogs, the excluded.

The machine serves a few, and grinds up the majority.

The machine is oiled by money and blood, greed and violence. Our
place? The machine, after all, dictates this—we are creators, maintainers, oilers of the machine.

The machine ultimately works well for no one; even for its creators
and maintainers.

The machine is doomed, self-destructing.

Machine images invade those who create the machine. They lose
all sense of humanity, of themselves and others. They lose all political sense, all sense of responsibility. And within, they turn to anomie,
emptiness.

The machine cannot imagine the machine. It is constructed, from outside. It is subject to the cruel criteria of efficiency, results, proofs, credentials. And to the violence of competition: Whose machine is better than mine? There follows a killing scramble for the top. The better and bigger, the richer, the more powerful become the only criteria of the human. The human is seized upon, subsumed, secondary. Enslaved.

The machine is also within us, unless we realize we are in lockstep, robots.

We are also within the machine, unless we refuse victimization, idolatry. As the psalmist explains, "Those who make the idols become like them."

Christ, on the other hand, names the world as a vine, names Himself as the Vine. This is the sense of Christ, of Himself, how He imagines Himself—always with us. Vitality, vitalism.

A priest once asked me, "What does your God look like? What do others look like? What do you look like, to yourself?"

We have implied in the vine image—growth, setback, pruning, sunlight, rain, winter, summer, planting, harvest. The image breathes life. We have the unpredictable of life itself; also the assured, the taste and savor and bouquet of things.

Imagine Christ as vine, ourselves as branches. And the wine! We are immediately in the realm of the vital, the living. And of sacrifice. The fruit of the vine both gladdens the heart—and portends death. A vast range, of emotion, of resolve, of heroism, of self-giving, "The cup of My blood, given for you."

To be on the vine implies life with others, life for others, to be alive and for life. The image is so compacted that separation, "going it alone," prospering at the expense of others, isolation — these are genetically impossible.

The image proposes a reaching out of branch and tendril, further, and further — the effortful energy of faith and love. (Note that the reaching is for support, mutuality.)

When Jesus says, "I am the vine," He plants Himself in deep soil, the Jewish soil of history, soil of betrayal and grandeur, bitterness and ecstasy.

Jeremiah and the psalmist agree: the people are recusant. They turn away from their only joy. They work injustice on the poor. They do the foul works of war. There are no more bitter denunciations in any literature than those gathered around the image of Israel as the vineyard. The people are thrice cursed. They have turned from God, from one another, and from their own conscience. They are a people of anomie, ignorant of the covenant, willfully given to darkness.

But there is another set of vineyard images. Images of joy in the fruit of the vine, harvest imagery, the scene and scope of the End Time. Here we conjure up the unwearied ecstasy of the grape pickers' song, banqueting.

Jesus is planted in that soil. The vine rises from that ground, from our own. His history is ours. Our history is His own.

He adds yet another image—that of sacrifice. "The cup of My blood, which is given for you."

Then alleluia!, the imagery of the wedding feast, and the wine that never fails, that never runs out. This is our eternity, verified in rare moments in time, verified at weddings, where the world is not put to the door, but included in a nuptial embrace, where we taste the wine of the vine.

27

Love One Another
as I Have Loved You

For the wedding of Art Laffin and Colleen McCarthy,
November 29, 2002

∼

As the Father loves Me, so I also love you. Remain in My love. If you keep
My commandments, you will remain in My love, just as I have kept My
Father's commandments and remain in His love. I have told you this so
that My joy might be in you and your joy might be complete. This is My
commandment: love one another as I love you. No one has greater love
than this, to lay down one's life for one's friends. You are My friends
if you do what I command you. I no longer call you slaves because a
slave does not know what his master is doing. I have called you friends
because I have told you everything I have heard from My Father. It was
not you who chose Me, but I who chose you and appointed you to go and
bear fruit that will remain. —John 15:9–16

OUR TEXT, dear friends, I thought of as a symphony whose themes
move grandly through time and eternity, from the love of God in Christ,
to the love of Christ for disciples, to the love of us disciples for one
another.

But don't forget the cost: Our world is fallen. Christianity is no frivolous hanging out in Eden. "Keep My commandments, abide in My love."
And the command is spelled out (even as it is revealed as one with
the rhythms of the heart): "That you love one another, even as I have
loved you."

Context, I think, is nearly everything. In the life of Christ, in our lives,
when do words of love befit an occasion, a crisis, a turning point?

I ponder the context of the command, precisely placed as it is for
endurance in an arduous time.

164

This urging of love for one another might have been folded into an earlier, less charged occasion, before opposition and frenzies had erupted—say, in the tranquil air of the Sermon on the Mount. It was not placed there, and for the best of reasons.

On reflection, it is clear that the instruction could make sense only here. It is a farewell, a legacy. Nowhere else could the words convey a like poignancy, a sense of finality, of tragedy impending. The last night of the mortal life of Jesus.

The next day, the Friday we name Good, will bring the end. Death will come about, well orchestrated, within the orbit of the law of the land, through the revolting savagery of capital punishment.

Thus the context, the atmosphere of our text. In the darkness outside the upper room, the world has turned brimstone against Christ. The final act is under way, the final surge and spasm of the principalities. The apparatus of temple and juridical Rome unite, to have done once for all, with this interloper, this interfering one, with his provocative healings, his insufferable welcoming of outcasts, his stories subverting the ironbound law of "things as they are."

"Things as they are." We pause over the colorless euphemism for a horrid system at work—then and now—religion gone to rot, voracious economics, an overbearing military and its judicial warnings, its thicket of crosses awaiting those who dare speak up — in sum, a voracious culture of death and death dealing—"things as they are."

The geography of "things as they are" was of course occupied Palestine. It is our geography as well. America is occupied, preoccupied, possessed by death as a social method, a hideous "final solution." America proposes to deal with human differences by eliminating humans. It proposes waging war without limits or moral boundaries, wars initiated against children and the aged, the ill, the refugees. Among other crimes, America throttles life and the living with a decade and more of hideous sanctions against the suffering people of Iraq. In a cruel mirror game, even as the two protagonists demonize one another, the tactics of Hussein are firmly in place in Washington, even as the tactics of Bush prevail in Baghdad.

Thus in so merciless a time, the love commended to us by Jesus will hardly go unchallenged. In His words a hint of the cost is laid down. Tomorrow He will enact in His own flesh the love He commends to us.

The command to us becomes the drama of His own undoing. The teaching of the Rabbi comes home to His own flesh. It is hammered fast in hands and feet and heart. This: "greater love has no one than this, that one lay down life itself for one's friends."

Art and Colleen are in small need of instruction on this capital and painful point. We summon the noble memory of Paul Laffin, Art's brother, killed while serving the poor in a soup kitchen in Connecticut. The words "greater love" clothed him and his family in their harsh and dreadful rubric.

And we recall today the less spectacular ways of "laying life down for friends." Indeed the words might be thought, in their broad application to life in the Catholic Worker, a key text, a summons to the discipline of prayer, service of others, and resistance against the overbearing superstate.

I may be pardoned a personal note. In this horrid year since 9/11, the *Catholic Worker* papers across the country, and the New York *Catholic Worker* paper, have each offered me a notable gift. While other Catholic publications fudged and wobbled and lost their way in the thicket of just war casuistry, the *Catholic Worker* papers from Los Angeles to New York were steady and clear. "Love one another as I have loved you." The Gospel was the point: Keep it open, honor its words, venture where they lead.

And in New York, the Catholic Worker has walked the walk. With other peace groups in the city, the Worker maintains weekly vigils against the beat of war drums, and has sponsored teach-ins and marches for peace, the protocol of the heart.

Colleen and Art, we thank you. Not only for this day and its loving reminder, but for all the days to follow; for fidelity, service, and resistance; for vigils and arrests; for imagining a world safe for the children; for creating such a world in the modest orbit of the Catholic Worker community.

28

Living as Though
the Text Were True

For the wedding of Jerry and Molly Mechtenberg-Berrigan
June 15, 2002

~

I tell you, do not worry about your life and what you will eat, or about your body and what you will wear. For life is more than food and the body more than clothing. Notice the birds of the air: they do not sow or reap; they have neither storehouse nor barn, yet God feeds them. How much more important are you than birds! Can any of you by worrying add a moment to your life span? If even the smallest things are beyond your control, why are you anxious about the rest? Notice how the lilies grow. They do not toil or spin. But I tell you, not even Solomon in all his splendor was dressed like one of these. If God so clothes the grass in the field that grows today and is thrown into the oven tomorrow, will God not provide much more for you, O you of little faith? As for you, do not seek what you are to eat and what you are to drink and do not worry anymore. All the nations of the world seek for these things, and your God knows that you need them. Instead, seek God's reign and these other things will be given to you as well. —Luke 12:22–30

W<small>E HAVE HEARD</small> the words of Jesus, chosen by Molly and Jerry on their day of days. This is how they purpose to live in the world—in community, in voluntary poverty, in the life of faith.

And to complete the picture, let's add another ingredient, abrasive as it is. They intend to live in resistance to the overbearing, anti-human, Babylonian, self-destructing, warmaking state.

Community, poverty, and faith, as they well know, must continually embrace and be measured by acts of divine obedience. Such choices our wicked times make crucial.

But we start with Jesus' words. They bespeak the generosity of the Creator. In metaphors both sublime and homely, God's goodness shines. Lilies neither spin nor weave. They are nonetheless beautiful beyond the splendors of that grand showman, Solomon. The Creative Hand also feeds the birds that neither sow nor reap, have neither cellars nor barns.

What then of ourselves? We are creatures who spin and weave, who have cellars and barns, and all to the good. And the Creator of lilies and birds knows our need as well—clothing, food, shelter, the ingredients of the common life.

But we humans also furrow our brows with worry, and seek to accumulate. (Many resemble, in fact, the mad accumulator and worrier in the previous story. This one, as Jesus tells, tore down his grain bins and built larger ones. He was a "fool" if ever one was born, for that same night, his life was snatched from him.)

But wait. "Don't worry . . . your heavenly Parent knows your needs." The advice is rounded off in a question that could be borrowed from a Zen handbook: "Which of you by worrying can add a moment to your life span?"

In all honesty, let us test the question. Let us put it to an Iraqi mother, holding in her arms a dying child. Put it to an Afghan refugee family, fleeing American bombs in the fury of winter.

"Stop worrying. Your parent knows that you need such things." Tell Sudanese slaves to "stop worrying." Urge it to South African blacks, Nicaraguan or Colombian peasants, victims of apartheid and torture and death squads. Tell it to the drought ridden, the flooded out, the victims of earthquakes, tidal waves, climate shifts, and unnatural disasters of every kind.

Are the words of Jesus to be thought a pointless, weightless paternalism from on high, a pablum for true believers, promising big, but failing people in horrid crisis? I suggest the contrary. I think our text offers a solid teaching, words that stand firm in face of brutality, greed, and warmaking. Words that stand firm against America.

Jesus infers it. The original blessing of Genesis was abundance, food, clothing, shelter for every human born, enough for every sensible modest need. Jesus is underscoring that original blessing, conferring it on ourselves. "Live in accord with it," he urges. The original blessing is the realm of God come to earth, the ethos that governs and binds creation.

But alas, through the depravity of the powerful, the blessing has turned to a curse.

The task then! "Make of the realm of God a verb, an imperative. Pursue it against odds. Build it anew, from rubble and betrayal. Live it, cherish it." He insists that the realm of God is our calling, that it answers our deepest longing.

We restore the original blessing by living as though it were true.

Meantime, the curse has enormous virulence and power. We witness to our daily bitterness and chagrin, the wasting and despoiling of creation. The original blessing is pillaged, looted. There is not enough for everyone—and for warmaking.

This, as I learned years ago, was the stunning insight of Dorothy Day. There is enough for everyone, but not enough for everyone — and for war as well. It struck me like a bolt of lightning, this scriptural insight, hopeful and exigent. Marvelously, it connected the work of mercy with the work of peacemaking. The hands that serve human need are also bidden to turn thumbs down on war. The hands of Christ that served and healed also beckoned to Peter, "Put up your sword." The hands that multiplied bread also said over the bread, in plain view of the cross, "This is My body, given for you."

War rages. The food is stolen from the child, the dwelling is bombed or bulldozed, the wounds of the innocent are untended.

War rages—to hell with humans. Throttle the community, waste the world. Make war, not love.

In the Fall, blessing has turned to curse.

And yet, the original blessing, once bestowed, was never recanted. It met every sensible, modest need of humans. And it can be restored. In community, in resistance, in faith. This, despite the crimes that followed and proliferated. In our Bible, many who seized the reins of power (kings, mostly, and their generals) proved neither sensible nor modest. In fact, Saul, David, Solomon, Hezekiah, and their clones and adjutants madly pursued booty and power. (Does it sound familiar?) They invaded, enslaved, betrayed, imprisoned, tortured, exterminated. They thus transfused a generational poison in the veins of history, "normalizing" ethically outrageous behavior. (Does it sound familiar?)

They even created a god in their own image, a celestial ventriloquist, who would approve, even initiate their politics of violence and contempt.

Yet God's hope for our beleaguered tribe is not extinguished. It shines forth in our text. Enough for everyone, for all of creation, and nothing for war!

Thank you, Molly and Jerry, and your community, for living as though the text were true.

Thank you for heartening us. We too would live as though the text were true.

29

The Gods of the Millennium

*The following poem was offered at an interfaith prayer service at
St. Francis Xavier Church in New York City, on September 17, 2001,
a week after the attacks on the World Trade Center.*

⌣

THE GOD OF EXPECTATIONS made money like mad, made money like butter in a churn, poured it out like butter over popcorn, on the deserving and covetous alike. For this, the god of expectations was blessed and applauded.

And that was a good year.

The god of approximations made the kingdom almost come. Granted, there were brush wars, small wars, minor contusions on the world map. There were bombings and sanctions and expendable children. And at home, a general mood of discontent and "Get the bastards."

But still. By and large the sanctuaries were full and the preachers preached and the collections came in and the leaders sat straight in the front pews of the national cathedral. And the president entered a bully pulpit to intone an infallible irrefutable doctrine of tit for tat.

And that was a good year.

The god of contemplation made humans spin like spinning prayer wheels. Seated on a bed of gold like a lotus in perfumed water, he intoned, "You think, therefore, you are. Think, think!" So they thought and thought and they were and were.

And that was a good year.

The God of Christians staggered up a hill, dragging a plank of wood, heavy as a plowshare. Like a plowshare, the plank made a furrow. From

171

the furrow sprang armed warriors, redundant lives, talking skulls, disconsolate dragons, teeth on edge. These were followed by a multitude of martyrs, clothed in their blood. And a girl named Cassandra brought up the rear, raving into the wind.

That procession? It was of small moment and went all but unnoticed.

Except for this: with regard to money, bully pulpits, prayer wheels, armed warriors—that was a very bad year.

V

Christians in a Warmaking State

Peacemaking is hard
hard almost as war
the difference being one
we can stake life upon
and limb and thought and love.

I stake this poem out
dead man to a dead stick
to tempt an Easter chance—
if faith may be
truth, our evil chance
penultimate at last

not last. We are not lost.

When these lines gathered
of no resource at all
serenity and strength,
it dawned on me—

a man stood on his nails

as ash like dew, a sweat
smelling of death and life.
Our evil Friday fled,
the blind face gently turned
another way, toward life

a man walks in his shroud

30

The Prophetic, Peacemaking Church

Now it will be necessary simply to hold on, to light the fires of truth here and there, so that eventually the entire structure will collapse.
— Dietrich Bonhoeffer, from prison, 1943

BIBLICALLY SPEAKING, the "future," as commonly understood, is of little interest. Prophecy is hardly to be classed with a phenomenon known in our own demented times as "futurology."

Indeed one is tempted to compare practitioners of the latter to astrologists and necrologists and other probers of dark arts. Each is interested in death, as metaphor and fact. Each insists in one way or another that it is in the stars, not in ourselves, that we are underlings, which is to say, that we are stuck in the world, in war, in a world inevitably at war.

Prophecy is an entirely different matter. Prophecy is interested in vocation. To what, ask the prophets, does God summon the church, the state (more precisely, the imperial state), and the makers of peace?

The term "vocation" is not to be confused, as it commonly is, with a successful outcome, with proving something or other, with self-justification, glory, good repute — the bastardized paraphernalia by which a given culture seeks to claim, seduce, detour, enlist believers.

Vocation stands on its own, before God. St. Ignatius put the matter for Jesuits and others in the "Spiritual Exercises." (The passage reads like a marriage vow, which in a sense, it is.) Long life or short, good health or ill, poverty or affluence—we are not to prefer the one to the other. We are to stand somewhere, and let come what may.

More nearly to our matter, the biblical vocation of the imperial state is unequivocal and devastating, implying a catastrophic outcome, a curse, a judgment. For the empire is, in fact, the chief evidence in history of the Fall of creation. Miming the Fall, it becomes the ape of God. It presents

175

itself in history as omnipotent, eternal, all wise, the one to which all must pay fealty.

In its blindness as to its own crimes, its tenacious violence, it must be named for what it is: the foremost agent and provocateur of death in the world. It makes death (as fact and metaphor) prolific, attractive, and above all necessary.

Therefore its vocation, this ape and agent of a kind of specious immortality, is unutterably ironic. Its vocation is to Fall. And be it further noted, to be the agent of its own downfall.

The presumed immortality of the empire has a horrid price attached. If the empire is to flourish (we remember the boast of "the thousand-year Reich"), then many must die.

And the death, even of great numbers, even of the innocent, must be rendered plausible, even normal. So the victims are variously demonized or stripped of their dignity, their very faces. They are abstractions, "the enemy," "the tyrant," and so on. They are expendable.

To the numbed citizenry, such lethal behavior on the part of authorities becomes a kind of wearisome abstraction. Another war? It matters not at all, or little. What matters, if we can judge from the petrified forest of flags that all but blot out the sun, is — glory, vindication, clout, scores settled. As we have seen again and again in our lifetime, in our own country: Vietnam, Grenada, Panama, Nicaragua, Afghanistan and Iraq.

It is really astonishing, that from Babylon to Assyria to Egypt to Rome, the biblical history is the same. The empires rise, the empire does unutterable harm in the world, then the empire declines and falls. That pattern was recently verified again in the fall of the former Soviet Union. It is the same pattern which is daily unfolding in these United States, which is being covered up at all costs by the bloody distraction of periodic war, domestic rot and ruin, and brazen chicanery.

But what of the vocation of the church? The church is called to something other than immortality. The church is summoned to death and resurrection. Therefore the church is to endure, submit, be disgraced and martyred, but also to outlast, to prevail over its tormentors and seducers . . . "until He comes."

As peacemakers, as those presumably called to the integral work of the church, the heart of the church, we are simply to keep at the essentials, "until He comes" — prayer, sacrament, public witness, arrests, court, jail.

And at the Lord's coming, the term "peace church" will be shown to be almost laughably redundant. (To some, it seems so now.) And the opposite term (surely so curious a phrase implies an opposite, perhaps "just war church") will be shown to be shameful.

Prophecy offers an unkillable hope, a promise, a kind of final act of the human drama. From Isaiah to Mary it sounds, "on that day," swords into plowshares, the mighty toppled from their thrones, the hungry fed at last.

Peacemakers are called to live in what one might call "the first act," the here and now. This is a purifying and difficult prelude. In it, commonly, little or nothing happens that might serve to justify the promise (let alone the peacemaker!). In fact the evidence, a veritable barrage of ideology, propaganda, sound bites, renegade media, polls and pollsters, goes to show that anything like a prophetic outcome, a peaceable world, is absurd. "Swords into plowshares? The poor of the world succored? Come now!"

Bonhoeffer, Merton, Dorothy Day, Gandhi, Romero, King, the murdered Jesuits and churchwomen of El Salvador (and shall we not say first of all, Christ our Lord) —these keep the promise. They delved to the heart of reality, confidently awaiting a world which (according to the world) cannot be. They are the maestros of the "nothingness" of God; they tarried at the "still point" where hope is all but obliterated.

Peacemakers such as these know a kind of peace. They taste it on the tongue, they offer it to others. But there is an irony here. The peace they experience is never publicly honored or ever seriously sought.

Isaiah, we are told, fell a martyr to the same powers who had earlier sought his counsel; swords into plowshares became a hot political item, not to be tolerated by the warrior state. Mary uttered her prophecy, but Herods and Pilates and their ilk sat secure on thrones, and the poor went unfed. No matter, the prophets say: In God's time that will come to pass which we are helpless to bring to pass.

And what of the "meantime," our own time? We are to keep at it, at prayer and sacrament, at public witness. When nothing changes (except for the worse!), when nothing happens (except the worst), no matter. The promise stands.

Keep at it.

31

Prophecy

THE WAY I SEE the world is strictly
illegal
to wit, through my eyes

is illegal yes;
to wit, I live
like a pickpocket, like the sun
like the hand that writes this, by my wits

This is not permitted
that I look about the world
and worse, insist that I see

what I see
—a conundrum, a fury, a burning bush

and with 5 fingers, where my eyes fail
that I trace—

with a blackened brush
on butcher sheets, black on white
(black for blood, white for death
where the light fails)

that I trace
that face which is not my own
(and my own)
that death which is not my own
(and my own)

This is strictly illegal
and will land me in trouble

as somewhere now, in a precinct
in a dock, the statutes
thrash in fury, hear them—HEAR YE!—

the majestic jaws
of crocodiles in black shrouds
the laws
forbidding me
the world, the truth
under blood oath

forbidding
row upon row
of razors, of statutes
of molars, of grinders—

those bloodshot eyes
legal, sleepless, maneating

—not letting me
not
let blood

32

The Handbook
of Christian Refusers

I₮ HAS BEEN OF HELP in pursuing the subject of God's peaceable realm to take note of a quite peculiar document, the handbook of the early Christian refusers, their visionary alternative, the book of Revelation.

I have lived long enough to witness utterly varied uses (and misuses) of the book. During the Vietnam years, the book of Revelation was largely closed, ignored by Christian resisters. Questions raised in the book had yet to become our own. Indeed, it seemed as though we were still too young, too naive, to suffer nightmares, much less to learn from them. More accurate to say, we took little note of the nightmares we secretly sweated through. Least of all could we imagine that so recondite a book as Revelation might shed light on a world that seemed overrun with savage fauna.

If in going counter to the tides of a monstrous war, we were out of our depth (and in our more lucid moments, we knew it), if we often felt helpless, beset, at sea—we were inclined to keep the news to ourselves. Were we ashamed? Grown men [*sic*], and Christians to boot, and peacemakers above all! Our credentials were unassailable; they forbade confession of weakness or sin in our midst. Even those who acknowledged the Bible as God's Word suspected that the book could shed little or no light on the horrid present.

With most, childhood faith was done with in any case; it was commonly regarded as—perhaps "unbalanced" is the most charitable word. Its morality was merciless toward weakness of the flesh, tilted favorably toward the rich and powerful, indifferent to moral questions raised by war.

No wonder, the book of Revelation (not to speak of the entire Christian testament), was for the most part a closed book.

More, we were Americans. As such we were the children of war, of some war or other. War was imbedded in our history. Peace, in any real sense, was not. Many had soldiered in former wars, or their relatives had. Everyone knew someone who had died in war; all, as a matter of course, paid taxes for war.

Such as we could become peacemakers only with the greatest difficulty. Whatever resources we could draw on were meager indeed, and religion was not among them.

How then confront our own monsters and nightmares — so awful a history, so claimant and violent a church and state? It was a birth struggle, it was like a death. No wonder we came along, slow and reluctant. We had yet to learn what a cold eye was cast by scripture on American specimens—whether peacemakers or warmakers!

Scripture was rife with far different episodes and images of the human than the ones we had been instructed in. Scripture spoke of us in ways that broke the heart and froze the mind — admissions of helplessness, shouting matches, despair, interventions, non-interventions. The shout of God, the silence of God. And as for humans, far different icons than ourselves dwelt in those pages, and suffered, and believed and died, and won their place in history.

They could not be silenced, finally, even by our indifference and ignorance. They wore the laurel of divine approval; God's Word spoke of them as a blessing to the nations. Thus they challenged our assumptions about the human condition. Were these saints, prophets, martyrs not far more human than we?

And then, by implication—was not the biblical God far different than we had imagined?

We took the long way round this hermetic, unsettling tome named Revelation. Self-knowledge still evaded us. Or perhaps we feared, knowing more of our weakness and folly than we dared admit.

The book remained closed, for years. And meantime, who or what could teach us that violence, dread, despair, lay not just in corporate and military America, or Vietnam—but in ourselves as well?

Who was to teach us that we who fought for peace, and even went to prison for our convictions, held a stake, large or minuscule, in the kingdom of war? Or that in our communities, depth charges lay hidden—hostilities and divisions, unaccountability ("Don't be judgmental" seemed the only commandment), shabby treatment of women, mistakes unregretted, fantasies unexorcised?

And what might the book of Revelation, with its weird ebb and flow of daymares and nightmares, its ecstasies and violence, spirits angelic and demonic—what might it offer our plight?

Some were to learn the hard way, and by and large, the wrong way. Shortly, in the 1970s, the neglected book was flung open literally with a vengeance. Suddenly the book was "in." It was scanned with a kind of fundamental fierceness by eyes that positively blazed as they read. The eyes lit on images of horror, vengeance, vindication. Ah, that was it! Purportedly, the images, the apparitions, invited believers to settle accounts, to clean up the messy world, once for all. Into such hands, just and justifying, hands eagerly reaching for the sword of Jehovah, the book was placed, like a sword.

I have another image. American culture is like a helmet of reprisal and vengeance, of God on our side and we on God's, of blazing intractable innocence, the innocence that kills. The helmet is lowered over the head of Christians. The visor is lowered upon this seeker after illumination. And eureka! the seeker sees. Or so we were told.

Such light, so offered, became only a more afflicting darkness. The seeker prided himself that he saw. And thereupon grew blinder than ever. America — fury, anomie, fear, violence, the war — all these the reader brought to the book.

A warmaking culture shrouded the book in darkness, disguised its mercies, isolated and distorted its images. The reader, rapt in that strange garment woven of many strands, culture, self-justified, instant salvation at hand—seized on this or that image, with a spasm of recognition, images of showdown, war in the heavens, no peace on earth. He had seen all this before, it was the climate and landscape of America.

And now, a moment of Greek recognition! He rode with the horsemen, he forgot the rest. He rode in the night and called it day. The outcome was a cultural triumph, nicely disguising a biblical disaster.

According to this (peculiarly American) reading, the book offered a perennial blessing on war. The blessing was bestowed anew. Nuclear weapons were blessed; and, push come to shove, nuclear war itself.

March to Armageddon, Christians, bring it to pass! Rapture will follow, for you and a number of others of like mind and justification.

Thus the culture seized on the book, the code was cracked. The culture declared itself owner of the book. Back to the job, the drawing board, the laboratories, the bunkers and bases and airstrips—wherever the last day of the human race was being calculated.

Back also to the churches, at least to a number of them, where the tolling bell of humanity was hailed as a blessed event, thrice blessed in anticipation.

There was heard, as though arising from the text itself, the shield of Mars vibrating with the stroke of his sword. It was like the last heartbeat of dying time. For if these revisionist Revelationists were correct, not only nukes, but a nuclear finis to the human adventure was the very will of God.

It might be adduced, and here and there it was, that such a reading of the book implied more than met the eye. That behind the reading, a very plague of fantasies, all unacknowledged, festered. That such fantasies, drawn as they were from a cultural matrix at odds with the word of God, barred access to truth.

The fantasies were weighted with malign power. Seldom such voices, such enticing exegetes as buzzed about the ears of believers! Under that spell, Christians could be certain beyond doubt, and were not shy in declaring—who the beast was, who the rampageous horsemen, the locusts that rained fire on the world, the steeds with their not quite human faces. One and all, these were images of the enemy, of the enemies' devious intentions, crimes, wickedness.

We were informed further that nuclear war was inevitable. The point of Christianity was thereby clarified. Christians were to raise no outcry, no resistance. They were called to "stand on the right side" in "the war of the just." And past all argument, the cause was just, for it was American. Thus, in many circles, prayer groups, prayer breakfasts, prayer rooms, retreats—thus went the reading of Revelation.

Had such an outpouring of piety ever moved the powerful in such directions? The closed book was open, its throat blazed with judgment and justification. Stage by stage, true believers moved with the message, from stupendous innocence to cultural collusion. And thence to a consorting with false gods.

I thought of such matters, I heard such talk, such premises and conclu-
sions drawn from the book. For years I studied Revelation, meditated,
consulted experts, appalled as I was at the drummers of doom, the mis-
handling of texts, the assumptions, the deadly frivolity. Surely there
existed a better way.

It must be possible, I thought, to reconcile the Christ of Revelation
and the Christ of the Gospels, the warrior image of Christ with the meek
and compassionate One of the Sermon on the Mount. A way to reconcile
the violent images of Revelation with the prohibition of violence in the
Gospels. There must in sum be one Christ, not two, if we were not to
suppose that our God is as divided in mind as Her stupefied votaries.

I concluded at last that we must reclaim the book from the violent hands
of the culture. Nothing must be allowed to subvert the text, no optimism
springing from political chauvinism or national frenzies; no pessimism,
issuing from the fall of this or that cherished ideology. And above all, no
false gods, prating of our moral excellence, probity, good name, pros-
perity, enticing us toward the violence that precedes entrance into a
secular nirvana. No gods of America ventriloquizing, aping, displacing
true God.

We must flee them all. They smell of death.

The word of the book is harsh; the harshness begins with the author.
John, one tradition held, wrote down his vision on a prison island,
Patmos, condemned there, as he testifies, for fidelity to God.

Must we also plant ourselves in a wilderness, a desert, a prison —
where the soul might grow literate, might *tolle et lege?* In such unlikely
places, a vision might be granted, as was granted to the prisoner John.
A modest and serviceable vision to be sure, something so modest as a
sane reading of a simple text.

Indeed, as my study went forward, the book appeared to dovetail
with the entire testament. Revelation offered a vision of peace. Offered
also believable images of the human, images of holiness, images that
named and then banished the superhuman and the bestial. To put the
matter in another way, Revelation exorcised the ruling images of my
culture.

The book offered true images of ourselves, our gods, our obsessions,
the spirits that reign in us. And that truthfulness became the rub. We
could not bear its abrasions. So we cast upon the God of Jesus our
own vengefulness, our hatreds, the wars that reach from earth to high

heaven. We cast upon another the imagery of the hell we bore within, and were busily bringing to pass on earth.

The book was a series of images about humans, about political structures, about secret appetites and crimes. Images also of God's judgment on human conduct.

Revelation showed us our gods. The images corresponded exactly and ironically with national shrines and cults and tributes and invocations and prayer rooms, corresponded with the beast we worshiped, the horses we rode straight toward disaster.

We had been worshiping false gods for generations. Thus the Armageddonists became our prophets, the prophets of the culture. And Revelation was transformed to a madman's handbook, filled with gleeful chaos, telling of a creation doomed to end in radiated dust.

John offers us something else—a setting, and a state of soul. His Revelation was not granted in some prosperous enclave of the world. It blazed forth on an ancient Devil's Island.

Access to the book, as would seem logical, continues in unexpected and unpleasant places: in prisons, ghettoes, base communities under assault. In such an unpromising geography, the book continues to steady the soul. It offers cold comfort but true; the unmasking, to the confusion of the mighty, of the puny and penultimate face of death.

The vision occurs amid the thankless, humiliated tasks of survival under fire. It is granted the disenfranchised and suspect, the exiles, the conscientious outlaws, the unrehabilitated misfits; the foursquare pegs, so to speak, who resist being plunged in the world's potholes.

Soul is the inner landscape of the teachable of God. Those who, as John describes them, "have ears, and hear." They take their stand in the shadow of the frown of Caesar. Their mark is fidelity, witness; they are afflicted and exalted by the relentless Word of God.

John knows his times and the politics that kill. He assembled bits and pieces, bones and rags, griffins and flying gods of Babylon, Assyria, Egypt, in order to limn the bestial physiognomy of Rome, his persecutor, the maker and breaker of martyrs. There is a noble irony at work here, an admirable understanding. He has grasped the perennial cliche called empire. Rome, in John's vision, is a near nothing, decked out as an entity great and noble, preening, pretentious, a moral void, overweening, a killer, a rider on rampage, a beast never seen on land or sea.

Indeed, Rome sums up and embodies a certain conception of power. It is the cunning convergence of all former tyrannies, executioners, fools, pretenders. Thus a history of empires is implied in the image of one empire.

And Revelation is no exercise in taxidermy, but a way of grasping the meaning, entropy, ideology of one's own times.

The vision is a summing up, with a strong implication left to ourselves. The cliche called Rome is never quite finished with. Tyranny is the constant and sedulous ape of Christ. It resurrects, takes new form, seats itself in power, seizes new weapons. And inevitably, tyranny seeks out and befriends religion, its ally, a blessing on the enterprise, a bargaining partner, a power broker, winked at and winking back.

But not this community. Christians, John reminds us, are to name the old names anew—Babylon, Assyria, Egypt. These take new names—Washington, London, whatever.

Name them for what they are, and suffer the consequence, in some latter-day Patmos or gulag.

Revelation is neither magical nor evasive. It is penetration, meaning, light in dark times. Our own. Now, John insists, is the hour of martyrs, of resistance against tyranny, a time that is by turns brutal or seductive, but inevitably exerts a life-and-death claim.

Thus the book implies a call to responsible action. The martyrs are the only adversary that enter history and offer relief. The revelation of the power of God is at hand in the powerlessness of the faithful.

John summons the past, whether of secular history or the Jewish testament. Martyrs and prophets are invoked, and most of all Christ, martyred and risen from the dead, all for the sake of an enlarged understanding of the present summons, the "way" of the believers.

Revelation is thus placed in our hands as a handbook of faith, of the believing journey through the maze of the world. But how shall we steadfastly refuse the accepted and acceptable reading of the times, in which power is the only password, and powerlessness the only curse? How let go the clutch of money, nation, security, bloodline? And deeper, more impenetrable than the brow of Caesar, further questions: Does God witness the plight of the just? Does God take the torment and blood in account? And if not, why endure at all?

The future too is respected and summoned: "I will show you what things are to be." What things, what future? Surely not the future contrived by magic men, by the pseudo-prophets of the empire, today by technologists in a like servitude.

In Revelation, there is apparently no interest, either on the part of the revealing angel or the afflicted exile, in the common understanding of "future." Of mere time-to-come, John needs no revelation. He knows quite well what lies ahead for such as he. For his compatriots in the faith, death has been the outcome. For himself, indefinite exile.

But such considerations are beside the point. The seer believed that he was in the hands of God, hands more merciful, he trusted, than the clenched fists of the emperor.

Thus, biblically, the "future" was of a different order than that of chancy fortune or misfortune. The new community might be groaning, humiliated, only half born in the world. No matter. Its vitality and continuity were assured in the death, rising, and witness of the Savior. Mere factitious sequence, inevitability, blind destiny, these are of no moment. Things visible are torn asunder. The heavens open. The faithful Witness, Christ, stands at the side of the afflicted, speaks for them, strengthens and heartens. That is all they need to know, all they are allowed to know. The rest is tinkering, magic, forbidden games.

John's vision is neither Orwellian nor Faustian. The beast, in murdering the faithful, has by no means resolved his own trouble. Death is no deterrent; indeed, the blood of martyrs heartens the living, and draws more converts to the "way."

And with regard to "the world," which according to the beast lies under his rule—things also fall apart. He is in command neither of this world nor of any other. He looms big, poses as superhuman, deceives adroitly, cuts a broad swath of violence, but all this is no more than the thrashing about of a cornered killer; dangerous indeed, but only because endangered.

What is the fate of the empire, that glittering amalgam of ego, avarice, sophistication, duplicity, high culture, contempt for life? The end is short and unhappy. A supreme irony indeed! The empire is in need of no external enemy to accomplish its downfall. The death of the saints brings the topless towers down. This is the theme of the angel bearing the bowl of wrath:

"Just
are You
in these
your judgments,

You
who are and were,

O Holy One.
For they
have shed
the blood

of saints
and prophets,

and You
have given them

blood
to drink.

It is
their due."

—Revelation 14:4–6

The empire, in the direst sense, has disposed of the saints. And yet they are by no means disposed of. Their work in this world stands unfinished.

A curiously disturbing sequence points to this (6:9–11). The scene is one of anguish and victory both. The noble dead are in fact living, their voices are heard. But no hint is offered either of beatific vision or ecstasy.

The setting is strange, reminiscent of the crowded holding cells that everywhere in the world shove into one constricted place the violent, the larcenous—and the heroes. In such a place of confinement the martyrs are sequestered. More, the cell lies under an altar, we are told, a place of sacrifice.

There the martyrs linger, by no means comforted—or for that matter, silenced.

Is God their deliverer or their jailer? Either—or both. No hint is offered that the face of God is manifest, that the Comforter is revealed to the noble dead—any more than on earth.

Their estate is altered, but their suffering has taken no new turn. They are God-haunted. God remains opaque, distant, absent.

And all the old wounding questions, questions with which we mortals comfort ourselves or distance ourselves or make minimal sense of the absurdity or cruelty of life — all these hover in the air. The scene has the bitter savor of our world, no other, no better. "How long, O Lord?" Lives of unexampled valor have won no revelation, whether of justice, of God's purpose, of the value of their terrible deaths. The innocent die, the powerful walk free. The dead know it, and the knowledge is a torment.

Heaven, like this? The scene is staggering. The martyrs, their contest won, cry out once more, as they cried out on the scaffold, before the beasts and torturers. "How long, O Lord, until your holy ones are vindicated?"

They are not given to know, any more than ourselves, in the year 90 or in the second millennium. Indeed in such matters of injustice, the murder of the innocent, the silence of God, a silence like a void — with regard to these, the valiant dead stand in our own tracks, no wiser than our ignorant selves.

They raise their cry, a voice responds. It is one of the striking non-answers of history. They are told — precisely nothing. In effect, "Be content." Or failing that, "Be patient. The time of knowing is not yet. And though you have brought the End Time closer, there is more to come."

Then or now, as we can presume, the martyrs do not bring on the end. Still, one thing is clear: They are the measure of the end, its sign and warning. Like a pot dipped in a stream, like clay fired in the furnace, their lives must be filled to the brim, fired to full strength. Then the stream will run dry, the vessel be broken. And God in the godly will be all in all.

Exalted matters, nonetheless heartrending for those who in so many places of the world perish today. Martyrs—the one constant of history, whether in synagogue, church, or world. Indeed it seems that for literally millions, there is no other vocation but untimely and violent death.

The warnings come early. From birth, multitudes are denied access to a minimally human life. They are hardly born, and they die; and that is all. Or they struggle free of moral infancy, vague discontent, misery that clings like an acid to the flesh. They raise an outcry, and their voice is quenched. It is heartrending, beyond all accounting.

And what of ourselves? We stand there, near. A hand wields the sword that cuts the martyrs down. And we also are helpless.

Or we hear the sound of a clock. Someone has described it as "a clock with a single hand, a hand that is a sword." Can we alter the times, beat the sword to a plowshare, summon true kairos?

We can do something. We can pray. Now and again we can salvage a life. Now and then offer moral gestures that impede the path of Mars. Still, we know to our dismay that the world and its malice, its rush toward oblivion, are seemingly beyond all effort and avail.

Indeed, at times, ours is a sense of standing like young Saul, holding the garments of those who slay the heroes.

Will the future be measured by that clock, a sword for a hand? God has assured us that there is a better timepiece.

The true kairos, the "right time," is to be announced, not by a few heroes only — but by all. Indeed it might be called a "mark" of the church: the ability simply to tell the time, to read the times aright, to interpret, judge, announce, denounce.

Saul, we are told, in virtue of God's mercy, became Paul. And yet before he was transformed, he was the fiercest of persecutors. His was not merely the crime of silence; he thirsted for the blood of the innocent.

And yet, and yet. Saul's transformation illustrates something both unlikely and hopeful, for our time, a change perhaps already under way, tentatively, in the church.

Let us recall. During the Vietnam War, the American church was, by and large, the church of Saul, of collaboration and silence. Was North Vietnam bombed? Were Laos and Cambodia invaded? Were the dikes broken and Hanoi carpet bombed? Each week, during seven and a half years, was an equivalent Nagasaki bomb exploded against the "enemy"?

The church knew, or should have known; it came to the same thing. The bishops stood there, holding the garments of an international lynch mob.

Shame, we are told, is a great emetic. It helps vomit up the collusion and crimes of the past, at least sometimes. And despite all, here and there in the land, we may hope that shame and confusion of spirit are under way.

I offer an image. At the start, let us say, it accords with common practice and expectation.

In the image, men (it can only be men, it concerns the Catholic church, and our recent past) — men of dignity and pride of place form a procession. This impeccable entourage of churchmen [*sic*] gets under way. Garments, icons, incense, gold and jewels — all are remarked. The splendor, we have been taught, is a reminder of spiritual maturation, of the honor due to God, of the kingdom come. In the noblest among the dignitaries, the color purple sounds like a trumpet. The wearers are princes of the church. They are to a man [*sic*], ready to die for the faith; hence their clothing blazes, the color of blood.

The majestic procession is under way. The question never rises: Are these exalted gentlemen merely stand-ins for secular authority (which is to say, the militarized and moneyed elite), decked out in the relics of a grand tradition, playing godly, playing human, playing Christ?

Processions like this have been wending their splendid way for centuries. And few, very few of the princes of the church have died in the way prescribed—for anyone or anything.

Then, in our procession, something happens.

In accord with immemorial ritual, the dignitaries have walked a certain distance. Beyond all accounting, things stop short. Great ones, here and there, drop out of rank. Decked out as they are in princely vesture, they fall to knee. Now one, then another of the princely marchers is crawling along on hands and knees. Pride of place? The procession was like a glacier moving grandly through frigid seas. Then unaccountably, it drifted into southern waters. And it broke up, fell away under a torrid sun.

Their majesties? They became a public show, a procession of shame, inching along in the dust. Toward what? vocation, holiness, truth?

It is as though the cry of the martyrs had sounded in our midst, had become a great summons to the church, the church of Saul, of silence, of moral majorities, crystal cathedrals, hatred of gays, contemning of women; the church of shady deals, of racism and pride, of property and tax exemption and central planning and sound investment and nuclear terror.

And what of the citizens, onlookers, churchgoers? They are appalled or dumbfounded or bemused at the humiliation of "their men," a humiliation to all evidence willful and self-imposed.

Many among the bystanders are visibly outraged. They came for a holiday, came in their throngs, brought the children along. To watch, to be edified, to be blessed, assured that all is as usual, all is well. Which is to say—to be asperged, befogged, to be told nothing of Gospel or prophets, to hear no nation (least of all their own) reproved. No judgment, no repentance.

"A terrible beauty is born." Among the onlookers, amid the cloud of confusion, the dust, the ruinous reversal of roles and fortunes and future, some raise an outcry. They call for the law to deal with these churchmen turned motley fools, these disrupters of the normal, of traffic and trade, bread and circuses, normal religion.

The church that marched in pride of place, heel to toe with the generals, presidents, secretaries of war and commerce, with the tycoons and robber barons, with the cronies and clients of these, the juntas and shahs, the torturers and oligarchs—why, the princes of the church are brought low, a progress of fools, the progeny of the Gedarenes! Their robes are befouled. They inch along with the dogs and swine. And they are we.

What can it mean, this abasement, this flagellation of spirit? A prince raises his head from the dust. He murmurs, "I heard an outcry, and a summons." Another sighs, "How blind we were, and for how long!"

They have come to understand that there are not two Christs, one of power and place, another of infamy and scorn, of prisons and torture. They have come to understand that if there exists such an entity in our world as the church of Christ, it is by no means the church of empire, the NATO church.

And yet, and yet. Our crimes, our malfeasance and blindness and cowardice notwithstanding, there are not two Christs, but one. The realization is humiliating in the extreme. We, the true believers, have been in the wrong, in sin. Up to this hour, and including all those triumphant yesterdays, the centuries when we rode high and mighty.

Yet Saul became Paul. He was stripped of his fondest hope, his proudest possession, his ego, his intractable pride.

It may yet come to this. After we have learned something of life and death, something of letting go and making do, there will be a finis worth it all. Our second coming, toward the One who comes.

Another image. We will mingle with a second procession, as it comes toward us. We have heard an outcry, faint at first, then more urgent. The cry that long before brought us to knee, shrove us of selfishness, reproved our numbed spirits. We heard before we saw; the cry of the martyrs was the prelude. But as events proved, it was prelude only. Then we met those others, saw those faces, and knew them for our own.

You should see us now, redeemed. The faces of the suffering mingle with ours. We see in them all that is possible, even to such as ourselves.

You should see us now, they and ourselves. They await us, we crawl along. Then they come toward us. They kneel, embrace us, lift us to their side. And we know, at last many things once hidden from our eyes. It is all one, the humiliation and the glory, the blood and the outcome. And we are one. The chastened church, the church of martyrs. The imperial church is redeemed by the suffering church. Indeed it could be said that the imperial church too has learned a little—to suffer, to endure, and to prevail.

Saul, Paul, and you holy martyrs, pray for us.

33

The Trouble with Our State

THE TROUBLE with our state
was not civil disobedience,
which in any case, was hesitant and rare.

Civil disobedience was rare as kidney stone—
no, rarer; it was disappearing like immigrants' disease.

You've heard of a war on cancer?
There is no war like the plague of media
There is no war like routine
There is no war like 3 square meals
There is no war like a prevailing wind

it blows softly, whispers
DON'T ROCK THE BOAT!
The sails obey, the ship of state rolls on.

The trouble with our state
—we learned it only afterward
when the dead resembled the living who resembled the dead
and civil virtue shone like paint on tin
and tin citizens and tin soldiers marched to the common whip

—our trouble
the trouble with our state
with our state of soul
our state of siege—
was
civil
obedience.

34

A Chancy Encounter
with an Angel

*I took the scroll from the angel's hand and ate it. It was honey sweet in
my mouth, but when I swallowed, my stomach turned sour.*

—Revelation 10:10

LET'S TAKE the episode with a kind of rueful literalness, the times being
evil. Conceivably, things went like this:

Myself: What, EAT a scroll? But why, what's the message?

Angel: Say for starters, Matthew, chapters 5–7, especially that chewiest,
least digestible bit of all, the one that sticks in the throat, gags, positively
will not go down. The one about "loving enemies."

M.: Sweet on the tongue, you said?

A.: Well you, ourselves. Pacifists, but only between wars. Like veggies,
but only between meals. All that sweet talk, all those infant formula
sermons. Then all that cozening up to money and the power boys. Very
little remembering, so much forgetting. No context.

Now it's said, we have guns and butter, guns melting into butter!
Marines as angels of mercy! Smart bombs on providential missions!

But what about the Word, the Word? It grows weightless, a wafer on
the tongue. It melts into white spit. Never reaches the gut, the heart, the
bloodstream.

M.: Sour in the stomach, you say. What an image—someone crouching
in a corner, half mad maybe, chewing away at an inky foolscap.

A.: A touch of madness in a mad time. Try it. It might drive you sane.

M.: Sanity maybe, catastrophe for sure. *Contra naturam,* that diet. Followed by belching. Vomiting even.

A.: Eat the scroll. Something might happen. Imagine it. The Word gets inside you, down and down. An emetic. Maybe that's the meaning here. You rid yourself of a slow-working, permeating poison. Call it moral paralysis, inhibition, dead images, conscience gone to rot.

Who knows, maybe you'll see something for the first time — the formidable resourcefulness of dark minds, the sweet talk of the powers, the latest hard sell of a war!

How right Socrates was; old sophists never die, they just go on "making the worse the better argument."

You've heard it all: "kingdom of darkness," "some people beyond redemption." The demon of Baghdad. Or, "first guns, then butter." Or, worse and worse, "those rapist ethnic cleansers! Now you've got to admit, beyond the shadow of a sane doubt, this time we've got the absolute, virtuous, necessary, salvific, compassionate, surgical project, just waiting for our get up and go, our grit, our bombs."

M.: My aching gut!

A.: Remember the old spiritual? "Everybody want' to go to heaven, nobody want' to die."

Remember, remember. A peace camp in the Iraqi desert. Witness for Peace in Central America. South Africans facing the guns and dogs. Buddhists impeding the tanks in Hue. Selma, Dr. King, the USA maybe, just maybe shaking off our sleeping sickness. Now let's remember something else — the future.

There must be at least ten thousand young people around the world ready, willing, and able to refuse military induction/seduction. They've swallowed the scroll!

Now suppose they heard a story, how St. Francis trekked across the world, seeking a meeting with the "enemy," the Muslim Sultan. And suppose these resisters came unarmed to the border of a war zone, fasted there, prayed, marched right in. In sum, risked their lives. With one thing in mind: to bring sanity, an alternative, to a mad impasse.

Suppose they hung in, refused to go away, eventually, reluctantly, were invited to sit down with those bristling, untrusting leaders.

M.: Wait a minute. Suppose they failed. Suppose they were gunned down.

A.: (Breaks into song.) "Everybody want' to go to heaven; nobody want' to die."

35

The Strange Case of the Man
Who Could Not Please Anyone

Т HERE WAS NO INKLING, hearing the story as a child, that it was to have more than passing interest. The story told of a man and his son and a donkey, going to market. The boy rode the beast, the father walked alongside. They met other folk heading in the same direction. Someone said, "Just look at that lazy boy riding the donkey, while his father walks."

So the boy got down, and the father mounted the beast. But someone on the road was again displeased, "Just look at that grown man, taking things easy, while his poor boy trudges along beside!"

So the father beckoned the boy up, and the two rode together. That didn't work either. Someone yelled, "Look at that poor donkey, weighed down by two lazy louts!"

At wits' end, the father and son dismounted. They made the donkey lie down, tied his legs together, front left to right, back left to right, and thrust a pole between. Then the two shouldered the beast and carried him off to market.

The story was my first inkling of the Catch-22 nature of things. It all came home during the Vietnam War years. I was saying in public that the war was a horror. No right-minded person should pay for it, enlist in it, kill for it, die for it, in any way justify it.

How dare he! Such bizarre views got me in trouble with multitudes of Catholics. "Who was this upstart priest anyway, refusing the immemorial party line, our dear and revered just war theory. Why, he even goes around breaking the law!"

Then the abortion issue heated up. I said at the time, and later, and still say, abortion is a horror, as war is a horror, as capital punishment is a horror. A civilized people has no business disposing of others, no matter who, no matter at what stage of life — whether such be "almost people," heinously guilty people, domestic people, distant people — whether Vietnamese, Grenadian, Panamanian, Afghanistani, or Iraqi.

Let us dare generalize in such grave matters. A civilized culture is known for cherishing, rather than obliterating, the lives in its midst, "midst" understood as a kind of unbroken line, a lifeline. Call it conscience, call it moral understanding. It extends from the womb to death row to Iraq.

Such opinions as these, need I say, were also found offensive, this time by the secular left. The rules of the game were all against me. According to the Catholics, you had to oppose abortion and support war. In the Vietnam decade, the biggest ecclesiastical gun of all, Cardinal Spellman, was saying so.

And according to the seculars, you had to oppose the war and support abortion on demand. This went without saying (though it was said rather frequently, and loudly).

Catch-22, and me right in there, caught there. Some would have me riding the donkey, some wanted me to climb down, some wanted me riding tandem, others wanted me carrying the beast! There was no pleasing everyone.

I reflected ruefully, wisdom comes hard. I mean the unconventional kind we call "biblical," or "morally adult," or "consistent." It seemed to me that another kind of wisdom, the conventional kind, whether of the religious or secular mode, is graced with little of the above.

It came to this, as far as I could understand matters. Most of us were willing, as the price of salvaging something, some theory, some flag, some ideology — to give someone up. In this way, most of us in one sense or another took hostages. Or traded in lives.

Such wisdom was "conventional." I use the word deliberately; it is not meant as a compliment. It implies convenience or custom or routine. It is not greatly given to independent judgment or compassion. And more often than not, it implies (and exacts) violence against others.

Conventional wisdom places its wager (a bloody one at that) on the merits of a quick fix. Improve the human lot by getting rid of someone — or many! It is the opposite of humane, radical, heartfelt, patient wisdom.

In a literally deadly way, such "conventional wisdom" reflects the schizoid culture back upon itself. In one form it would save the Iraqis but could not so arrange domestic structures as to welcome the unborn to a safe haven. Or (as in the case of Catholics), such "wisdom" proclaims,

"All who are conceived must be brought to birth; but on reaching adult-hood, the safely born are degraded; they become the expendables. The next war beckons, it is justified, my country right or wrong, follow the flag."

Almost everyone is willing to give someone up. That is the bloody rub. It's no news to anyone these days that Catholic women, a multitude of them, are in a high voltage of anger at church authorities. One can say — justifiably so. And at the same time, one registers a caveat: Anger is not the recommended fuel for moral clarity. Indeed anger tends quite often to distract and becloud, implying as it does a dearth of tenderness and trust, a breakdown on both sides of willingness to listen. A cold war in fact, threatening to explode into a hot. An impasse.

Alas for all that. The consequences are damnably hard to live with. Many women, feeling more and more isolated in church and state, claim the abortion issue as their own. Thereby they succeed, I think, only in further isolating and burdening themselves. Communality is out, responsibility unshared.

Likewise some insist that war is a male issue. The logic in both cases escapes me. I had thought that in a far deeper (and perhaps more helpful) sense, warmaking and abortion were simply human issues. Women and men together make babies; women and men (though in far different ways) make war.

The banning of bombs, and the cherishing of the unborn, as of all living beings — this is the urgent moral business of ourselves. All of us, woven into, weaving anew the wondrous web of life. Graced with the burden and glory of the human vocation. We are stewards of life, never hucksters of death.

36

The Catholic Bishops
Approve Bush's War
(November 2001)

Lᴇsᴛ I ᴍᴇʀɢᴇ
with mountains that surely will fall,
their decrepitude my own—

Lest I walk shod
in blood of Abel, crying from the earth,
"My tantamount, my brother, my undoer"—

Lest eons I must carry
Rachel's sacrifice, her tears my albatross—

Lest I the Christ
disavow,
and Him who shackled there
I drag through sludge
of cowardice and dismay—

Lest weighed, I be found
wanting—
no guest of heaven,
a ghost, and no egress
from foolish trumpery of time—

Lest I disappear, down down
the 110th escalation
of pride,

and truncated, eyeless, soulless,
be found

unfit for armed might,
for rubble and America—

Lest I be sifted
like wheat or chaff,

and under a pall
(the appalling flag)

am borne away
piecemeal

to broken doorways
of sheol or limbo,

(the divergencies
not large, nor mine to choose) —

Lest I

37

The Faith That Seeks Justice
and Makes Peace

WE LIVE IN A CULTURE both faithless and fervent in the works of injustice and war. Racism, wars small and large (but seemingly never
ending), gross interference in the affairs of others, manipulation and
murder; these and the urban violence that tears at the domestic fabric
of decency and hope have created a political atmosphere of betrayal,
greed, and violence. Little of justice is in the air; race and color and
gender and (most of all) income, these determine who rides high and
who is ground under. It seems as though the nation were intent on self-
destruction, as though a force beyond rational control were spinning us
about, morally lost and incoherent.

Despite all, many good people do not give up. Many have a sense,
drawn from religious tradition, that they are summoned to a faith that
does justice. Together with others drawing on other traditions, they long
to create a social fabric woven to the benefit of all, a society marked by
compassion and altruism, with special attention paid to the powerless
and disenfranchised.

We Americans can hardly claim as an inheritance a common memory
of peace; quite the contrary! Peacemakers and poets, we shortly discover that we must make peace from scratch, in close conflict with a
blood-ridden history. We must confront structures that bespeak faith-
lessness and violence, whose apogee are vast, close-guarded military
installations.

That confrontation must take a multitude of forms, in which poetry
holds an honored place. It always has in my lifetime. I recall with gratitude the scene in Danbury Federal Prison, where my brother Philip and
I were held during the Vietnam War. Our little band of resisters became
close friends, and poetry forged an important bond. On Sunday morn-
ings we would meet in the yard, and each would offer a poem composed
or memorized during the week.

We were saying in effect: Big Brother does not own us. Or, We are here on our own terms, not yours. Or, We reject the sterile, lockstepping, prosaic routine that would break steady will to bits. Or, We find and celebrate beauty, verve, éclat—even in your sterile wilderness. Or, We shall make the desert break in unlikely vociferous bloom. We shall create even here the original human being, in a peaceable realm.

If we are serious, we will be taken seriously and hailed into courts and jails.

In this effort of peacemaking, my family and friends are abruptly linked with the unequals. We stand in court and jail side by side with the poor, the minority folk who in one way or another have fallen afoul of the law. This transplanting of our class and gender and education and social expectation might, despite all, work to a larger advantage. Together, we and the disadvantaged (thus goes our hope) might even construct a modest model of the larger, distant ideal, a community worthy of the name invoked by Dr. King, "beloved." If we and our friends are lucky, and astute and enduring, then our small numbers and smaller effect may reasonably be thought a worthy image of a larger world-to-come.

Still, even as our beloved community approaches the biblical blueprint, influential thumbs turn down—the media, the courts, the military, the politicians—and yes, the official church. A chorus sounds: "The law, the law, they have broken the law!"

We are a species of squatters, to be evicted or rounded up. Do we claim the right to enter a military area and express our outrage at the waste, the secrecy, the limitless violence enshrined there? If we do, we are summoned before judges, those paramilitary acolytes, turning a frosty eye on the likes of ourselves. The court is autonomous, the judges automatons. The outcome is automatic, the only unknown being the degree of judicial outrage to be inferred in the jail sentence.

No wonder we defendants glance at one another ruefully. Indeed peacemaking is a chancy undertaking, given the bellicose world. Punishment is attached to it, and the shaking of a fragile community, rooftree to foundation.

In time I came to understand that our offense, in the eye of the beholder, was this: We were challenging certain myths and assumptions concerning the human itself, its capacities, drives, needs, appetites, spirituality. How is the human to be defined in a most inhuman time? What might a prohuman politics look like?

Undoubtedly the culture and the Gospel hold wildly divergent views on the subject. Is "equality" in America a shibboleth, indicating little more than a vast leveling of appetite and instinct? Is peacemaking, on the other hand, a practical synonym for the human vocation? Does the Gospel teach us so? What is a human being? What is a human community? How are these verified in a most inhuman time?

We kept raising the questions, as though (so went the rejoinder) such questions had not long since been answered. Those who perished in the wars of our lifetime, the (finally "equalized") dead of Hiroshima, Dresden, Auschwitz, Hanoi, Belfast, San Salvador, Baghdad, and a host of others "equalized" on other killing fields, the tortured, bombed, disappeared, radiated, winners and losers alike — these had settled the matter. The victims as well as the destroyers, once for all (in the serious way of blood both shed and exacted), the dead as well as the living, these had answered the questions we harped on.

Raising such questions? The effort was as vain and vainglorious as seeking to raise the dead. Our brand of peacemaking, far from shedding light on the question of the human, was laughed out of court. Or found guilty in court.

Thus, out of a bloody time, a dictum was tested, and assumed the form of a dogma. Violence, not peacemaking, was synonymous with the human. We humans were a species of animal, gifted with a particular skill at settling scores.

In the process many died, and some prospered. And both the dead and the living, in their different ways, gave testimony to the same truth. The truth was an "equalizer," its symbol a gun; we humans are a genetically violent species.

The dead know this, we were told, if they know anything. By presumption, the dead have settled all scores. Or the scores were settled on their behalf. Which comes to much the same thing.

So also with the living. No point of talking forgiveness, remorse, guilt, remission of debts, starting over. Such might correctly be indulged after, not before, an unconditional victory, or an unconditional surrender.

To preempt the process, to deny its viability and validity, smacked of weakness, and invited incursion and conquest. No, settle a score first; after we have shown the power of the sword, we can sheathe it (for awhile). But first, an eye (if not two) for an eye.

The war drums sound, always the same throb: just war, necessary war, inevitable war. In answering the beat, victor and loser alike settle their scores and attain a kind of grandeur. So it is drummed into us: dying and killing are the only game. Taking blows as shrewd as the blows dealt, finally (warriors, civilians too, a few or a multitude) by choice or default, nameless or celebrated — they, we, go under. Finally equal, each to all. Thus the drama, ad infinitum. Thus, underscored in blood, a definition of the human remains unassailably glorious. *Dulce et decorum.* "How sweet and befitting to die for one's country." No one has put matters better or more seductively than the old Roman poet.

And the peacemakers? The culture grants us this: We may choose, for various reasons peculiar to ourselves, to offer other, far different versions of the human. We may appeal to Christ, to Gandhi, to saints and heroes and martyrs, ancient and modern. But the contrary evidence is formidable. Anthropology and history and psychology, the conduct of politics and the normal teachings of religion — in sum, the skills and disciplines, even the gods we summon to justify our behavior — these move through time and the world, teaching, prodding, insisting, dramatizing, a vast phalanx, a persuasive field of force.

Peacemakers? They are like forlorn survivors on a battlefield.

To the question once more. What is a human being, a human community? The prevailing answer issues from the barrel of a gun. The answer is rational, sensible, pragmatic. It has been tested in fire and blood. It is the warrior, the warrior nation, that makes sense, makes history. Deductively, even metaphysically assured, the victors, the vanquished, the weapons' hucksters, spectators, TV watchers, the "intellectual neutrals," the citizens and churchgoers, all agree.

The war itself is the star credential. It guarantees the legitimacy of public authority. The polls rise and rise. The media are dazzled, the objectors vilified, the citizens in a stupor. "The president," writes the *New York Times,* "underwent his rite of passage by invading Panama." And again, "The president shed his wimp image in the sands of Saudi Arabia."

As to academe, war is prime grist for the mills. Whether on the winning or losing side, "experts" are heard from. They seize upon history (synonymous, according to them, with the history of war and its handmaiden arts, the psychology of winners and losers, the history of diplomacy, power politics and economics). They appeal to psychology, sociology, anthropology, social sciences, the history of Western religions. What tools, what an arsenal! They take aim, bend their disciplines to the task, fire. Behold the trophy, an unchallengeable theory of the human.

Violence as human, human as violent. The force of the theory carries all before it. Its power, be it noted, is in no way dependent on who won the last round of war, or who lost. Or on the continual flux of power and might, as yesterday's loser speedily joins the winning team, having learned an unspeakably harsh lesson.

The point is infallible deduction from experience. From the widest experience short of death itself—winner, loser, observer, warrior, churchgoer. Warmaking humans are the norm. Therefore warmaking is eminently human, an entirely normal, "equalizing," indeed laudable form of conduct. Let us wage war, and be found just—since we have waged a just war.

Thus the world was arranged, or disarranged, long before any of us present appeared. Violence is of the essence; nonviolence is both unimaginable and unworkable. Scientifically it can only be termed unbiological.

The Sermon on the Mount? All well and good, and admirable in its own way, and useful for normal times. But the times are hardly normal. A war is under way. In clear opposition to the war, do the plain example, words, life and death of Christ stand vindicated?

In the heat and horror of wartime, the story of Christ appears as a kind of primitive relic, unrealizable, unworkable, discredited in practice. This is how the Gospel is viewed during wartime, if the truth were spoken (it is hardly ever spoken). And we are left a legacy both desiccated and looted. It is known as "a point of view," "an interim ethic," quibbling, nonviolent velleities half realized, feebly tested, lamely presented. No heroism, no clarity. No Christ.

One American Jesuit wrote in highly critical vein of such as ourselves. He insisted on the fragile character of nonviolent activity, its meager showing in the column of achievement; this latter, one grants, with reason. He paid more or less conscious tribute to the theory and practice of war, whose chief ideologue he quite correctly identified, and without a tinge of regret, as Western Christianity. What remained unclear throughout his essay were his own convictions. Did he cast his lot with fragile nonviolence, or with the Christian Excalibur? With a disarmed Christ, or with a sword (if one is to give credence to the Gospel), which has been imbedded for centuries in the body of Christ?

Imagine a nonnuclear world? Whatever vision might be thought to inspire its creation, whatever ploy or concession might bring it to pass— these must be consigned to the political loony bin. Where madness is in command, the sane must tread softly.

Questions, questions. Faith, justice? Christian faith, Western justice? Did these perish at Hiroshima? Was a posthuman history born there, did our history die there? Was the "new human" conceived there? Did the human perish there, radiated, our future rendered freakish? Did a precious tradition die, did religious understanding vanish, dust on the terrible winds? Did civilization itself go under, did Christianity spawn its own demise, did the demonic extinguish the holy, did Mephistopheles and Satan laugh up their fiery sleeves? Were the gnostics proven right, and the armageddonists? Was the rapture of Revelation vindicated, our only hope (my hope that is, and the devil take yours)?

The lurid glare of 1945, much magnified since, has shed meager light on such questions, questions that might be described, in an age less morally beclouded, as properly spiritual. It can be reported, however, that though the nuclear gods are frequently invoked, they remain, like the great standing forms of Easter Island, mum indeed.

The Bomb fell, and we were told that it won the war. More, the Bomb settled the question of war itself, once for all. In 1945, Americans were in sole possession of the Bomb. It followed that we were not only victors, but makers of a grand new eon. We had started things over, in the way of the Creator or of Christ. Year One of the Bomb. We and the Bomb would terrorize terror out of countenance. We and our secret were something grand, something of a healing team, the homeopaths of the future.

The errant nonsense was shortly exposed, along with the pretense that the Bomb could be named beneficent. Terror, it appeared, though propagated under virtuous auspices, remained terror, and honored no borders. Japan was not the only victim whose bones lay scattered in the plain of Jericho. We too would know the terror that stalks by day.

A cruel history, a crueler present. We had thought the Bomb could be contained, a genie in a bottle, guardian and servant of Pax Americana. Then we discovered that our creation was unendowed with what might be called "ideological commitment." The Bomb knew no loyalties. A playboy of the Western world, it lightheartedly sold its services to the highest bidder. Shortly, if one can so speak without odium, the original nuclear terrorists became the terrorized. As Bomb cloned Bomb, Year One of the Bomb stretched into Year Fifty and beyond. Terror, like the demon in the Gospel story, ranged far and wide, thirsted, refused to return pacifically to its dwelling.

When it finally returned, it was accompanied by forty demons more terrible than itself.

And yet, we grant something to these, our Years of the Bomb. The questions that arose out of the doom of Hiroshima were indeed late and lamely posed, frequently stifled, softened, evaded, by all manner of myth, promise, sweet talk, frictions and enmities, ignorance multiplied, frivolity and distraction.

And yet, and yet, the questions held. They would not go away. They hung in the air, like a woven thread suspending the nuclear sword, unimaginably precarious in midair.

People began to wake up, to look up. What they saw was unthinkable. Many turned away in disbelief at the evidence of their own eyes. The end of things, the end of the world?

Some few took courage and a second look. In Europe and America, they raised questions, loud and clear; questions that signaled a fresh sense of a common predicament. Questions that might even signal the stirring of grace.

At least in some cases, the questions implied more than moral fatuity, perpetually furrowed brows, perplexity unlimited. If such questions were pursued passionately, and if they were inherently valid, might not answers be discovered? The questions beckoned; a new path opened, unexplored, unknown, and grievously neglected.

A new definition of the human, it seemed, was also a very old one. The nuclear dilemma had brought the old and the new together. Dr. Martin Luther King said it best, "The choice before us is nonviolence or nonexistence." The human as nonviolent, temperate, on the move in quest of justice and peace. A glimmer of light, the gift of light, better than darkness.

Then, from questioning the limitless nuclear folly, timorously and yet with new will, some repented and took action. Military centers were marked with blood. People fasted in public, sat in and were arrested. The Plowshares movement was heard from, domestically at first, then in western Europe, even in Australia. The actions multiplied, despite (or perhaps because of) the severe sentences leveled against nonviolent actors. And this for two decades, and beyond. It was a fair start. If the demons in possession of the house were not routed, they had at least been served notice of eviction.

We opened a very old handbook of the human, known as the Bible. And there we read again a few truths long neglected: Humans do not own the universe. We are forbidden to foreclose on its future. Creation is not "ours" to insult and dominate. All things are loaned to us—from ancestors, for the sake of the unborn, in the great hand-me-on of the dance. We are parties to a spiritual, genetic covenant.

A long, long look is in order. What do we hand down? Shall we manacle the hand of the unborn to a nuke, as an only inheritance?

Early on in Christian history, peacemakers were stigmatized by the state. Popular culture, state religion, secular history agreed in portraying them as bizarre. Overmastered by strange longings, it was as though they were commanding the ocean tide, the tide of empire, to turn in its track. They introduced "strange gods." Had that been all their crime, it remained a small matter; the empire was tolerant of theological novelties. But this God of the Christians was like no other. God, they insisted, was incarnate, clear eyed, passionate, political. He felt the plight of his people to the bone. He pronounced stern judgment on perfectly normal, perennial imperial misconduct, exploitation, terror.

Then came his death, which might be thought to have settled matters. But shortly thereafter sanity itself seemed to have fled the earth. One after another, unimaginable events tumbled out of rumor — epiphanies, healings, prophecies, denunciations. Most bizarre of all, a faith that proved consequential in the extreme took root. An ethic, a style in the world, flowered. With regard to imperial law and order, the faith shortly took the form of a Great Refusal.

These Christians were votaries of a dead man who walked out of his tomb. Through teaching and example and the stories that sprang up, his followers dared announce a new version of the human — gentle, compassionate, self-giving, just, nonviolent, peaceable. They were a company of equals; their bond was prayer, hospitality, goods held in common.

Up to a point they were judged with benign contempt as harmless. But the most benign secular eye, like that of the historian Josephus, lit on their conduct vis-à-vis temporal power. He declared them grudging, even mischievous subjects.

Indeed. They had only a thinly veiled contempt for the imperial cliche, "what your country can do for you, what you can do for your country." Their spirit was gyrovague, their center of gravity and grace was simply elsewhere.

This was the rub, which could not be rubbed away. They dwelt at the edge of society, where benefits and emoluments were thin to nonexistent. Their numbers multiplied, unaccountably. As they grew in number and influence, it became evident that their behavior was, to put matters simply, incompatible with the prospering of empire.

There followed, in the nature of imperial logic, the gravest civil, political, economic, military consequences. The disciples were condemned in large numbers as a clan of unruly subversives. They were finical in their loyalties, loud in their claims of otherworldly bonds. They demoralized the commonweal, opposed as they were to taxpaying, military service, the law, courts. Detained, tried, and condemned to the direst sanctions, they remained fanatic and joyful.

Worst of all, they attracted to their way all manner of malcontents, drifters, naifs, the high and mighty as well as the anonymous poor, the great, and the unknown.

So the plague grew, and grows to this day.

In South Africa, the Philippines, Central America, Northern Ireland, Sudan, Iraq, Palestine, Colombia, throughout the tormented world, even in the United States — the ancient faith summons believers to works of peace and justice. To a sense of equality and mutuality that brooks no domination, no killing. To nonviolence.

A faith that remains consequential. A faith that more or less equably bears with the consequence of an ethic of resurrection — scorn, obloquy, judges, and jails.

Let us offer a muted Alleluia.

38

Advent

IT IS NOT TRUE that creation and the human family are doomed
to destruction and loss—
This is true: For God so loved the world that he gave his only
begotten Son,
that whoever believes in him shall not perish, but have
everlasting life.

It is not true that we must accept inhumanity and discrimination,
hunger and poverty, death and destruction—
This is true: I have come that they may have life, and that
abundantly.

It is not true that violence and hatred should have the last word,
and that war and destruction rule forever—
This is true: For unto us a child is born, and unto us a Son is given,
and the government shall be upon his shoulder,
And his name shall be called Wonderful Counselor, Mighty God,
the Everlasting, the Prince of Peace.

It is not true that we are simply victims of the powers of evil who
seek to rule the world—
This is true: To me is given authority in heaven and on earth,
and lo, I am with you, even unto the end of the world.

It is not true that we have to wait for those who are specially
gifted,
who are the prophets of the church, before we can be peacemakers.
This is true: I will pour out my Spirit on all flesh,
and your sons and daughters shall prophesy,
your young shall see visions,
and your old shall have dreams.

It is not true that our hopes for liberation of humankind, of justice,
      of human dignity, of peace
are not meant for this earth and for this history—
This is true: The hour comes, and it is now, that true worshipers
shall worship the Father in spirit and in truth.

So let us enter Advent in hope, even hope against hope.
Let us see visions of love and peace and justice.

Let us affirm with humility, with joy, with faith, with courage:
Jesus Christ—the Life of the world.

39

Our Hope in Christ

I WOULD LIKE TO RAISE two questions in regard to hope: a question of symbol, and a question of what I call "conduct."

Biblical prophets were expert in use of symbol. They were, moreover, entrepreneurs of symbolic action. And this I take it, not from arbitrary willfulness, but because they were simply pushed to such measures and means. Pushed, that is to say, by the temper of their times, which they invariably and accurately viewed as in no sense "normal," but morally abominable. Pushed also by the dynamic of hope, which (as we too were to learn) is best understood as an irony—hope against itself, hope wrestling not only with its apes and counterfeits, but with its own lesser prior, as yet immature forms.

In other words, hope as a kind of virtue of extremes, a virtue *malgré lui.* A virtue pushed to the edge. The edge of society, edge of respectability? Let us say — to the edge of the rational; edged out, derided as incompetent, irrelevant, bizarre even.

Nevertheless. The work of hope begins, here and now, in a most unlikely time and place. The task being — to expose and declare the lie. The lie? The claim on the part of public authority that right reason is in command, an available resource; that nuclear weapons are in effect a rational undertaking. The truth being—and only hope can announce it—that rationality, coherence, not to speak of ethical understanding, are in desperately short supply. Moreover, incoherence, irrationality, are all but a credential of high office, and a badge of office, once assumed. Bankrupt power, vacant academe, offer only straight-faced insanity — functional, self-persuaded, all but unreachable. They talk high-toned nonsense—deterrence, MAD, peacekeeping warheads, star wars, smart bombs, defense shields, and the rest. It is at this point, when words convey only insanity, reveal nothing of truth, conceal almost totally the intent of the speaker — and so debase the powers of the soul, and more, when such language, taken seriously, does like damage to the hearer—at such a point the prophet, the Christian, must seek another method. For the sake of sanity, yes, for the sake of one's soul, for the salvaging of others.

This is our situation — bankruptcy of language, the destruction of truth, the despair of our people, the works of death. I have recurred again and again, not to words, words, words, but to an edgy, nonverbal exploratory power of the soul. In order to free ourselves from public insanity, we construct a kind of sign language. We play mute in the presence of the madly verbose. We gather to ourselves the natural forces and primordial realities of the earth—water, fire, ashes, blood, living flora, all varied vessels and elements of life. Planted, scattered abroad, blessed, invoked, breathed upon, dug up, anointed, outpoured, in the very tic and spasm of crisis, with these we seek to dramatize the truth about our condition, our violated and violating humanity. They may even serve to rebuke our inhumanity.

It all seems quite simple, in line with tradition, as we learn in reading the Jewish prophets. But nothing, it seems, is more complex than the effort to simplify. The effort, I judge, requires that one set aside, at the very beginning, all such considerations as effectiveness, results, costs, goals, the gimlet glance of the technocrat, even the technocrat of the spirit—the lackluster litany composed by those whose "rational discourse," alas, reveals only the rot of the mind.

In such activity, one remains in the dark about its effect. As to results and goals, a like darkness prevails. We engage in symbolic activity in a spirit of hope. We scatter ashes. We pour our blood abroad (formerly on draft files, now on nuclear weapons). We stage dramatic events like "die-ins" or "sit-ins" or "kneel-ins." We plant trees and present flowers at military bases. We would dramatize, make vividly present the hellish realities of nuclear war—realities which the military, the corporations, the courts, the jails, the Pentagon, the president, the Congress, most academics, and most churches, for reasons of their own, have rendered abstract, distant, impregnable to understanding and conscience. Realities of life and death.

Death as a social method, preempting all other human skills, claiming the field, claiming all life—we cannot abide that death be so proud. And life — life as absolute gift, inviolate, the life of the mind, the lives of children, the aged, the unwanted and dispensable poor—we cannot abide that life be cheapened, bartered, given up on, weighed against money and ego, and inevitably found wanting.

So we devise these liturgies of hope, formalized, rehearsed to a degree, but with their own spontaneity too. We ground them in the liturgical year, in its life–death–new life rhythms, in the rhythm of the scripture story and prayer. Literally beyond words, the actions dramatize the waste, want, moral perfidy, of nuclear war. And the alternatives that lurk just below surface and appearance, when the heart and eye are aware—joy, truthfulness, the sublime worth of life.

We are told something of this in the book of Jeremiah. On one occasion (in chapter 19) he was instructed to buy an earthen flask, to proceed in company with the authorities to a public place, a gate named for the refuse and offal dumped there. Standing in that place, he was instructed solemnly to warn the people of impending doom. In a sign thereof, he was to break the flask to pieces, as the people would soon be broken, along with their cities, their culture, their future, their spirit.

The little drama has a liturgical flavor—a procession of personages, the bearing along of a symbol, to be destroyed as instrument of memory and truth; finally, a fierce diatribe to bring matters home.

Prior to the event, matters in Israel had evidently gone mad. Rights were trampled under, idolatry and oppression were on rampage. Some new way of revealing the truth of things was required. So recourse was made to symbolic action. Which in the event, succeeded, but ironically. The truth was conveyed, but the prophet also paid up. Jeremiah was scourged and placed in the stocks. For such an outcome, good sense surely forbids longing. But one can be sure that punishment of those who initiate such actions has not greatly altered in intervening centuries, as we see with Dr. King and Dorothy Day. Witness the sentences meted against the Plowshares activists, and others who cross the line against the culture of war.

Jeremiah's act was hopeful. He simply did not give up, though evil rode high and corruption turned pure air foul. When words went nowhere, he found another way to convey the truth, an act that was risky, bound to confound and displease, but in the event, grasped.

As we reflect on our hope in Christ, we need to reflect on something more than the moral energy required to make our way through an average day in a mad world. Something more momentous and mysterious is in question.

Let us speak first of the world of His time. Certainly, it was out of joint. Hope must have been a difficult burden, not always gracefully borne. The country was occupied by imperial soldiers and authorities; the people were humiliated and resentful. Jesus appears on the scene as a healer, friend of outcast and leper and prostitute. His powers win a following; contrary forces get in gear. The cosmic character of his mission, elaborated later in terms such as redemption, universal salvation, expiation, sacrifice — these take their start from quite modest events, connections, His quotidian conduct, discourse, self-understanding, as revealed one to one, or in small groups. Teacher, wonder worker, critic of religious and civil conduct, we are told that bitter opposition was alerted, and quickly moved against Him.

The tone of life darkens. He has performed what one can only call the wrong moves of God. Indeed, it appears that He simply does not belong to this world of power, to its plays and ploys. He lacks skills necessary to the game; worse, He rashly challenges the game. And yet, His moves are made deliberately, thoughtfully. He does not present himself as a romantic whose appeal lies in an offhand or out-of-hand rejection of society, its mores, structures, authorities. Nothing as simply or as simpleminded as that. No solutions randomly or hastily arrived at, no sterile answers in place of fruitful questions. In how many instances, refusing to generalize, casting the carefully loaded question out of orbit, confounding a self-serving inquiry by insinuating a different one, playing sage, playing fool, playing dumb, He hints at the rigors and resources native to greatness.

I sense deep and wide-ranging hope in such conduct. From a stark point of view, hope implies this, though Christ must enter the dark regions of death (hostility, rejection, betrayal, injustice, torture) — still He did not give up on life itself. Which is to say, Christ persisted in the defense and vindication of the powerless and the victim. He persisted in the most thankless task of all—in telling the truth.

The pampered children of a culture that strives, like a foolish parent, to keep the truth of death from "the youngsters" —we had best go slow here. For we are as distant from, say, the life and death of a Salvadoran peasant or an Iraqi mother as we are from the bloody last chapters of the evangelists. The connections are, to say the least, weak; the simpatico in consequence, though declared frequently in worship and in print, may justly be considered suspect, and not only by the peasant or the mother or Christ.

Let me confess my ignorance. I cannot easily conjure the images that touch on what it means "not to give up on life." I have only the faintest inklings, through many sojourns in jail, through standing in many docks. No great claim, on the scale of the world and suffering humanity, if we agree that moral stature arises through suffering, mine is indeed a minor report.

Still, an inkling. Chiefly through friends and family who walk with me through the thick and thin of my life, I gain a hint now and again of grace under pressure — grace, pressure, the two in loving conflict. Friends who endure death, endure and come through, the death of love, their own death.

Such reflections occurring in pondering Christ's hope. He refused to give up on life. He refused, though evil claimed him for its prey, to give up on goodness. He unmasked injustice and hypocrisy. And He paid the price.

> *"Then leaving Him, they all fled."*

> *"One of you is about to betray Me."*

> *"And Peter swore, 'I do not know the man!'"*

> *"My God, My God, why have You forsaken Me?"*

Surely these are among the darkest words of our sorrowful history. Mercifully regarded (and we had best be merciful here, the words concern ourselves), they imply the despair of those surrounding Christ, of His inner circle; under pressure, His friends became former friends. But a question lingers, a question larger even than their or our questionable humanity. Larger, more hopeful even than the sad fact; we read those words of despair, betrayal, abandonment, and see our own reneging, our vile second-guessing on the high worth of goodness, truth, nonviolence.

The question might be framed something like this: How did Christ regard such evident default, such literal running out on the debts and burdens of friendship?

If He answered despair with despair, it seems to me something momentous follows. We are indeed stuck where we so often choose to be. But what if, in midst of such provocation, the default of the good amid the (far more easily borne) default of the wicked—what if He were able to absorb that mindless as well as terribly mindful evil, to absorb it, to turn it around? Granted that under its assault, He quakes, cries out, sweats blood, suffers what can be seen only as a dreadful execution, meantime undergoing not only the cutting of social lifeline, but the death of reasoned expectation. Tested to the uttermost, He dies. And wonderfully, the ending is peaceful, a kind of Buddhist diminuendo, horror purged.

Something extraordinary here, for us. Hope cut to the bone, vindicated in Him. He hoped as He died that friends might be faithful, enemies reconciled. Was the hope verified?

The hope of Christ is our testing. But not all of life is testing, nor all of hope, or we Christians would be a grimmer company than we are, in a wintrier world.

Let us think not only of the hope of Christ cut to the bone, cut to the shape of the cross, but of earlier, more sunny hope, such as shed light and warmth upon beginnings. Prior to setback, prior to dampening or disillusion, hope gathered strength at the start of His public life. A youthful hope, untried, it looked fervently on life's possibility; its skill was that of a lively imagination. Christ imagined, truly and well, the life He was undertaking in the world. Was He to be a healer? Then He must imagine healing—what would a healed human, a healed humanity, look like? Would He be a teacher? What images, stories, parables, would make the truth available, attractive? Would He raise the dead? What then was death? What is claim? And could He raise others, a stupendous toppling of the empery of death, without undergoing death in His own body? Without descending into very hell, and so leading the enslaved back to life?

He healed, He told the truth, He vindicated life. The illness, the untruth, the captivity to death — He understood these not so much as moral deviance (except in the conduct of envious power) but as radical inability to understand and to love.

Mistrust of love, failure of imagination. These are the icy and torrid poles of the human impasse; too hot to handle, too cold for comfort. Around these poles, His spirit plays, cooling the one, warming the other. I use the word "plays" deliberately; for His imagined world is one in which no school, including His own, is without its recess, no drudgery without its dance.

He would have about Him awakened minds, mindful hearts. He is uninterested, even scornful and off-putting, toward immature, unquestioning disciples. He hopes that humans, even the most shy and mistrustful of self, become not robots, even sanctified ones; nor followers, even ecstatic ones.

But He offers a friendship respectful of temperaments, of gifts weighty and gifts scant. Granted friendship and reasonable good luck, Christians may discover not only that they are awakening to the hope of Christ, but more, that in becoming themselves, they are beginning to resemble Him.

40

An Ethic of Resurrection

ONE THING seems reasonably certain. Our ethic is a gift of the God who rolled the stone back, who beat death at its own game. If that be true, something would seem to follow. The death game is not our game. We are called to undergo death, rather than inflict death. And in so acting, to cherish life. And the vocation is no less urgent or valid in our stalled and death-ridden culture. A calling to works of solace and rescue.

The ethic of Jesus, as I understand it, issues from the ever so slight edge He grants to life, in the "life vs. death" conflict of the Easter hymn. He grants the edge (better, He wins the edge) from the edge. From His chosen place in the world.

The drama, in its raw original form, opened during the week we call holy. It has had a long run, and tragic. To these years of war and turmoil and sanctions and the death of children.

We are not to ignore the fierce "reversal of fortune" in the drama of Jesus, as history misses His point, and yet stages His story again and again. The script has been seized on, bowdlerized, deformed. We have a new script, different stage directions, and up to the bloody present, a far different outcome. Which is to say, the prevailing and victory of the Hero of life has been everywhere and at all times denied, proven absurd, shunted aside. His nonviolence, patience, reconciling love—these are deemed unworkable, impractical, unrealistic. In power politics, on death rows, in abortion mills, in a defunct and discredited just war theory, in the churches as well. The word is—Out with all that!

Thus briefly, Friday to Sunday, the Lord of life is thrust offstage. We have a new and darker hero, icon, model. Death is our great protagonist. The power of death is the *motor mundi*, the driving force and fuel of event. This is what the world and its amortized religion have made of the drama. It is the legend stitched on the flag of every nation and principality, the Tao of death, the ethic of death, the ideology

220

of death, the victory and prevailing of death. An infection at the heart of things.

Is it just at this point that the church is called to break and enter? To say no to death in virtue of, in hope of, a larger yes to life?

By and large, one must conclude in shame and confusion of spirit, we Christians intervene in the death game (if at all), with sparse understanding, grudgingly, with a foggy maybe on our lips, with a "just war theory." The clear words of our Gospel, "Blessed are the peacemakers," "Love your enemies, do good to those who do ill to you," "Peter, put up your sword," "This is the cup of My blood, given for you" — such words are among the first casualties of war. War is declared. We are suddenly inducted along with everyone else. We cannot utter a forthright, unmistakable no.

I propose that we reflect on the implications of that no in virtue of a larger yes, that we undertake an ethic of resurrection, and live according to the slight edge of life over death:

- Ideologies of "the nations," political or economic arrangements however enlightened or democratic, can never be equated with the Realm of God. Indeed the Word of God addressed to the nations, as well as to revolutions whether of right or left, is always and everywhere the same: "Not yet. Not yet the Realm of God."

- And especially and always and irrevocably, the community of faith grants no compatibility, none, between the Gospel and the sanctioned slaughter known as war.

- The "just war theory" is in fact a cruel oxymoron. War, no matter its provocation or justification, is of its essence and nature supremely unjust. The injustice of war implies a blasphemous inflation of human authority, that humans are allowed to decree who shall live and who shall die, to dispose of human differences by disposing of humans. We are done with that theory forever.

- Imperial ideologies always reduce themselves to this — the vindication, indeed the honoring of death as a social method.

- The ethic of Jesus is distrustful of any theory or praxis of social change that does not exact risk and sacrifice of Christians.

- Our faith confesses no debt to the law of the land, when that law is protective of the realm of death and its artifacts, its courts, jails, taxes, armed forces. When Christians enter such precincts, they are to reflect the skepticism of scripture. Can worldly powers attain, dispense, or honor justice? They cannot.

- As to law courts, Christians enter them under rigor of the law, as defendants and resisters. They enter in jeopardy, at the mercy of death's servants and sycophants, like the One they follow. But never in debt to the law, not a farthing.

- The best time for Christians, the most enlightened time, the time when ethical hairsplitting is halted and the Gospel rings clear, is the time of the martyrs. On the other hand, complicity with secular power, commonly and absurdly known as "normal times," implies only Christian decadence. We are to learn from, and follow, our martyred sisters and brothers.

- The Christian response to imperial death-dealing is in effect a non-response. We refuse the terms of the argument. To weigh the value of lives would imply that military or paramilitary solutions had been grotesquely validated by Christians. There is no cause, however noble, which justifies the taking of a single human life, much less millions of them.

- Our no, uttered in face of imperial violence, takes the form of a nonanswer. Our appeal, more often than not wordless, like the silent Christ before Pilate, is precisely to Christ Crucified. Which is to say, to God in trouble for being Godly. God under capital sentence. God sentenced to death, executed for being God, for being human. The crime—such acts, miracles, healings, stories, refusals, as serve to vindicate, honor, and celebrate human life.

- The no to the state, uttered by the unarmed Christ, is vindicated in the resurrection. Of this, the world can never be a witness. (The military, be it noted, were in attendance at the event. The soldiers were struck to earth, and subsequently entered in collusion with the authorities, to lie about the occurrence [Matt. 28:11ff.].)

- In contrast, "witness of the resurrection" was a title of honor, self-conferred by the twelve (Acts 1:21–22). The meaning of the phrase is simple. The apostles were called to take their stand on behalf of life, to the point of undergoing death, as well as death's analogies—scorn and rejection, floggings and jail.

- This is our glory. From Peter and Paul to Martin King and Romero, Christians have known something which the "nations" as such can never know or teach—how to live and how to die. We are witnesses of the resurrection. We practice resurrection. We risk resurrection.

- We Christians have our own language and symbols. These properly understood are charged with life. They are life-giving, vessels of life. A few examples may be in order. When we pour blood at the Pentagon, we in effect renounce ideological bickering, concerning, truth told, who shall live and who die. We declare in fear and trembling our willingness to die rather than to take life. In granting and dramatizing the thin edge and advantage of life, we rest our case. The drama contains the entirety of our ethic.

When we spread ashes at the Pentagon, we mime the death-ridden pollution of the place. The drama contains the ethic.

When we dig graves on the White House lawn, we pay tribute to the empty grave of Easter, even as we show forth the universal grave to whose brink humanity is being pushed. The drama is the ethic.

Such acts as these are ventured in favor of life, even as they say more loudly than words our no to the inflation of death.

Let me illustrate two phenomena—ideologized religion, and an ethical breakthrough.

Twenty years ago the Catholic bishops set about preparing a letter to the church concerning the morality of nuclear weapons. In the course of their inquiry, they requested a meeting with Alexander Haig, the then secretary of state. Haig, a principality of awesome arrogance and univocal mind, at first agreed to the meeting. Then he abruptly left town, unavailable. It was a gesture of contempt. It was also, given the circumstance, entirely predictable. Who forsooth were these bishops, attempting to place imperial polity under their scrutiny?

Whether, on the other hand, the bishops acted properly in requesting the meeting remains moot at the least. I incline to the opinion that the bishops' consulting Haig on the ethics of nuclear weapons would be roughly equivalent to Jesus' consulting Pilate on the scenario of holy week. Meanwhile, the bishops never asked to speak with those Christians who for years had been on the front lines of Gospel nonviolence.

A different ethic, a breakthrough. Walter Sullivan, bishop of Richmond, Virginia, spoke briefly at St. Paul's Church in New York on the same subject. The gist of his thought was simple and to the point: "No nuclear weapons anywhere in the world, in the hands of any worldly power. Period." An eminently Christian position, a translation against all odds, of the counsel to "love enemies," "walk another mile," "reconcile," an ethic of resurrection.

My teachers, among others, have been Martin Luther King, Dorothy Day, Gandhi, Thomas Merton, and my brother Philip, a continuity of nonviolence and nonideology, stemming from the early church and the prophets, from Jesus Himself.

My teachers are nonideologues. They are attached to no self or special interest, including the self-interest commonly considered most legitimate of all, their own lives. Simply put, they know how to live and how to die. They draw on the great earth-time symbols that offer both "mimesis" and "praxis" — "the image" and "the movement." Gandhi walked to the sea and took up the forbidden salt of the poor. King declared, "The church is the place you go from." He started in the church and went from there, breaking down segregation, economic injustice, and denouncing the Vietnam War.

Incomparably the greatest of these is Jesus, who for His part took bread, broke it, and said, "This is My body, given for you." Then He took a cup and said, "This is My blood, given for you." The ethic of the body given, of the blood outpoured! The act led straight to the scaffold and to that "beyond" we name for want of a better word, resurrection.

We have not, in this century or any other, improved on this. More, being equally fearful of living and dying, we have yet to experience resurrection, which I translate, "the hope that hopes on."

A blasphemy against this hope is named deterrence, or Trident submarine, or star wars, or preemptive strike, or simply, any nuclear weapon. These are in direct violation of the commandment of Jesus: "Your ancestors said, 'An eye for an eye,' but I say to you, offer no violent resistance to evil. Love your enemies."

That is why we speak again and again of 1980 and all the Plowshares actions since, how some of us continue to labor to break the demonic clutch on our souls of the ethic of Mars, of wars and rumor of wars, inevitable wars, just wars, necessary wars, victorious wars, and say our no in acts of hope. For us, all these repeated arrests, the interminable jailings, the life of our small communities, the discipline of nonviolence, these have embodied an ethic of resurrection.

Simply put, we long to taste that event, its thunders and quakes, its great yes. We want to test the resurrection in our bones. To see if we might live in hope, instead of in the *silva oscura,* the thicket of cultural despair, nuclear despair, a world of perpetual war. We want to taste the resurrection.

May I say we have not been disappointed.

41

Hope, That Intransitive Being

THIS OCCURRED TO ME
that faith is prose
and love is music
but hope is—poetry.
Something evades   the net of logic
something hums   along in the mind
only half aware
. . .
What do we hope for?
the times   reduce us
lilliputians   among idiot giants
We shift   the burden of life   (if only a moment)
a sack of rocks   borne uphill—
O to get through   one day   without catastrophe!
We look skyward—
Hope to hell it doesn't fall on us!
No firm ground   who is on firm ground?
we huddle   on a creaking ice floe   on the volcano's tooth
for all sophistries   snooty talk   military puffing
religious hype
for all   that a tight knot of survivors
barely making it
Come now   admit
We're scraping bottom—
acedia   despair   willfulness   discontent   greed
. . .
In contrast to which
HOPE
steps softly   elusively
like a mouse in Swiss cheese

tunneling as it goes
gentle   elusive
I like that!

    . . .

HOPE
intransitive being   which is to say
hope   hopes for—nothing
like poetry   like Zen   like God
neither justifies   nor explains
No   hope stands there   noiseless as a mouse
in a cheese   made of   moonlight
infinitesimal eye   all alight
a diamond chip   a catch of moon
when the wind stirs a leaf alarmingly

    . . .

Then we admit
Of course   let us hope   for something!
that the sky   doesn't fall in   or
the waves   whelm us utterly   or
a volcano   consume us   like firebrands.

    . . .

And yet, and yet
were these to befall
I hope   we would hope on

    . . .

Then   let us pray
Christ   our avatar of hope
whose heart   in spite of all
hopes on for us   in spite of us—
rain   rain on us
untamed   unconstrained
your wildfire   storm of hope